YUGOSLAVIA

Marxist Regimes Series

Series editor: Bogdan Szajkowski,
Department of Sociology,
University College, Cardiff

Afghanistan Bhabani Sen Gupta
Angola Keith Somerville
Bulgaria Robert J. McIntyre
China Marc Blecher
Ethiopia Peter Schwab
German Democratic Republic Mike Dennis
Ghana Donald I. Ray
Grenada Tony Thorndike
Guinea-Bissau Rosemary E. Galli and Jocelyn Jones
Guyana Colin Baber and Henry B. Jeffrey
Hungary Hans-Georg Heinrich
Kampuchea Michael Vickery
Laos Martin Stuart-Fox
Madagascar Maureen Covell
Marxist Local Governments in Western Europe and Japan ed. Bogdan Szajkowski
Mongolia Alan J. K. Sanders
Nicaragua David Close
P.D.R. Yemen Tareq and Jacqueline Ismael
Romania Michael Shafir
Soviet Union Ronald J. Hill
Surinam Henk E. Chin and Hans Buddingh'
Vietnam Melanie Beresford
Yugoslavia Bruce McFarlane

Further Titles

Albania
Benin and The Congo
Cape Verde, São Tomé and Príncipe
Cuba
Czechoslovakia
Democratic People's Republic of Korea
Marxist State Governments in India
Mozambique
Poland
Zimbabwe
Adaptations of Communism
Comparative Analysis
Cumulative Index

YUGOSLAVIA

Politics, Economics and Society

Bruce McFarlane

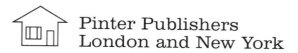

Pinter Publishers
London and New York

First published in Great Britain in 1988 by
Pinter Publishers Limited
25 Floral Street, London WC2E 9DS

British Library Cataloguing in Publication Data

A CIP catalogue record for this book is available from the British Library.
ISBN 0-86187-452-8 hardback
ISBN 0-86187-453-6 paperback

Library of Congress Cataloging-in-Publication Data

McFarlane, Bruce J.
    Yugoslavia: politics, economics, and society/Bruce McFarlane.
    p.   cm.—(Marxist regimes)
    Bibliography: p.
    Includes index.
    ISBN 0-86187-452-8   ISBN 0-86187-453-6 (pbk.)
    1. Yugoslavia—Politics and government—1945-   2. Yugoslavia—
Economic conditions—1945-   3. Yugoslavia—Social conditions.
I. Title.   II. Series: Marxist regimes series.
DR1302.M4   1988
949.7´02—dc 19   88-5845
                                                        CIP

Typeset by Joshua Associates Limited, Oxford
Printed in Great Britain by SRP Ltd, Exeter

Editor's Preface

Yugoslavia is one of the most socially and politically complex of Marxist regimes, containing within its borders a variety of peoples, cultures, languages and religions. For over forty years the successive rulers of the country have been dealing with the constant and ever-increasing challenges and demands of the distinctive sections of the various societies which form contemporary Yugoslavia. But not only this: during the postwar years the country found itself at times isolated and under pressure from its ideological opponents as well as its socialist allies, including the Soviet Union, and forced to embark on a set of unique, wide-ranging economic and political experiments.

This comprehensive and penetrating study not only explains the roots and rationale of the Yugoslav model of socialism but even more importantly evaluates critically its successes, shortcomings and failures.

The study of Marxist regimes has commonly been equated with the study of communist political systems. There were several historical and methodological reasons for this. For many years it was not difficult to distinguish the eight regimes in Eastern Europe and four in Asia which resoundingly claimed adherence to the tenets of Marxism and more particularly to their Soviet interpretation—Marxism-Leninism. These regimes, variously called 'People's Republic', 'People's Democratic Republic', or 'Democratic Republic', claimed to have derived their inspiration from the Soviet Union to which, indeed, in the overwhelming number of cases they owed their establishment.

To many scholars and analysts these regimes represented a multiplication of and geographical extension of the 'Soviet model' and consequently of the Soviet sphere of influence. Although there were clearly substantial similarities between the Soviet Union and the people's democracies, especially in the initial phases of their development, these were often overstressed at the expense of noticing the differences between these political systems.

It took a few years for scholars to realize that generalizing the particular, i.e., applying the Soviet experience to other states ruled by elites which claimed to be guided by 'scientific socialism', was not good enough. The relative simplicity of the assumption of a cohesive communist bloc was questioned after the expulsion of Yugoslavia from the Communist Information Bureau in 1948 and in particular after the workers' riots in Poznań in 1956 and the Hungarian revolution of the same year. By the mid-1960s, the totalitarian model of communist politics, which until then had been very much in force, began to crumble. As some of these regimes articulated demands for a distinctive path of socialist development, many specialists studying these systems began to notice that the cohesiveness of the communist bloc was less apparent than had been claimed before.

Also by the mid-1960s, in the newly independent African states 'democratic' multi-party states were turning into one-party states or military dictatorships, thus questioning the inherent superiority of liberal democracy, capitalism and the values that went with it. Scholars now began to ponder on the simple contrast between multi-party democracy and a one-party totalitarian rule that had satisfied an earlier generation.

More importantly, however, by the beginning of that decade Cuba had a revolution without Soviet help, a revolution which subsequently became to many political elites in the Third World not only an inspiration but a clear military, political and ideological example to follow. Apart from its romantic appeal, to many nationalist movements the Cuban revolution also demonstrated a novel way of conducting and winning a nationalist, anti-imperialist war and accepting Marxism as the state ideology without a vanguard communist party. The Cuban precedent was subsequently followed in one respect or another by scores of Third World regimes, which used the adoption of 'scientific socialism' tied to the tradition of Marxist thought as a form of mobilization, legitimation or association with the prestigious symbols and powerful high-status regimes such as the Soviet Union, China, Cuba and Vietnam.

Despite all these changes the study of Marxist regimes remains in its infancy and continues to be hampered by constant and not always pertinent comparison with the Soviet Union, thus somewhat blurring the important underlying common theme—the 'scientific theory' of the laws of development of human society and human history. This doctrine is claimed by the leadership of these regimes to consist of the discovery of objective causal relationships; it is used to analyse the contradictions which arise between goals and actuality in the pursuit of a common destiny. Thus the political elites of these countries have been and continue to be influenced in both their ideology and their political practice by Marxism more than any other current of social thought and political practice.

The growth in the number and global significance, as well as the ideological, political and economic impact, of Marxist regimes has presented scholars and students with an increasing challenge. In meeting this challenge, social scientists on both sides of the political divide have put forward a dazzling profusion of terms, models, programmes and varieties of interpretation. It is against the background of this profusion that the present comprehensive series on Marxist regimes is offered.

This collection of monographs is envisaged as a series of multi-disciplinary textbooks on the governments, politics, economics and society of these countries. Each of the monographs was prepared by a specialist on the country concerned. Thus, over fifty scholars from all over the world have contributed monographs which were based on first-hand knowledge. The geographical diversity of the authors, combined with the fact that as a group they represent many disciplines of social science, gives their individual analyses and the series as a whole an additional dimension.

Each of the scholars who contributed to this series was asked to analyse such topics as the political culture, the governmental structure, the ruling party, other mass organizations, party-state relations, the policy process, the economy, domestic and foreign relations together with any features peculiar to the country under discussion.

This series does not aim at assigning authenticity or authority to any single one of the political systems included in it. It shows that, depending on a variety of historical, cultural, ethnic and political factors, the pursuit of goals derived from the tenets of Marxism has produced different political forms at different times and in different places. It also illustrates the rich diversity among these societies, where attempts to achieve a synthesis between goals derived from Marxism on the one hand, and national realities on the other, have often meant distinctive approaches and solutions to the problems of social, political and economic development.

University College   *Bogdan Szajkowski*
Cardiff

Contents

List of Illustrations and Tables

Map

Figures

Tables

Preface

The Country

Yugoslavia is a country featured by stark contrasts. The pristine waters of the Drina River near Mostar are more pleasing to the eye than a series of garish billboards on the coastal road from Rijeka to Dubrovnik. A coatless worker may show you around the federal parliament in Belgrade, but that city also has its curtained black limousines for the privileged political figures once satirized by former Vice-President Djilas in his *Anatomy of a Moral* (Djilas, 1959). In Yugoslav parks chess players have a working knowledge of Marx and monopoly-capitalism, yet there are parts of Bosnia where female illiteracy is 80 per cent and infantile mortality amongst the highest in Europe.

On paper, working people in this Marxist regime have wide powers of 'self-management' over the assets of firms and offices in which they work. Yet one is told by many workers that professional management submit and re-submit proposals until they get their way. The economy is described as being under the influence of planning; yet the market, rather than production and distribution for social need, is the dynamic hub of economic movement. The peoples' welfare is part of the government's objectives function; yet subsidies to the performing arts and even to hospitals are cut because 'productivity' is the criterion officially used in the superstructure as well as in the economic base. While 'effectiveness', 'productivity' and other technical coefficients proliferate, everyone knows that the Yugoslav economy is wracked by inefficiencies.

Finally, there are few countries in the world which contain within their borders such a variety of peoples and language (Croats, Serbs, Slovenes, Macedonians, Bosnians, Montenegrins, as well as minorities formed by Albanians, Turks, Romanians and Hungarians). Yet the unity of the country has been maintained for forty years despite Soviet economic blockade and pressure of all sorts from Western powers.

This book, apart from outlining the basic attitudes and mechanisms that have emerged in socialist Yugoslavia, attempts to probe the sources and the results of Yugoslavia's contrasts.

Sources and Their Use

This book is based on a wide range of materials in the Serbo-Croatian language: documents of the Federal Planning Office, statistics from the Bureau of Statistics, bank publications, journals of the academy such as *Ekonomist* or wider political journals like *Naša Stvarnost* ('Our Reality') and newspapers. For many years an irregular bulletin in English reprinted important speeches and economic statements called Information Service Yugoslavia. The Yugoslavs publish more detailed statistics than other marxist regimes and a major source for such statistics on demography and the economy is *Statistički Godišnjak*, Statistical Yearbook. The Federal Bureau of Statistics publishes as well 'Pocketbooks' of Statistics in English. Figures are also published in a monthly, *Yugoslovensk Pregled*, of which the summarized quarterly in English is *Yugoslav Survey*. *Službeni List*, the official government gazette, is issued in Serbo-Croation.

Among newspapers, the main sources are *Borba* (the equivalent of *Pravda* in the Soviet Union), which had been the official daily organ of the Communist Party until 1954 when it was handed over to the broader 'popular front', the Socialist Alliance of Working People of Yugoslavia. The other organ of daily news is *Politika*, a semi-government newspaper. The daily paper of the Alliance of Working People of Croatia is *Vjesnik*, and the equivalent in Slovenia is *Slovenski Potočevaleč*. The Communists' own weekly paper is *Komunist*. The economic weekly published in Belgrade is *Ekonomska Politika* and in Zagreb *Ekonomski Pregled*.

International affairs are discussed from a Yugoslav government viewpoint in a regular English language publication *Review of International Affairs* and in *Međunarodni Problemi* issued by the Institute of International Politics and Economy, Belgrade.

Periodicals of a general political-social kind include *Gledišta*, *Naša Stvarnost* and *Socijalizam* (in Serbo-Croatian) and *Socialist Thought and Practice* (in English), while academic economic journals consulted for this book included *Ekonomska Analiza*, *Finansje*, *Ekonomist*, *Ekonomska Revija* and *Ekonomski Pregled*. I have also consulted some 'rebel' journals published in Yugoslavia such as *Praxis*.

Mimeographed materials are issued in Belgrade by the Agricultural Economics Institute, the Faculty of Economics of Belgrade University, the Institute of Foreign Trade, the People's Bank of Yugoslavia, the Yugoslav Investment Bank, the Institute of Economic Investments, and the Institute for Economic Research.

Pamphlets and books (quite a number in English) are also published by the Confederation of Trade Unions of Yugoslavia. Due appreciation is also made of a group of secondary works published by people of Yugoslav origin living abroad. The author was a post-graduate student at Belgrade University in 1958 while on a scholarship of the Yugoslav government, and has visited the country on many occasions since then.

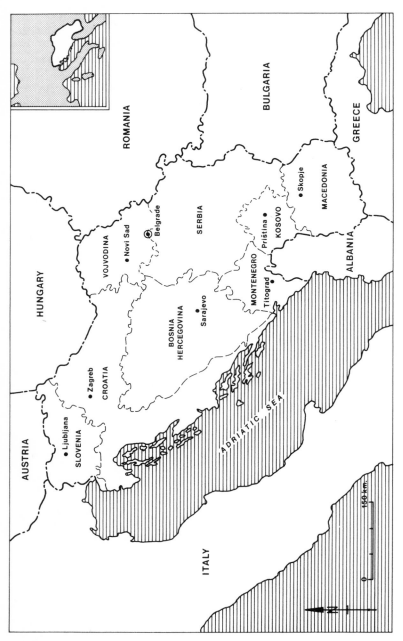

Yugoslavia: regions and autonomous provinces

Basic Data

Official name	Socialist Federal Republic of Yugoslavia
Population	23.1 million (1985)
density	90 per sq. km.; 155 persons per sq. km of agricultural land
Population growth	0.9 (1970)
Crude birth rate per 1,000	15.9 (1985)
Crude death rate per 1,000	9.1 (1985)
Fertility rate	100.8 (1955); 65.8 (1985)
Mortality rate	
Men	11.7 (1955); 9.7 (1982)
Women	11.1 (1955); 8.3 (1985)
Life expectancy	Male: 64 years (1965), 67.7 years (1981); female: 67.7 years (1965), 73.2 years (1981)
Agricultural population	4.27m. (1981)
Agricultural population as % of total	1948 67.2%; 1981 19.9%
Ethnic groups	Serbs, Croats, Macedonians, Montenegrins, Bosnians, Slovenes; ethnic minorities include gypsies, Albanians, Hungarians, Italians, Romanians
Capital	Belgrade
Area	255,804 sq. km.
Official language	Serbo-Croatian

Administrative Divisions
Share of regions in territories and population of
Yugoslavia

	Territory	Population
Serbia	34.5%	41.5%
Croatia	22.1%	20.1%
Bosnia–Hercegovina	20.0%	18.7%
Macedonia	10.1%	8.2%
Slovenia	7.9%	8.3%
Montenegro	5.4%	2.7%

Plus two autonomous provinces: Kosovo Metohia and

Vojvodina

Membership of International Organisations	UN since 1946; Founding Member of Non-Aligned group of nations; Member of IMF, World Bank; Observer at CMEA general sessions; member of Balkan Pact (now dormant) with Greece and Turkey

Political structure
Constitution	3rd (1974)
Highest legislative body	Federal People's Assembly
Highest executive body	Presidency (collective)
Prime Minister	Branko Mikulić
President	Lazar Mojsev
Ruling party	League of Communists of Yugoslavia
Secretary General	B. Krunič
Political Organisations	League of Communists, 2.16m.; Socialist Alliance of Working People, 15.0m.; League of Trade Unions of Yugoslavia, 5.9m.

Economy
GDP	62 billion dinars
Growth rate of GDP (1972 prices)	1948–85, 5.3% per annum; 1981–85, 0.6% per annum
Growth rate of GDP per head (1972 prices)	1948-85, 4.4% per annum; 1981–85, −0.3% per annum

Foreign debt	19 billion dinars (33% GDP)
Total exports	2,258 billion dinars (1985); 50% raw materials and semi-finished goods; 17% machinery; 33% food, textiles, medicines
Destination of exports	European Economic Community, 30.5%; EFTA, 4.8%; Socialist countries, 50.2%; developing countries, 15%
Production of electric energy per head	3,235 kwh (1985)
Flats and houses per 1000 inhabitants	59 (1985)
Size of work-force	Socialist sector, 6.5 million; private sector, 0.14 million
Structure of work-force (1985)	38% in industry; 38.5% women; 51% women in private sector

Culture

Number of professional theatres	70
Number of cinemas	1,298

Education

Adult literacy rate	85%
Primary school enrolment	100%
Secondary School enrolment	79%
Secondary school leavers	258,826 (1985)
Tertiary education graduates	22,648 (1985)
Workers in socialist sector with middle school qualification	1.5m.
Workers in socialist sector with high school qualification	317,000

Share of Gross Social Product going to defence   3.9% (1984)

Health

Population per physician	795 (1979); 601 (1984)
Population per hospital bed	167 (1979); 164 (1984)
Daily calorie supply per capita	3,575 (1983)
As % of requirements	141% (1983)

Population Forecasting

The following data are projections produced by Poptran, University College Cardiff Population Centre, from United Nations Assessment Data published in 1980, and are reproduced here to provide some basis of comparison with other countries covered by the Marxist Regimes Series.

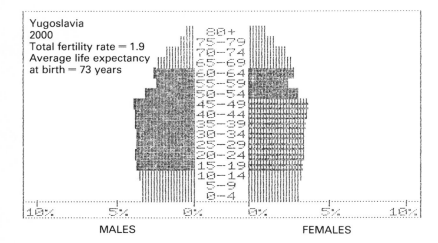

Yugoslavia
2000
Total fertility rate = 1.9
Average life expectancy
at birth = 73 years

MALES   FEMALES

Projected Data for Yugoslavia 2000

Total population ('000)	25,167
Males ('000)	12,478
Females ('000)	12,689
Total fertility rate	1.95
Life expectancy (male)	70.1 years
Life expectancy (female)	75.8 years
Crude birth rate	13.8
Crude death rate	9.0
Annual growth rate	0.48%
Under 15s	19.85%
Over 65s	13.12%
Women aged 15–49	24.83%
Doubling time	145 years
Population density	98 per sq. km.
Urban population	57.5%

Abbreviations and Glossary

AVNOJ	Anti-Fascist Committee of National Liberation of Yugoslavia
CMEA	Council of Mutual Economic Assistance
COMECON	See CMEA
CPC	Communist Party of China
CPY	Communist Party of Yugoslavia
CPSU	Communist Party of the Soviet Union
EEC	European Economic Community
FEC	Federal Executive Council (Cabinet of Yugoslavia)
FPRJ	Federal Peoples Republic of Yugoslavia
IMF	International Monetary Fund
NATO	North Atlantic Treaty Organisation
NFRJ	People's Federal Republic of Yugoslavia
OECD	Organisation of Economic Cooperation and Development
SDS	State Security Service (see also UDB-a)
SFRJ	Socialist Federal Republic of Yugoslavia
SFSN	Death to Fascism, Freedom of the People (war-time slogan of partisans)
SG	Statistical Yearbook
SKJ	Savez Kommunista Yugoslavija (League of Yugoslav Communists)
SKOJ	Savez Kommunista Omladine Yugoslavije (National Youth Organization of Yugoslavia)
SSRNJ	Socialist Alliance of Working People of Yugoslavia
SZZPP	Federal Planning Commission
UDB-a	Internal Security Police, replaced by SDS

Glossary of Terms

associated labour	General Yugoslav term to describe those enterprises and offices that use or hire socially-owned means of production and function on self-management lines
birokratizam	bureaucracy (as social phenomenon)
Borba	Daily newspaper ('struggle')
delegation system	System of indirect election to political assemblies from 'delegations' elected themselves from economic units and other 'bodies of associated labour'. Other political and social

	organizations, including trade unions, send their delegates to the assemblies directly
dinar	Yugoslav currency unit
integracija	Vertical integration in industry
Kosmet	An underdeveloped region and autonomous province of Yugoslavia, Kosovo–Metohia, populated largely by Šiptars (Albanians)
Nin	Newspaper (Belgrade)
Politika	Newspaper of Yugoslavia
Šiptar	Albanian
Skupština	Assembly, Parliament
Statistički Godišnjak	Statistical Yearbook
Zadruga	peasant cooperative

Part I
History, Political Traditions and Social Structure

1 Geographical Setting

Yugoslavia is situated in south-eastern Europe, mainly on the Balkan peninsula. Mainland frontiers are in the south west with Albania, the south with Greece, the east with Bulgaria, the north east with Romania, the north with Hungary and Austria and the west with Italy. In the sea zone along the Adriatic coast there are about 1,050 islands including seven exceeding 100 sq. km: Krk, Brač, Cres, Hvar, Pag, Korčula and Dugi Otok. The total length of Yugoslavia's frontiers is 2,969 km.

Due to the open nature of the northern frontiers the climate tends to be dominated more by cold continental air currents than warmer south ones. As a result its geographical position, between $46° \frac{1}{2}'$ and $40° 5'$ north latitude and $13° 23'$ and $23° 02'$ east longitude, which is part of the temperate zone, makes it colder than southern France or Naples.

Mountain areas (e.g., the Dinaric Alps) dominate the country, covering 60 per cent of its total area. This made communications between regions historically very difficult and also cut the arable land to a quarter of the total. Only in Vojvodina (near Hungary) was large-scale cultivation possible. However, forestry has been a major asset, with timber exported on a large scale.

The natural wealth of the country lies chiefly in agriculture and minerals such as coal, iron and non-ferrous ores, like bauxite and chrome. In the pre-Marxist period these constituted the overwhelming percentage of Yugoslavia's exports, but since 1946 the production of industrial raw materials and manufacturing have become the leading economic sectors.

Before the Second World War the proportion of the active population in agriculture was 79 per cent and did not fall below 50 per cent until the census of 1961. Hence the movement of population into non-agricultural pursuits has become a major demographic feature of Yugoslavia over the last fifty years: in 1948 the agricultural population was still 67.2 of the total, but by 1981 this had dropped to 19.9 per cent (*Statistical Pocketbook of Yugoslavia, 1986*, p. 35).

The Population

A leading feature of the Yugoslav nation is the heterogeneity of the population. The most important of the 22.4 million inhabitants at the 1981 census were Serbs (9.3 million) and Croats (4.6 million). There were also 4.1 million Bosnians and Hercegovinans, 1.9 million Macedonians, 1.8 million Slovenes and 590,000 Montenegrins. In addition there were ten national minorities of which the most important were Šiptars (Albanians) of 1.7 million, Hungarians (470,000), Turks (120,000), Slovaks (83,000), Romanians (58,000) and gypsies (70,485). The density of the population is below the European average at about 80 inhabitants per sq. km., Serbia being the most densely populated and Montenegro the least.

While Islam persists in Hercegovina, Bosnia and Kosovo–Metohia as a result of 500 years of Turkish occupation, Christianity was accepted by most south Slavs after the ninth and tenth centuries. The Slav apostles, Cyril and Methodius, created a new alphabet and a new south Slav literature while preaching Christianity. Today quite a few people retain some religious affiliation with the line-up being Croats and Slovenes (Catholic, 32 per cent), Serbs and Macedonians (Orthodox, 41 per cent), Bosnians and Hercegovinans plus Kosovo–Metohians and Turks (Muslim, 12 per cent).

Between the two World wars 45 per cent of the population was illiterate as a result of the backwardness of its economy in the years before 1940. Today there is improvement but lack of literacy still stood at 9.5 per cent overall at the Yugoslav census of 1981 (*Statistical Pocketbook of Yugoslavia*, 1986, p. 38). This figure included 14.7 per cent of women, while 23.3 per cent of women in Bosnia–Hercegovina were illiterate.

At the time of the ancient Romans, much of the coastal territory of modern Yugoslavia (contemporary Slovenia and Croatia) was called 'Illyria' while the eastern area was peopled by Thracians. In the fourth century BC the Illyrians were partly driven inland by the Celts who attacked from the coast and managed to found Singidunum (later Belgrade) and Taurunum (later Zemun). Next the Romans conquered Illyria's tribes and extended control over the peninsula represented by Yugoslavia's coast. With the decline of the Roman empire the peninsula was linked to the eastern Byzantine sphere of influence.

In the fifth century AD the first Slavs settled on the Balkans Peninsula, retreating from the Hun and Goth invasions of central Europe, and this immigration accelerated in the seventh century, during the period of civil wars in Byzantium. The mode of production at this time was similar to what Marx called 'the Germanic' mode. The Slavs lived a tribal life with *zupans* or chieftains leading the diverse tribes but paying political tribute to Byzantium. The Croat and Serbian states, formed by unions of tribes, developed and preserved their existence through various trials (the successful imposition of Frank rule), but the Slovene state lost its separate identity following a German invasion in 722 AD.

Croatia experienced serious difficulties when, at the beginning of the tenth century, it found itself squeezed between Hungarians advancing from the north to the Adriatic sea and the Venetians, a rising maritime power. Forced to manœuvre between these two expansionist peoples, the Croats were made to accept the suzerainty of the Hungarians until 1918, when Yugoslavia was formed.

Serbia continued its existence and even expanded first under Stevan Nemanji and later under Dushan the Mighty, when in 1345 it became an empire which included Thessaly, Epirus and Albania. After the death of Dushan the Serbian state was unable to withstand a Turkish invasion. Following defeat by the Turks at Marica (1371) and Kosovo (1389), Serbia endured five hundred years of vassalage under the Turks.

Turks left their stamp on the history of the region. They conquered Bosnia in 1403, Zeta in 1499 and the Croatian areas of Slavonia (north) and Dalmatia (coast). Only the port-republic of Ragusa (Dubrovnik) was able, by payment of heavy tribute to the Turks, to maintain independence up to 1806. At that date Napoleon's troops took it, along with Illyria. When the French succumbed to Russia and Austria, the Dalmatian coast was absorbed by the Austro-Hungarian monarchy which had already defeated the Turks in the decisive battle of Vienna (1683). The Turks, however, maintained control of Serbia, Macedonia and Montenegro until the nineteenth century.

At the beginning of the nineteenth century Karadjordja and then Obrenović led the Serbs into a united front against the Turks. They formed the state of Montenegro, recognized by the great powers as an independent state, along with Serbia, at the Berlin Congress in 1878. However, all the other Yugoslav regions remained under either Austrian or Turkish domination until 1918.

'Yugoslav' literally means 'South Slav' and Yugoslavia first appeared when former territories of Austria–Hungary were joined to Serbia in December 1918. Although the 1918 formation of a united Yugoslavia was a direct result of post-war settlements of the affairs of defeated Austria–Hungary and Turkey, it is important to note the longer-term influence of national liberation ideas throughout the nineteenth century, a force which inspired Yugoslav peoples. Already during 1918 Serbia and Montenegro had joined the 'Entente' group and fought the Central Powers.

It was, then, as an outcome of these underlying historical processes that a common state of Serbs, Croats and Slovenes (incorporating also Bosnians and Montenegrins) was formed under the Karadjordjević dynasty in 1918. Yugoslavia was becoming a national state of unified peoples. This had come after many trials for the people concerned.

During the 1920s only a limited form of parliamentary government and democracy existed in Yugoslavia, for class and national antagonisms were strong. In the 1921 elections the Communist Party won fifty-eight seats and became the third largest party in parliament. The first act of the parliament, after adopting the constitution (June 1921), was to outlaw the communists.

While some show was made of preserving the triune nature of Yugoslavia (Slovenia, Croatia and Serbia), friction was particularly strong between the Croats and the Serbs. These two peoples were of the same racial origin and spoke the same language, but the Croats were Catholic, used the Latin script, and had a different historical-cultural tradition to the Serbs, who were Eastern Orthodox in religion and used the Cyrillic script.

At first, French capital was dominant in Yugoslavia, for the native bourgeoisie was weak. The Serbian landlords and bourgeoisie attempted to dominate all of Yugoslavia, while what industry there was largely represented foreign interests. French military and political influence was strong in the 1920s. In the countryside capitalism had started to develop in the early nineteenth century. In the south, reforms in 1836 had established peasant proprietorship, while in the north the serfs had been freed in 1848. Large-scale landlords and the Church were important in rural areas. In 1931 some 68 per cent of peasant families owned only 30 per cent of the land, and there were a large number of landless labourers.

The component regions of Yugoslavia as they emerged from the First World War had sharply different standards of living. In Slovenia the standard was comparable with Austria and 20 per cent above the national average. Montenegro and the region of Kosovo–Metohia were at the level of Turkey, much below the national average. The sharp contrast in a country of different cultures was seen by communists and non-communists alike as a problem that would need to be tackled before sound economic development could be achieved but a successful solution to the task has proved elusive, as will be shown in Part III below.

With the 1930s depression the influence of French capital began to give way to British. The decline of French influence was hastened by the assassination of King Alexander, together with the French Foreign Minister, on the occasion of a visit to Marseilles. This was carried out by members of the Croat fascist Ustashi, an organization established by Pavelić in 1929 and which received assistance from Fascist Italy. What Italian influence there was in Yugoslavia, however, dwindled with the imposition of sanctions against Italy over the 1935 Abyssinian war. From 1935 to 1940 German and English investments grew. German capital, however, tripled, while English capital only doubled. The appointment of Stojadinović as premier in 1935 brought pro-German influence to the fore.

In the controlled elections of December 1938 Stojadinović suffered a rebuff and this fact, together with the growing international crisis, forced a modification in internal policy. The monopoly of power held by the Serbian group yielded to a Serb–Croat coalition when Maček, leader of the Croat Peasant Party since 1928, joined the Cvetković government in August 1939.

The modified monarchial system with representative legislative bodies sharing power had not succeeded in developing the economy or in dealing with the activities of the small Marxist and Social-Democrat groups that sprang up in the 1920s.

On 6 January 1929 democratic forums were formally abolished by King Alexander and a dictatorship proclaimed, in order, it was said, to safeguard national unity. After the Royal assassination (1934), a Council of Regents took over under Prince Paul. In 1939, this government signed an agreement with the Croat Peasant Party which gave autonomy to those parts of Yugoslavia in which Croats were in a majority; but this agreement was not recognized by

Serbian political parties. This state, in turn, collapsed in 1941, when, after many attempts to appease the fascists, Nazi invasion from the north and Italian invasion on the west coast occurred.[1]

The subsequent national uprising against Italy and Germany was accompanied by a civil war between the partisans and Mihailović's royalists or Chetniks, while both of these groups fought the Croat Ustashi. Mihailović had formed his group in May 1941, but the severity of German reprisals deterred him from undertaking much armed resistance. When the partisan movement started to make its presence felt, discussions were opened with Mihailović, but the Serbian royalists objected to the establishment of People's Committees by the communists and co-operation came to an end in November. Mihailović believed communism to be a greater danger than the Axis, and at times allied himself with the enemy in attacking Tito's forces (Marjanović, 1970).

The communist-led partisan movement was the only one in Yugoslavia which fought on the basis of the equality of all the component nations. This policy of national equality also explains the fact that Italians, Hungarians and even German partisans fought in Tito's army.

The partisans organized a National Congress of the National Liberation Committees in November 1942. According to the main biography of Tito (Dedijer, 1953, p. 187) it was intended to elect a provisional government, but this idea was given up at the Soviet Union's request. After the Italian surrender, September 1943, the National Liberation movement gained both in territory and in arms, and at the second National Congress of National Liberation Committees (29 November 1943) the Federal People's Republic of Yugoslavia was officially established.

A British delegate reached Tito's headquarters in May 1942 (Maclean, 1966) but the Russians, anxious not to disturb their relations with their Western allies, did not send a mission until February 1944. From 1943 some military aid started to arrive from the Soviet Union, and a lot more from the West in the following year. From February 1944 Britain stopped sending aid to Mihailović, realizing that he was not resisting the Germans.

Right from the start Tito acted the part of an independent force with considerable political power, and before Soviet troops actually crossed into Yugoslav territory an agreement was signed between the Soviet Command and the National Committee of Yugoslavia (September 1944). However, in October Churchill and Stalin reached an agreement in Moscow over the future of the Balkans. The Soviet Union was to have the predominant voice in Romania, Bulgaria and Hungary, and Britain in Greece. Yugoslavia was to be a shared sphere of influence. This arrangement ignored the fact that Tito's regime, after bitter fighting, had moved from a partisan detachment of 300,000 in 1943 to one million by the time Yugoslavia's national partisan army entered Belgrade in 1945 (Tito, 1971, p. 175). Eventually, the British in practice allowed Tito's ascendancy.

3 Modern Political History

The Rise of the Communists and Partisans

In April 1919, while Tito was abroad and not yet a Communist, various groups merged into a United Workers' Party at a Conference in Belgrade. This soon became the Yugoslav Communist Party after a further conference at Vukovar in June 1920. They were divided from the beginning over attitudes to the Comintern, whether to support illegal methods of work to overthrow the Kingdom, whether any new socialist state would be under Serbian leadership or a federation with equal status for Slovenes, Croats and Serbs. Despite divisions, about 20,000 people joined the Party.

From the 1920s the Yugoslav left attempted to come to terms with the undemocratic situation within their own country and with Moscow's influence over the Comintern and hence the politics of all Communist parties. Thus the Serbian socialist party between the wars came under the strong influence of Lenin, or Rakowski and the Bulgarian revolutionary Tesnyaki and declared for communism. In Yugoslavia, after the defeat of the Communists, the Croatian Peasant Party, a Catholic opposition to centralizing tendencies in Belgrade advanced much; its leader Stepan Radić went to Moscow and joined the Peasant International. Although Tito's later rise changed much of the nature of the early party it is clear that Croatian Nationalism versus Serb Centralism has infected the Yugoslav left from the beginning. This makes some of the events of 1970–1 (see the section in Chapter 8 below on Croatian nationalism) much more comprehensible in historical perspective. It also foreshadowed the way that the fortunes and policies of the Party were affected by a series of interventions from the Moscow-based Comintern, for these *ad hoc* acts of interference were, in turn, the result of squabbling which reflected national rivalries within the YCP itself.

Those who survived persecution within Yugoslavia from 1926 were struggling to develop a semi-underground left. Membership of the Communist Party dropped from 60,000 in 1920 to a few thousand in 1928 (Auty, 1970, ch. 6; Dedijer, 1953). In August that year, Josip Broz Tito, future leader of the party, was arrested and served five years imprisonment. During this time, his fellow Communists in Moscow were falling foul of Stalin's ascendancy within the CPSU and the Comintern. The experience and testimony of a member of the Socialist Party of Croatia (later a Communist) in Russia of the 1920s, Anton Ciliga, is important here. In February 1929, he reported the Comintern called a general meeting to pacify all Yugoslav leftists living in Moscow who had condemned by ninety votes to five the conduct of the Yugloslav Party directors. These were people who were still backed by the Comintern in fleeing the military-political coup in Yugoslavia of January 1929 and the policy of supporting Serb nationalism. Later, most of the Yugoslavs in Russia were arrested and jailed (1928–31) for supporting the left opposition rather than Stalin (Ciliga, 1940, pp. 80–120).

Back in Yugoslavia, the second and third conferences of the Party showed that power was gradually falling into the hands of its left wing. One of these, Krsta Kaclerović, a Croat who was also close to the Comintern, became secretary in 1923. Sima Marković, however, criticized Stalin and argued for a Serbian-oriented centralized Communist machine whereas Stalin believed Croats might want to opt for national emancipation. The left supported the Croats and Marković was expelled, the Party centre moving to Zagreb. Here it was possible to recruit more workers from the industrial region of the country.

Divisions arose over illegal versus open work with the working class. Tito (at this time a delegate to the Zagreb Party conference from the Metal and Leather Workers' Union) opposed the two factions supporting these rival positions and asked the Comintern to mediate (Auty, 1970, p. 63). Tito then was elected secretary by the Zagreb Communists, while the Comintern appointed a new central committee for the Party as a whole headed by a Croat from Bosnia, Djuro Djaković. It followed the 'left-turn' of the Comintern and made a declaration of 'open War' by the Party on the Serbian bourgeoisie and the dictatorship. Broz was tried and gaoled in 1928 for hiding grenades, which featured in the new Comintern policy approving of armed action by Communists against the authorities in their countries. During these five years he met a tough Jewish intellectual, Moša Pijade, who became a life-long ally. Released from gaol, Tito was given Comintern moral and material support to reorganize and reinvigorate the party (Dedijer, 1953, p. 25). He started in Slovenia with Eduard Kardelj and Boris Kidrič, propounding the need to develop a 'popular front' and the inevitability of the Party having first to support a 'bourgeois–democratic revolution' before advocating socialist solutions. However, after a short time, he was sent to Moscow to a job in the Comintern, leaving the leading role to Gorkić (on Comintern orders), who followed a policy of 'low profile' for the Party, instead favouring working with and voting for united opposition candidates opposing the new regent, Prince Paul. As the Party leadership split over this

(Gorkić being opposed by Vladimir Čopić) it was dismissed by the Comintern and in October 1936 Tito was sent back, with Dmitrov's support, to reorganize the party again. He first made contact with left-wing circles in Paris, then managed to travel to most parts of Yugoslavia to rebuild Party cells and to make new contacts with the Croat Peasant Party and legal trade unions. After Gorkić 'disappeared' in Moscow, Tito became the undisputed leader, but had to avoid going to Moscow himself as long as possible. He finally went in 1939 after missing the purges and was officially appointed General Secretary of the Yugoslav Communist Party early in 1939. However, only 3,000 Party members remained.

As the war danger mounted, the Party attracted secret and growing support from some of the progressive bourgeoisie. Figures such as Dr Ivan Ribar who had many personal connections with students from families of his own class helped the Left. Many students were recruited into the Party youth organization and became leading cadres in the partisans when the Germans attacked Yugoslavia.

It is now proposed to deal with two major questions in this section of the book: what sort of Communist Party developed and how did it propose to tackle the tasks it set for itself—the transformation of the social structure of Yugoslavia?

Tito had succeeded by about 1942 in changing the whole nature of the Communist Party from its Moscow-leaning small group mentality to a tough and disciplined Marxist Party. His leadership core included the classical communist types like the intellectual Pijade and the worker Ranković. However, as the Germans attacked more and more villages, and killed more ordinary Yugoslavs, the partisans and their communist core were increasingly thrown open to ordinary citizens from all classes and social backgrounds. Patriotism and mass membership increased; the 'disciplinary core', while giving leadership in the anti-fascist struggle, had to dilute many of its 'harder' Marxist attitudes. There was no room, really, for the sort of views that had been exhibited (for example) by Stalinists in the Spanish Civil War—survival depended in Yugoslavia on winning support 'across the classes'.

The composition of the leadership and their social outlook reinforced this situation. In Montenegro, former student leader Djilas and others ignored instructions not to make communist revolution (Auty, 1970, p. 173). They organized a local 'government by soviets', killing-off opponents and wreaking vengeance on enemies with a violence that lost popularity. Another Montenegrin, S. Vukmanović-Tempo, was sent to curb excesses. In Slovenia and Macedonia it took much longer to organize partisan detachments, while there was a confused situation in Croatia, where some wanted to link up firmly with Tito while others, due to Croat nationalism fanned by a local Communist leader Andrija Hebrang, were less co-operative. This profile of leading Party members already indicates the sort of party that was emerging to take power. First, it was different from the pre-War groups in being remote from Kremlin palace intrigues, which tended to embroil foreigners-in-exile in Moscow. The Party was, therefore, now genuinely 'home grown'. Second, as the Montenegrin excesses indicate, the Party reflected very strongly the national differences between Serbs, Slovenes and Montenegrins in style, level of nationalism etc. Third, although some leaders (like Djilas, Kardelj, Bakarić) were intellectuals, the core leadership of Moša Pijade, Tito and Ranković were the 'self-educated' worker kind. This predisposed them to orthodoxy in relation to Marxism-Leninism and explains the long delay in gearing up to oppose Stalin after he had provoked them and had threatened the new socialist Yugoslavia's national sovereignty. Orthodoxy also implied a policy that was likely to be in favour of very rapid industrialization (despite the Soviet Union's insistence that 'we have everything you need industrially'). Despite the fact that the Party had a mass base including many peasants, its policies were not likely to be particularly sympathetic to peasants. The very rapid collectivization of agriculture and the high rates of investment of the early Five Year Plans seem to point in this direction. They, in turn, were designed (as shown in detail in Chapter 10 below) to transform the social structure, social conditions and class structure of pre-war Yugoslavia.

As the regime took office in 1945 the Supreme General Staff of the partisans became, in effect, the Politburo of the Party and the core of the new government. Pijade worked on legislation and the Constitution; Ranković became chief of security; Djilas became Vice-President with responsibility to propaganda; Kidrič became chief of economic policy; Kardelj conducted foreign affairs and Tito took the main leadership role.

Social Structure and Problems of Socialist Transformation

Pre-War Yugoslavia was a dependent economic satellite of Europe and a class society based on agrarian social relations. The task of transforming these twin aspects occupied the Yugoslav communists for the first decade of the regime. The large number of peasants (and ex-peasants working in new factories) set definite limits on how far the Party could go in any desire to be more 'liberal', to loosen planning and to accelerate growth. Moreover, national unity against Moscow demanded a softer policy on collectivization after 1948.

Croatia, in particular, represented a serious problem. It had been in the Hungarian part of the Austro-Hungarian empire. The Croats were treated harshly although they had their own parliament (Sabor) which met in Zagreb and their own President (appointed by Hungary). Some measures of local government self-rule had developed. Economic discrimination against Croatia (refusal to extend railways to the area) and neglect of commerce and industry, coupled with peasant unrest against military conscription and taxes, meant that industrial growth was delayed until the Austro-Hungarian empire collapsed. In the meantime the Church fanned Croatian nationalism.

In 1945 all republics were short of food. UNRRA supplies were accepted as a short-term measure, but peasants were immediately put under strong pressure from the new Yugoslav leaders (Auty, 1970, p. 271) without, however, any NEP-style incentives being allowed or applied. Prices were low, land holdings were fixed at a ceiling of ten hectares, fines and imprisonment were common.

As well as the generally hostile policy towards the peasantry (despite the fact that large numbers had been partisans), the YCP leadership saw the solution to the question of 'social relations' in agriculture to be rapid transformation of the peasantry into industrial workers by means of very rapid industrialization on the Stalin model of the 1930s. The severity of this policy as applied in Yugoslavia is outlined in Chapter 10 below and in Bićanić's study of these times (Bićanić, 1973, ch. 5). This change in the social structure would, it was hoped, accelerate general economic growth while generating a new mass base for the Party among industrial workers. The Soviet leaders were hostile to the overall thrust of 1945–8 economic policy in Yugoslavia. One Soviet leader said, 'What do you need industry for, in the Urals, we have everything you need' (quoted in Auty, 1970, p. 273).

The Yugoslav Communists, however, believed in the urgency of changing the social structure. They also seem to have hoped that a new class structure would minimize the older nationalist rivalries and gradually erode them. For both reasons their new political structures were adapted to meet the main task in hand: industrialization.

Politics in the First Decade of Socialist Yugoslavia

The Titoist forces enjoyed British support following the military missions of Deakin and Fitzroy Maclean to such an extent that the West acquiesced when a short-lived Šubasić-Tito government was replaced in January 1946, by a full-scale Marxist regime.

The new government was able to build on some basic forms of administration that had emerged in liberated zones during the War, and on aspects of the Soviet model. National Liberation Committees, practising a form of local self-management, were federated at the second session of AVNOJ (the Anti-Fascist Committee of National Liberation) held in Jajce on 29 November 1943. At this meeting the legal framework for a new 'Federal People's Republic of Yugoslavia' was established. A new constitution proclaiming equality of treatment for constituent nationalities as well as confirming the revolutionary achievements of the regime came into force on 31 January 1946.

German resistance in Yugoslavia lasted until 15 May 1945. Yugoslavia had suffered severely. Ten per cent of the population (1,706,000 people) had been killed—more than in France, Britain or America. The immediate post-war period was one of reconstruction. A Law on Nationalization had been passed in November 1944, covering all property held by enemy nationals, collaborators, and war criminals—in effect, 80 per cent of Yugoslav industry. A Law on Agrarian Reform was passed in August 1945. A constituent assembly, which met in November 1945, confirmed the republic, while by the following year initial reconstruction had ended and a Five Year Plan was commenced (April 1947).

From the beginning, Yugoslavia's relations with her neighbours were a pre-occupation and at the end of 1947 there was a move for Balkan federation, to include all the Balkan Communist countries. Pacts of friendship were signed between Yugoslavia and Bulgaria, Hungary and Romania, and Tito toured these Balkan states. This time the move was stopped by a statement in *Pravda* (January 1948) that 'these countries do not need a problematic and artificial federation, confederation, or customs union'. This was followed by Soviet treaties with Romania, Hungary and Bulgaria.

Another move for a Balkan Federation developed in March 1948, when Yugoslav and Bulgarian delegations were in Moscow. In reply, Stalin proposed a Bulgarian-Yugoslav federation only. The Yugoslavs were suspicious; their dispute with the CPSU had already started, and they thought this was a move to swamp the Yugoslav Communist Party, so they would not agree to this proposed union (Djilas, 1962).

The dispute over the Balkan Federation was only one of a number of points of friction which had been developing with the Soviet Union over a number of years. At the heart of the problem was the fact that Tito had come to power from the fruits of Yugoslavia's own efforts against fascism. Yugoslavia, Albania and Greece were the only countries in the Balkans in which communist revolutions occurred during the Second World War. Albania was a very small country under Yugoslav influence, the Greek revolution had been suppressed, so that Yugoslavia's relationship to the Soviet Union was quite unique; the Tito regime did not owe its existence to the Soviet Red Army. As early as 1942 the Yugoslav communists had complained a lack of assistance from the Soviet Union and of the over-friendly attitude of the Soviets to the Mihailovich–royalist group. When Soviet troops passed through Yugoslavia during 1944 and 1945 their behaviour towards the civilian population was sometimes bad; the Yugoslavs complained of rapes and robbery. Tito and Djilas mentioned these matters when in Moscow in April 1945 to sign a Yugoslav–Soviet treaty of alliance (Djilas, 1962), but Stalin remained unmoved.

Yugoslav troops occupied Trieste on 30 April 1946, but Anglo-American forces reached this city soon after and Yugoslavia was forced to withdraw her troops (12 June). In May, Tito annoyed the Soviet Union by protesting too angrily over the arrangements which the great powers had reached for the future of Trieste, but the main source of friction was undoubtedly the economic and political relations between the two countries. The Soviet Union tried to impose the same unequal relations on Yugoslavia as it had established with the dependent regimes in Eastern Europe. Proposals for Soviet-Yugoslav joint-stock companies favoured the Soviet economy rather than the Yugoslav; eventually the Yugoslavs agreed to the formation of only two such companies (air and river shipping, February 1947). The trade pattern also favoured Soviet needs rather than Yugoslav; Soviet technicians in Yugoslavia were paid higher salaries than the Yugoslavs wished.[1] Then, in the political field the Yugoslavs found that the Soviet Union had established its secret service in Yugoslavia. Yugoslavia's ambitions for a Balkan Federation would have established an area of 447,000 square miles with a population of 80,000,000 less responsive to Soviet influence; her ambitious Five Year Plan would have created an economic pattern orientated to Balkan needs rather than Soviet needs.

The open break with the Soviet Union commenced in March 1948, when the Soviet Union deferred a renewal of its trade agreement with Yugoslavia until December 1948. The Yugoslavs then limited the right of the Soviet trade representative in Yugoslavia to direct access to Yugoslav economic information without first obtaining top-level approval. In late March the Soviet Union withdrew all its military advisers and economic specialists from Yugoslavia, saying that they were surrounded by unfriendliness. An exchange of letters between the two Communist Parties now commenced. On 28 June 1948 the Cominform[2] expelled Yugoslavia from its ranks, accusing the CPY of having departed from Marxism, pursuing an unfriendly policy to the Soviet Union, neglecting the class struggle, submerging itself within the People's Front, practising bureaucracy, and so on. At the end of 1948 an economic blockade was imposed on Yugoslavia by her Communist neighbours with whom, up till this time, the major portion of her trade had been conducted.[3]

The 1948 expulsion isolated the Yugoslav Marxists from the Communist world, and massive disruption stemming from a total trade and investment blockade of Yugoslavia by the Soviet Union and East European states followed. As a direct consequence Yugoslavia had to do things: to embark on socio-economic experiments of its own and to expand trading relations with non-Communist countries (Tito, 1971, p. 158). These it proceeded to accomplish, and by 1953 was in a position to launch a Five Year Plan which was successful in economic terms.[4]

After the break with the Soviet Union, Yugoslavia faced economic crisis within and political pressure from abroad. Some foreign aid was obtained, first from the United States, which lifted its economic boycott[5] in February 1949 and gave a loan in September; later Britain and France also gave aid. But this would have been quite inadequate of itself. The government was thrown back on the need for mobilization of full popular support, and Yugoslavia was still sufficiently close in time to her revolution for revolutionary fervour and idealism to be a factor among both the leadership and the people. Had the Balkan Federation been formed in 1947 or had the break with Russia come later, say after the completion of the Five Year Plan, the chances are that the bureaucracy would have become so strong and the economy of the country sufficiently established that the self-management or workers' council experiment of 1950–3 either would have been very limited or would have taken some other form.

The first gesture towards greater popular participation was the June 1949 Law on People's Committees. These People's Committees had first appeared in 1941 during the uprising and had been organized in May 1946 on a country-wide and village scale. Now they were established on a regional scale and the state ministries surrendered many of their powers at the regional, county, and village level to the People's Committees. But the Executive Committees of the People's Committees were responsible both to those who elected them and to higher organs. This system of dual responsibility was a typically Soviet-Stalinist tradition.

A limited but significant development of freedom in the realm of ideas came next. Such a liberalization was a necessary precursor of changes which were to come. In a speech to the Slovene Academy of Sciences and Arts (December 1949), Kardelj criticized the tendency in the Soviet Union to deny the 'social limits of human perception in the conditions of socialism' and to make 'a fetish of the state' as 'the infallible interpreter of absolute truth'. He then stated:

We hold that our men of science must be free to create, for, without the struggle of opinions, and without scientific discussion, criticism, and the testing of theoretical postulates in practice, there can be neither progress in science nor a successful struggle against reactionary conceptions and dogmatism in science.

Kardelj made some qualifications in regard to the danger of going too far with 'destructive criticism', a typically Stalinist category. Yet, this was a beginning; and further advance was foreshadowed when the decision was made (also in December 1949) to establish workers' councils in the factories with advisory powers.

The advent of the 'second revolution' (as Yugoslav ideologists have since called it) was marked by the June 1950 law which extended the powers of workers' councils in the factories, with more influence given to administrative committees elected by the workers' committees. From 1951 managers were no longer to be appointed by the state but by a special elected committee governing all plants in one industry. 'State ownership', said Tito, 'is a lower form of social ownership and not the highest, as the rulers of the U.S.S.R. think' (Tito, 1971, pp. 89–90). State ownership was to be transformed into something better! These measures, he said, were not premature. If anything, they were a little late.[6]

It is late because our Party, until the announcement of the infamous Cominform Resolution, had too many illusions and was too uncritical on taking and replanting here everything that was being done in the Soviet Union, even those things which were not in harmony with our specific conditions, or in the spirit of the science of Marxism-Leninism. It was ready-made recipés that were wanted and that were imposed on us, or that we ourselves went after.

From this new step of legalizing workers' councils certain other changes followed of necessity. One was the ending of centralized planning on the Soviet model. The 1947 Five Year Plan was due to end in 1951; the economic blockade had already made its implementation difficult. It was extended to the end of 1952, but thereafter this method of planning was abandoned. From the beginning of 1952 an Annual Social Plan was introduced, permitting the government to guide the broad outlines of economic development, but giving the factory enterprises considerably more freedom. The price at which goods sold was determined by free competition. An essential difference with the Soviet system was that in Yugoslavia the product of the factory belonged to the factory collective, not the state.

In agriculture there was a parallel diminution of state authority and growth of freedom. The compulsory sale of foodstuffs to the state at fixed prices was suspended at the end of 1950, and the Machine Tractor Station system was abolished in this year. (In the Soviet Union the Machine Tractor Stations were an important agency for the domination of the collective farms by the state.) The tractors and other agricultural machinery were sold to the co-operatives. In 1952 the peasants were given the right to liquidate the work co-operatives if they wished to. The number of work co-operatives fell from 6,904 in December 1951 to 1,258 in December 1953. In May 1953 the maximum size of holdings in private possession was limited to 10 hectares (in less fertile areas 15 hectares) to prevent the rise of large-scale farmers.

An important by-product of the introduction of workers' self-management was administrative decentralization. The six republics making up the federation were given greater economic and political autonomy. Another political change was the renaming of the Yugoslav Communist Party in November 1952 when it became the 'League of Communists' (SKJ), while in February 1953 the People's Front was reorganized as the 'Socialist Alliance'.

The Modern Political System: Overview

From the viewpoint of 'delivering' a higher material living standard for a majority of citizens, the record of the Yugoslav regime since the 1950s, while erratic, remains impressive.

By 1974, as Tito remarked at the 10th Congress of the SKJ (Tito, 1974, pp. 24–9) the average life span had been extended from 48 years before the war to 67 years in 1970; 30,000 kilometres of roads and railway lines had been built and modernized; two million flats had been built so that every third family resided in an apartment constructed after 1954; more than 80 per cent of rural households had been connected to electricity.

According to later statistics, the percentage of households with a refrigerator rose from 25 per cent in 1968 to 70.4 per cent in 1978; those with radio from 66 per cent to 69.5 per cent; those with a television set from

28.1 per cent to 71.2 per cent; those with a washing machine from 10.9 per cent to 50.4 per cent, and those with a passenger car from 7.9 per cent to 29.2 per cent (*Statistical Pocketbook of Yugoslavia*, 1986, p. 57). At the more basic level of food consumption the per capita consumption of meat rose from 43.7 kilograms in 1974 to 56.5 kilograms in 1984; of milk from 86.9 litres in 1974 to 101.2 litres in 1984; while potatoes, the staple diet of low income groups, fell from 90.3 kilos per capita in 1974 to 55.4 kilos in 1984 (*Statistical Pocketbook of Yugoslavia*, 1986, p. 58).

Social consumption has also been catered for, with big improvement in adult education, science and technology, public health, social welfare (*Statistical Pocketbook of Yugoslavia*, 1986, pp. 118–19; 122–4; 138–41).

Overall the lot of the 'working man' as Tito liked to call him, had greatly improved over the last three decades. Yet serious problems arose in the course of achieving these results; uneven regional development; continuing and rising deficits on the international balance of payments; inflation (18 per cent annually 1976–80 and 40 to 60 per cent in the 1980s); unemployment (800,000 in the 1980s with 700,000 working abroad).

Phases of Development

The task of selecting cut-off dates for different phases of the socio-economic development of Yugoslavia since 1946 is complicated by the fact of cycles of production and investment (Čobelić & Stojanović, 1966; Horvart, 1971b). This has also been an issue in Eastern Europe (McFarlane, 1984a, pp. 189–91) and in China.[7] Such cycles differentiated the development into five cycles[8] up to the early 1970s (Horvart, 1971b, p. 92) and probably two since (1974–9 and 1980–5).

However, there are enough socio-political continuities occurring around the periods distinguished by economic cycles that to use cycles would only be a description of part of reality with concentration on economic policy/conditions. Important as this is, the political aspects, the legislative changes, probably make a wider perspective necessary. For the purpose of this book, I offer the following phases of development: (a) 1946–50: Stalinism; (b) 1950–6: beginnings of worker-council based system in industry and abandonment of collectivist agriculture; (c) 1957–61: successful Five Year Plan and period of liberalization following 5th Congress of Communists; (d) 1961–9: economic reforms up to Constitutional amendments issue; (e) 1969–74: crackdown on separatist tendencies, more say in economic matters for republics; (f) 1974–80: from 10th Congress of SKJ to Tito's death (May 1980); (g) 1980–4:

collective leadership under rules prepared during Tito's lifetime, onset of the economic crisis;[9] (h) 1984 to date: trend towards locus of power in republican government *and* serious deepening of the economic crisis, with cuts in real living standards.[10]

In the course of Parts II, III and IV of this book the main political, economic and legal developments in each of these periods will be critically reviewed.

Part II
Political Systems

4   The Party

The road travelled by the Party has been a tortuous one. It started as a small leftist group with most leaders training in Moscow and became the leader of a national revolutionary war. For ten years it was influenced to evolve into a structure similar to the CPSU as envisaged by Moscow. It suffered the blows of Stalin. It became a 'League' five years after that without giving up much power.

The various zig-zags that had become a familiar feature of Party life did not end with its transformation into a League. The 1958 Congress turned the Party into mainly an 'ideological force', even if a leading force. The economic experiments of the 1960s weakened the Party's hold on the economy. By the 1970s people were describing it as merely a debating club (Horvart, 1971a) while after Tito's death it experimented with new forms of inner-Party democracy, with recall and rotation of leaders, while struggling at the same time to preserve the basic unity of the nation at a time of turbulence and uncertainty.

How complete is the control of the League of Communists in Yugoslavia? What is the party's role? It is rather difficult to answer this question simply because the very nature of the Yugoslav communist movement has been changing. At the 6th Congress in November 1952 the name of the party was changed and a new course laid down. There was an attempt then to break down the Soviet type of 'monolithic' structure. The Communist Party then numbered 780,000 members. At the Congress of the People's front in February 1953 Kardelj tried to define the role of the League of Communists: 'The League of Communists does not profess to rule in place of the masses, but to inspire and educate the masses so that they themselves might be able to exercise their government, and manage their factories and all their other social bodies and organizations'.

In mid-1956 Kardelj wrote an article for the Moscow *Pravda* on 'The Leading Role of the League of Yugoslav Communists in the Building of Socialism' in which he argued that the communists had been persuaded to change their methods of work under conditions of decentralization. Initiative now rested on individual members of the League. Fractions were abolished.

The S.K.J. 'do not adopt preliminary concrete proposals for decisions independently and in principle communists are not obliged to be unanimous with regard to questions raised'. However, they were likely to be disciplined later if it is felt that their position had not been in accordance with socialist principles. Organization of the Party was not on a purely territorial basis (i.e., some branches were vocational or institutional).

The 7th Congress of the League of Communists provided another occasion for the public assessment of the role of the party. By this time (April 1958) party membership had fallen to 755,000. The League disclaimed in its programme any claim to a monopoly of political power. 'The League of Yugoslav Communists is also of the opinion that the proclamation of absolute monopoly by the Communist Party of political power as a universal and "perpetual" principle of the dictatorship of the proletariat and of socialist development is an untenable dogma'. They denied that the alternative under socialism were multi-party *or* one-party systems, saying that either alternative might be valid according to the particular situation of a socialist country. Political organization would not disappear under socialism; but in Yugoslavia, it was clear, the existence of 'direct democracy' and of two political organizations was considered enough.

The second political organization was the Socialist Alliance. Prior to the war, when the Communist Party was illegal, a 'People's Front' had been formed, and played a part in the popular demonstrations of 27 March 1941, which overthrew the government. It was not a coalition of parties, but a separate organization. At its 4th Congress, in February 1953, the name was changed to Socialist Alliance. Its membership in 1954 was 7,500,000. Of the twenty-six members of the Executive Committee of the Socialist Alliance in that year eleven were members of the Executive Committee of the League of Communists (the latter had an executive of fourteen).

The continued existence of the League of Communists and its monopoly of political power (despite the Socialist Alliance) was one obvious factor in limiting extension of political pluralism. Whatever may be said of the withering away of the state and the struggle against bureaucracy a great deal of the power of the political bureaucracy remained. Kardelj had argued in February 1953 that the formation of a multi-party system in Yugoslavia to replace the one-party system would be pointless and would even allow a strengthening of the old-style parliamentary system and of political bureaucracy. He looked forward to a withering away of all elements of political monopoly, gradually. But in the meantime, the Communist League remained and so did its political control.

An underlying problem was that some political centralization through a party was necessary if the economic decentralization was going to work. As an earlier commentator noted:

It can work, in short, if in the background there is a strong unitary party organisation, capable of stepping in and correcting the course of the economy if it threatens to get out of hand. This organisation exists, and the need for it explains the apparent contradiction between the tight political control which the communist machine still exerts at the centre and the looseness of the social and economic structure. [Norman MacKenzie, *New Statesman*, 14 June 1958]

There were inevitably narrower limits set to political and foreign policy discussion than to arguments about social or economic policy.

Another reason for the continuing strength of the Communist League was the personality of Tito (Auty, 1970, 252–88). It often happens that the prestige and affection attached to a great national leader gives him and the group he leads greater and more prolonged power than they might otherwise have. Yet, six crises at least faced the Party and the League and personality alone could not explain their outcome. We now turn to these.

Several splits of internal political crises have shaken the League of Communists: (a) the division over how to react to Stalin's pressure in 1948 and the expulsion of the Stalinist wing of the Yugoslav Party; (b) the removal of Milovan Djilas, the Vice-President, in 1954; (c) the removal from office of Alexander Ranković, Minister of State Security in June 1966; (d) the student revolt of June 1968; (e) the replacement of the whole leadership of the Croatian Communist Party in 1971–2 due to the upsurge in Croatian nationalism and the threat of secession from the Yugoslav federation that was widely canvassed in Zagreb during 1971;[1] (f) the death of Tito in 1980 and the political paralysis at the top that this caused; (g) severe quarrels between the Kosovo Serbs and Šiptars leading to splits in the Party over how to deal with it in 1981–7.

The 1948 Quarrel with the Cominform and the Expulsion of the Stalin Supporters

Relations between members of the Yugoslav left and Moscow had been difficult since the 1920s. In 1948 the two Parties parted company. These events have been outlined in Dedijer (1953, ch. 6), Auty (1970, ch. 16) and Djilas (1962, p. 175). Andrija Hebrang and Streten Žujović disagreed with taking a strong stand against the Russian moves when the Cominform attacked Tito in 1948. They, together with former chief of staff Arso

Jovanović, were removed and quite a few other people, many simply unable to alter unthinking loyalty to Moscow, were arrested. But Tito took the majority of the Party and the nation with him in rejecting Soviet and Cominform attacks during the period 1948–50. The idea of an independent road to socialism now became a reality.

The Case of Milovan Djilas

After the expulsion of Yugoslavia from the Cominform it became necessary for the Yugoslavs to account for this action and explain the attitude of the Soviet Union. Djilas, who ranked with Kardelj as the leading theorist in the Communist Party, examined the political issues involved in a sensational article 'The Soviet Union, Appearance and Reality' (*Borba*, 20 November 1950). He denounced the 'nationalistic obscurantism', the holding down of the satellite states, the exploitation of these countries, the 'grey and standardized' thought of the Soviet Union, the spy system, the cooked-up trials. He concluded that a new, entrenched system of state capitalism had developed there. This view was shared for a while by others, including Dedijer and Kardelj.

But while Kardelj later reverted to the position that the Soviet Union was merely a backward socialist state (a form of state capitalism) Djilas maintained his views, and, moreover, started to apply his analysis of the Soviet system to Yugoslavia. From September 1953 to January 1954 he wrote a number of articles in the party organ, *Borba*, on the basic problems of communist Yugoslavia (Djilas, 1959). In these he implicitly questioned the need of the Communists to monopolize political power, coming to the conclusion that the best way to prevent the development of a Soviet-type bureaucracy in Yugoslavia was to develop freedom of discussion and freedom of organization. In January 1954 he contributed an article to the magazine *Nova Misao* entitled 'Anatomy of a Moral' fiercely attacking the new ruling caste which, he argued, had now arisen in Yugoslavia (Djilas, 1959). The Central Committee of the LYC met and after two days of discussion reprimanded Djilas (18 January). Said Tito: 'I was the first . . . to speak of the withering of the state, of the withering of the League of Communists, but I did not say that this must happen within six months, a year or two, but that it was a long drawn out process' (Auty, 1970). The completely free discussion and freedom of organization advocated by Djilas would lead to a struggle for power, said Kardelj.

After his resignation from the Party in March 1954, Djilas retired to a

Belgrade suburb where he lived on a government pension. Vladimir Dedijer, another member of the Central Committee, continued contact with Djilas, although few others did so. In December 1954 both men gave interviews to foreign journalists calling for greater political freedom in Yugoslavia. Both were tried on the charge of invoking outside intervention in Yugoslav affairs, being given short sentences, which were suspended on their entering into bonds not to repeat this sort of offence.

In November 1956 Djilas published an article in the American magazine *New Leader* entitled 'The Storm in Eastern Europe', which *inter alia* denied any difference between Yugoslav 'national communism' and Soviet communism and looked forward to further political revolutions in Eastern Europe on the Hungarian model, which would bring political freedom. Djilas was then sentenced to three years imprisonment. His appeal against this was rejected by the Supreme Court of Serbia in January 1957.

Dedijer wrote 'An Open Letter to Tito', 22 November 1956 (published in the *New Leader*, 19 December 1956) asking Tito to defend the principle he had enunciated in the struggle against Stalinism, that the Yugoslav revolution would not devour its own children. Dedijer made a two months tour of northern and western Europe in the spring of 1957 giving a series of lectures in which he criticized the policy of the Soviet Union. His views were repudiated by the Yugoslav government, which subsequently refused him permission to leave Yugoslavia to take up a fellowship at Manchester University where he was to lecture on the partisan war in Yugoslavia (September 1957). Later he became an archivist of the national liberation war.

In August 1957 *The New Class* appeared in New York, written by Djilas between his first trial for propaganda against the state (January 1955) and his second trial on the same charge (December 1956). In October he was put on trial for the third time on a similar charge. In *The New Class* Djilas summed up and developed his previous ideas. The function of communist revolutions was to carry out the industrialization of backward countries. But they also throw up a new tyrannous class, the bureaucracy, which obtains power and privileges through collective ownership. At times, as in Yugoslavia after 1948, the new class may have to introduce reforms, but they do this merely to preserve their power. This power is exercised through the Communist party, which is bureaucratic and composed of wrangling cliques. Communism, he now believed, had many of the characteristics of state capitalism, but was really a new social system. Djilas was found guilty on 5 October and sentenced to seven years imprisonment in addition to the sentence he was already serving. The trial was held in camera.

Behind the Djilas affair was the growing contradiction (so dangerous to the party) between a certain degree of cultural freedom that had developed in Yugoslavia and a rather lesser degree of political freedom. This lesser degree of political freedom arose out of the poor economic position and the low standard of living. As Kardelj remarked in December 1956, 'it is impossible to pursue a very strained economic policy which demands great efforts of the whole people and to simultaneously ensure an uninterrupted advance of democracy in the social and political system'.

In the late 1960s Djilas took his views further with a polemic on Marxist philosophy in *The Unperfect Society*, despite being under a ban not to publish before 1972. However, Djilas did *not* see that the Party itself was changing— in composition and in policies—the technocrats, experts and professional men were already dominating Party bodies, Ministries and enterprises. Expertise and qualifications were replacing closeness to the leadership as the road to privilege. Instead, he lashed out at the Communist League's continuing monopoly of power and its 'ideological economy', ideas already present in *The New Class*: 'Party bureaucracy remains the bugbear of Yugoslavia. Until the Communist's monopoly of political power is broken, reforms—however well intended—will have no real value' (Djilas, 1969). Continuing his attack, and widening it, Djilas maintained that 'the present Yugoslav regime is not capable of surviving any major crisis'.

However, Djilas' advocacy of a Western-style of pluralist democracy did not attract wide support. He had become essentially a dissident, writing in Belgrade, but publishing abroad. While his works were significant contributions to the study of Marxist regimes, his earlier role of the 1950s, that of 'conscience of the Revolution' was gradually dissipated as the new men after Tito's death implemented enough controlled liberalism to keep the technocracy happy and they moved to develop the system of workers self-management along more businesslike lines, eroding the 'social relations' of production (from the viewpoint of syndicalism) but putting a brake on declining productivity in Yugoslav industry.

The Ranković Affair

In the summer of 1966 Tito parted company with one of his oldest colleagues, when Alexander Ranković was charged with obstructing Party policy (which was then encouraging a more liberal attitude to intellectuals and to Šiptar unrest in Kosovo, and more decentralization in the economy). Ranković was further accused of maintaining a parallel network of control down to commune and factory level manned by security police and their associates, and as well was accused of phone-tapping Party leaders. He was stripped of office but was not imprisoned or expelled from the Party.

At the heart of the Ranković affair was the issue of how to retain the authority of the League of Communists while at the same time meeting the demands of the public, intellectuals and many Party members for greater freedom, more democracy and less bureaucracy. Ranković had provided one answer: to strictly ration these 'gifts' that the Party might bestow, and to hang on to centralized mechanisms to protect what he saw to be the power base of the post-war Marxist regime. Tito, however, had mellowed and softened; he sensed that Ranković's Serbian-based political machine was antagonizing the Šiptars and Croats; and he needed the unity of public and Party in case of a renewed threat from the Soviet Union. For that reason he insisted on a controlled, but unmistakeable liberalism, and therefore Ranković had to go.

The Student Revolt, June 1968

On 2 June 1968 student demonstrations erupted in Belgrade. In part they were fanned by events in France, and by a general influence from the New Left groups, which were anti-capitalist but also opposed to the Communist bureaucracy of the East. In a 'self-management' society this protest was bound to take its own form (Perlman, 1973, p. 3). Those who occupied the Law Faculty and many of the staff expressed views that were democratic-socialist. Some students and staff (M. Marković, N. Pečuljic, L. Tadić) later published their ideas in the campus paper, *Student* and in the rebel journal *Praxis*. Others made intellectual links with the 'new Budapest school' and Czech dissidents.

The regime however, 'contained' the unrest by the technique of adopting the slogans raised by student dissidents for itself and promising to meet the students' demands (Perlman, 1973, p. 11). They relied, ultimately, however, on the same weakness of the student movement on which de Gaulle counted in Paris: the isolation of student protest from the interests and the organization of the workers (Perlman, 1973, p. 23). A number of student leaders were later quietly promoted into the bureaucracy of the University administrations.

The Croatian Revolt

Mrs Dabčević-Kucar, an economist, tried to restrain (on behalf of the Communist League of Croatia) the virulent nationalism which swept Croatian intellectual and political circles during 1970 and 1971. She failed to blunt the sharp edge of the upsurge and eventually was dismissed, along with most of her executive. The underlying cause of unrest was a feeling that Belgrade, dominated by Serbs, was taking too big a share of revenues and foreign exchange earnings accruing to the booming tourist industry along the Dalmatian coast. At this time, Hrvatska Matica, a traditional Croatian cultural organization, experienced a remarkable upsurge, while student groups sang patriotic Croatian songs in restaurants.

Tito was very, very, concerned at the time about a real danger of separate Croatian membership of the United Nations, one of the most serious consequences of the programme of the nationalists. This was the key reason for his harsh line of cracking down on Croatian nationalism generally and his strong action against the official communist leaders in Zagreb. More detail on the broader effects on Yugoslav politics of the Croatian Revolt are given in Chapter 8.

Party Problems after 1971

In all of the crises after the SKJ Congress of 1958 a background problem was that the Party *was* becoming less monolithic than before; even if it refused to commit *hari-kari*. It did practice 'rotation' of elected Communist delegates and leaders, it did 'recall' unworthy cadres and it did (especially after the new constitution of 1963) practise a separation of Party and state, breaking up the joint state–Party committees of control which were the hallmark of the East European system.[2]

Moves towards finding some sort of relevant role for Party bodies were, however, still around in 1971–2. A plan which succeeded for a short time (1974–9) restored the institution of a Central Committee for the SKJ, an institution abandoned back in 1963. It was to have 166 members, evenly divided among the republics, plus a dozen members representing the army. The Central Committee would elect a 34-member Presidium which in turn would elect an executive committee. This brought the internal structure closer to a body like the Chinese CP and reflected the concern that the 1971–2 events had wrought.

From the Seventh Congress in particular the League of Communists expressed a desire to be primarily an *ideological* force rather than an *instrument of power*, controlling a monopoly of decision making. The reason here was that the Party (or League) came to the conclusion that only in the constitutionalist movement could it find the economic dynamism and political stability that Yugoslav socialism needed to survive and to grow. Another vexing issue was the continuing 'fall-out' from the expulsion of the leadership of the Croatian Communist League in 1972. During the run-up to the SKJ Congress of 1974 a series of Party congresses were held in all republics. The Serbian Party Congress expelled Marko Nikežić and Latinka Perović who were, respectively, President and Secretary in 1971. They lost their party cards for opposing Tito's actions against Croat and Slovene leaders in the autumn of 1972. At the Slovenian Party Congress, President Franc Popit criticized bureaucratic-étatism, dogmatism, centralism and unitarianism saying that all of these phenomena would lead in the final analysis to the abandonment of 'the non-aligned position of socialist self-managing Yugoslavia', clearly a reference to the danger of the crackdown on Croatia and Slovenia leading to a closer alliance with the Soviet Union.

The Yugoslav Party leadership took serious stock of the state of Marxist ideology in their country at the Tenth Congress of the League of Communists held in Belgrade 29–30 May 1974.[3] Tito saw a positive trend of the 1960s when he noted that 'with its Marxist analysis of the role of the state, with its criticism of statism and bureaucracy, the League of Communists dispelled many a doubt and error in theoretical thought and steered the action of socialist forces towards cutting the roots of statism and the bureaucratisation of social relations' (Tito, 1974, p. 75). However, some ideological disarray was apparently persisting, for he noted:

Along with the results scored in developing and applying Marxist theory, there were also a number of weaknesses, breakthroughs of theoretical theses without a sufficiently clear and determined class orientation. In particular, serious stagnation occurred in the development of Marxist-oriented criticism. Current policy came to be cut off from theoretical knowledge and criteria, and a pragmatic attitude towards the tasks of socialist development was adopted. This spurred anti-socialist attempts to discard the revolutionary essence of Marxism from the social sciences. [Tito, 1974, p. 75]

The solution to 'ideological weaknesses' as suggested by Tito was a two-fold action: first, 'to study more closely the experiences of *other* workers', communist and liberation movements far more than we have done to date' and second 'to draw up a long-term program of ideological education in *all* spheres of social life' (Tito, 1974, pp. 75–9). Clearly this meant that the League of Communists had not been playing its 'leading educational role', which had, after all, been the chief function given to the League after the older Leninist-vanguard Party role had been abandoned at the Seventh Party Congress in 1958.

The Constitutional debates of 1961–3 and in 1974 prevented any trend towards total liquidation of the Communist League. While Tito was alive the Party persisted in its belief that social classes were ultimately more significant in social development than nationalities (Tito, 1974). After Tito's death this view was certainly modified but has been overtaken by the view that a monolithic party simply cannot, on its own, run a modern industrial state. It needed the intelligentsia and the unions to back Party initiatives and it needed some kind of unified market to bind the republics together by economic links. It has been discovered, since Tito's Constitutional amendments of 1974 have made their impact on politics and on economic management, that this cannot be done in the present system. Why?

In the first place, regionalism has developed to such an extent in the 1980s that the national market has splintered.[4] In the second place, the trade unions have become more and more irrelevant in the context of enterprises 'doing their own thing' and a general anarchy in relations between enterprises across republican borders.

In the third place, the intelligentsia has continued to be very critical of Party policy and of Party inaction in relation to corruption, regional étatism and events such as the Agro-Commerc affair.[5] This occasionally has spread to the official intelligentsia with the Serbian Academy of Sciences, in 1986, criticizing the failure of the Party to ensure the implementation of the long-term adjustment and stabilization program agreed to by Parliament in December 1985. For doing this, the Academy was severely rebuked by Party leaders and the celebration of its centenary was cancelled.[6]

Party relations with their own supporters have not been easy, as problems of foreign debt (now 40 per cent of Gross National Product) hyper-inflation, financial scandals, and inter-regional tensions have all come together to pose a socio-political crisis in the wake of the worsening economic situation. Displays of public dissatisfaction in two provinces, Bosnia and Croatia, have generally been met with heavy-handed measures. The Mikulić–Poždaric group in Bosnia not only 'rolled-over' all protests from those disrupted by the staging of the Winter Olympics but it has a record of 'cover-up' and of expelling those Party members raising doubts about the quality of leadership and the degree of *glasnost* in the running of the Bosnian economy.

In Croatia, a petition of citizens to protest against projected atomic power stations was accepted by the Parliament,[7] but generally petitions have been followed by police crackdowns ever since 1981.

If the problem in Bosnia was that it had become a semi-independent kingdom, the problem for the Serbian Party has been to prevent the old 'heartland' of Serbia (i.e. Kosovo) from obtaining either independent Republican status under the Constitution or an eventual union with Albania. With 1.5 million Albanians and 0.5 million Serbians living in the area, with the high birth rates among the Šiptars (Albanians) and clashes between Serbs and Šiptars, the Serbian Party finally split wide open in September 1987. A minority led by Dr Dragiša Pavlović, long-time member of the Praesidium of the Central Committee of the League of Communists of Serbia, Ivan Stojanović of the mass-media organ *Politika* and Radmila Kljajić (secretary of the Belgrade Party Committee) were expelled.[8] This was done at the insistence of Slobodan Milosević, and was a result of Party disagreement on how to deal with the Kosovo issue.[9]

The Serbian split, result of the Kosovo affair, was symptomatic of the rise of nationalism in Party circles. Dr Pavlović, who was expelled, was in favour of undermining Albanian unrest by developing the material base for modifying it. The majority faction, on the other hand, simply wanted to assert Serbian nationalism over Albanian nationalism and to use coercive administrative methods, which might not only exacerbate matters in Kosovo but could also discredit the Party with the population of Yugoslavia outside of Serbia.

Fragmentation of the Party along nationalistic lines will mean it will not be able to play the role of a unifying force in Yugoslav society, resolutely overcoming the centrifugal pressures leading to a Balkanization of the country.

Overview

In Chapter 3 the early development of the Party with its combination of diluted Marxism (to help popular frontism) and a mania for rapid industrial-ization, was sketched. In this chapter the Party handling of three crises—the student revolt; the Croatia–Slovenia disaffection of 1971–2 and reaction to the Kosovo explosions of 1981 and 1987—were used to draw the conclusion that it has been the fate of the SKJ to get caught between two stools. In order to decentralize the economy and allow enough democracy to quieten the intelligentsia, the self-managing workers' boards and the student movement, the Party has to withdraw from interfering in the management of the economy and from cultural and artistic tutelage. When, instead, it tries to take on a purely 'educational' role to promote socialism, the police or the judiciary or some 'Serbian unitarian groups' have taken advantage of the vacuum to insert their own administrative rule. The Party (as after the 1958 SKJ Congress, after the death of Tito and after the hyper-inflation of 1986) eventually rues its unwillingness to rule as politics explode and it reflects that it has failed to turn its 'educational function' into a new effective 'leadership' role. The result in the 1980s has been a political paralysis and the serious weakening of the two pillars of the former Titoist Party line: development of a federation through the growth of a national market and use of central controls where 'self-management' leads to abuse of power.

5   The Constitution

After an Act of 1 February 1945 issued by AVNOJ annulling all legislation in force between the World Wars, work began on a new Constitution which was proclaimed on 31 January 1946 along with the creation of the Federated People's Republic of Yugoslavia. Legal Status was conferred, under Article 6 of the Constitution, on the People's Committees that had been set up during the National Liberation War.

The original constitution endorsed the practice that had grown up in 1945 in which the 'unity of the people's power' was exercised through a hierarchy of councils and assemblies running from the local communes up to either the republican governments created by the Constitution or directly up to the federal government. The federated structure of the state and the public ownership of major means of production were other features; they were given real focus by the existence of a single party inserting itself (in joint Party–state Committees) to oversee all public affairs, and by the rapid proliferation of centralized economic planning agencies.

However, the original Constitution was overtaken by two events. First was the expulsion of Yugoslavia in 1948 from the Cominform, which began a process of rethinking about the political and economic structures that had been set up, as well as rethinking (Kidrić, 1950) about the lack of incentives and excessive reliance on administrative measures and penalties in the economic system as a whole. The second, partly stemming from the first,[1] was the decision to introduce a new system of workers' management, completed after major speeches in 1949–50 by Tito (Tito, 1971, pp. 78–90) and by growing experiments in workers' management already appearing in practice, stimulated by an Act of 27 June 1950.

If the 1950 Law on Workers' Control started a socialist experiment within the unfolding socio-economic system, the new Law on the Constitution of January 1953 may be regarded as ending the intense phase of this transformation. This Constitution contained a number of new features. Here we will only mention the main changes. The Federal People's Assembly was to consist of two houses, the Federal Council based on territorial electorates with universal, equal and direct suffrage, and the Council of Producers, representing specific economic organizations and working collectives. In this latter House, professional workers, individual peasants and private entrepreneurs were thus not represented. The administrative role of the state presumably was somewhat weakened in that there were now only five federal state secretariats—Foreign Affairs, Defence, Internal Affairs, National Economy, and State Administration. In the six republics the state secretariats were Home Affairs, Economy, Budget, and Administration. The republican governing organs were to be legally independent of the federal.

Under the Constitution of 1953 only five ministries were left to the federal government; three of these—Foreign Affairs, National Defence, and National Economy—were concerned to a greater or lesser degree with foreign affairs. Foreign affairs became the major field of preoccupation of the federal government. Moreover, it is a sphere in which the Federal Executive Council has the predominant role, rather than the National Assembly or the Ministry of Foreign Affairs itself.

The Federal Executive Council (FEC) was the executive organ of the National Assembly. The Ministers for Foreign Affairs and National Defence were appointed from among the members of the Federal Executive Council (the other three ministers were not members of this Council, though they were responsible to it). Because of the special representation of Foreign Affairs and National Defence on the FEC and because foreign policy was not one of the major powers of the National Assembly, the parliament had less influence on the formation of foreign policy than on internal policy.

The President, under the Constitution, represented state sovereignty at home as President of the Federal Executive Council and state sovereignty abroad. Tito was elected President for the second time on 29 January 1954.

Kardelj's peroration to his January 1953 speech in the Federal People's Assembly (Skupština) on the new constitution is worth citing in order to see the ideological influences at work.[2] At this time Kardelj was promulgating the view, later abandoned, that the system in the Soviet Union was one of state capitalism. He told the federal Skupština in a major constitutional review:

The political significance of all these efforts of ours is extraordinarily great, not only for our country, but also for international socialism in general. With our concrete experience—and not with political and ideological arguments alone—we are each day more convincingly proving not only that Soviet despotism is not a necessary form of socialism, but that it is not socialism at all. With such experience—and not only with theoretical arguments—we are removing the stigma from the socialist and communist name, a stigma which Stalin has placed upon it by using this name to mask and justify state capitalist despotism and imperialist hegemony. And finally, with our deeds we are proving step by step not only that democracy is not a monopoly of capitalism, but on the contrary that only under socialist conditions can democracy really become the common good of all the people.

We can say, then, that the events of the Tito–Stalin quarrel and the economic blockade of Yugoslavia overtook the Constitution within a few years. As well, the new experiments in workers' control and the expanding role that it was desired to give local government (communes) soon forced a debate on the need for a new Constitution. This was to develop into the Constitution of 1963 embodying new principles and a new role for the party in influencing Yugoslav civil society.

Work on the new institutional arrangements continued vigorously between 1953 and 1958, encouraged by analysis of weak points in the system of economic planning and especially in the rules relating to workers' councils' distribution of the net income of enterprises as they emerged during the Five Year Plan 1953–7. The main changes recommended were sanctioned by a new Constitutional draft tabled for discussion in 1961 and formally accepted by the Federal Assembly in 1963. Further Constitutional amendments were adopted in 1967, 1968, 1971 and 1974.

The 1963 Constitutional Changes

When the Yugoslav leaders announced in December 1960 that the country's top political and legal personalities were to begin work on the new constitution it was said that the draft would be completed within a year and that the new Yugoslav constitution would be formally approved by the Skupština (Federal Assembly) in the spring. However, the diversity of views and opinions caused hitches and delays; and the fact that the draft was not submitted for public dicussion until June suggests differences were severe, and the new constitution was finally submitted to the Skupština only in late September 1961 but not ratified until 1963.

Though the two-year long debate was conducted behind closed doors and any differences of view rarely reached a wider public, it seems that one of the controversial issues had been to define the relationship of the republics to the federation and to agree on the economic role of the republics. Ever since 1953, as the by-product of economic decentralization, Yugoslavia's six republics had been allowed a greater degree of autonomy, new national rivalries and frictions on issues such as investment allocations and compulsory contributions by Slovenia and Croatia to the lesser developed areas (especially Kosovo–Metohia) had been growing.

This problem seems to have provoked considerable controversy during constitutional debates. The economic experts favoured more central controls and less economic competence in the republics, while the representatives of national republican interests urged greater economic autonomy for the republics. It appears that a compromise was found whereby the republics retained their economic powers but absorbed clear commitments to the federation whence subsidies for the underdeveloped republics were drawn. The aim was to put to an end the annual friction and bickering whenever republics were called upon to pay their contributions into the federal fund that was earmarked for the development of the South.

These particular problems were frankly and openly discussed in 1963. Prominent Yugoslavs argued that the degree of economic autonomy extended to the republics was harmful, that in view of investment and other problems, the country should have one economy and one economic policy. Criticism of educational 'decentralization', which means that practically each one of the six republics pursued a different educational programme, was not prompted solely by practical reasoning but also because they perpetuated national divisions. This debate was resumed in 1974 and even more strongly in the 1980s.

Another novelty which the 1963 constitution introduced, reflecting the wish of the leadership to extend the affairs of the state to more people and rejuvenate the regime, was the *rotation principle* proposed both on lower as well as on higher levels of the executive. The principle that nobody will be eligible for re-election after two terms of four years became established, though an exception was permitted in the case of the President.

Something that might be called decentralization began to take place at the very top. The functions of the President of the republic and of the head of the executive council (i.e., the Government) were now to be separated. Until 1961 both functions—that of the head of state and of government—were formally in the hands of President Tito, though the day to day affairs of the executive council were left more and more to two vice-presidents, Kardelj and Ranković. By separating the two posts the new constitution in fact prepared the way for succession.

Although the political monopoly of the Communist Party was not at this stage affected, the new constitution enabled the process of political liberalization to continue, and 1960 in particular had clearly shown that decentralization was not being confined to economics and administration.

The main problem that persisted in the period after the 1963 constitution was that the greater degree of autonomy extended to the constituent republics allowed them to assert themselves and old rivalries, though in a different form, now began to emerge. In 1968 these antagonisms became so serious that a Constitutional amendment concerning levies on richer republics to finance the under developed regions, and access of republics to foreign exchange, became necessary.

The Constitutional Amendments of 1969-71

There were a number of features of these amendments. The first aimed to satisfy non-Serb aspirations and to head off Croatian separatist sentiment in particular. The amendment giving republics more say in the distribution of foreign exchange earnings (especially from tourism), in the operations of the national banking system and in decisions about levies struck to finance the underdeveloped areas were suggested by Macedonian party leader Krsta Crvenkovski. The confidence of the Party in the Constitution and the stability of the federation were again badly shaken, first when the Croats thought (in May) that the Serbs were going back on the main political and economic bargains struck in 1969 (*The Economist*, 1971) and later when Croat nationalism was at its peak in 1971. Serb paranoia increased with the singing by Croat students of anti-Serb songs, and the suspicion that the Croats were in touch with the Albanians for joint pressure on Serbia.

The Constitutional amendment made in 1971 (Articles 244 to 281) on 'relations within the federation' also came under criticism from economists and bankers (*The Economist*, 1971). They feared the national market would be broken up into seven regional-Republican ones, that the Constitutional amendments, by providing a formal obligation to harmonize the views of the Republics before major national decisions were taken, would slow down the processes of government and the planning of national development. Some tension was eased with the success of a large loan floated by the Serbian government to complete the Belgrade to Bar railway, for, the federal government having withdrawn as the main investor, it had been feared that republics other than Slovenia and Croatia might suffer.

Supporters of the Constitutional amendments were able to argue that the processes of government had, at any rate, stalled during periods of bitter inter-Republican rivalry over the source and expenditures of funds for republics and that with the federal government withdrawing subsidies and centralized investment funds, reckless capital investment and 'political factories' in the South and East, would now be curbed. As part of the 'deal' around the Constitutional amendments, the powers of the Belgrade-based Yugoslav Investment Bank, the Agricultural Bank and the Foreign Trade Bank were clipped. Commercial Banks, too, were pressed to direct more of their credit towards Croatia.

These tensions show clearly enough that the Yugoslav Marxist regime had politicized economic decisions in such a way that nationality and ethnic differences *were* exacerbated. The Constitution was trying to construct a synthesis between national diversity and the idea of socialist unity, trying to provide an ideology which would fit in with the Yugoslav Marxist regime's concept of contemporary political reality. However, because economic problems were at the centre of Yugoslavia's political strains the synthesis was at best a fragile one.

The second major aspect of the Constitutional amendments, especially Articles 237-3 dealing with defence, was that, along with the Defence Law of 1969, the unity of the army forces was re-established and people were forbidden to surrender in times of war. The principle of a 'territorial army' was re-established on a federal basis (Article 235), the military having been under pressure to decentralize to several 'republic-based' armies during the Croatian–Slovenian revolt of 1968–71. General Ljubičić (Ljubičić, 1974, p. 102) told the Tenth Congress of the League of Communists:

We have constantly endeavoured to preserve the unity of the army and the armed forces in their entirety, because inimical forces have constantly resorted to powerful propaganda in the endeavour to weaken our morale, to sow mistrust, to disrupt our fraternity and unity and thereby to debilitate the strength of our defences. At the same time the LCY in the Yugoslav People's Army, in all commands, has combated all attempts at penetration by various nationalist, liberalistic, separatist, centralist, bureaucratic and technocratic forces.

With this authoritative statement we can deduce that the armed forces were deeply concerned by events of 1968–71 (Ljubičić, 1974, p. 102) and the decision to dismiss the Croatian leaders was made with strong army support. The pay-off was the new Constitutional position given to the 'nationwide' army.

The third aspect of the Constitutional amendments was that there was a new stress on the delegation principle and the rights of groups of 'associated labour'. By mid-1974 Tito was proclaiming the crucial importance of the new 1974 Constitution of the Socialist Federal Republic of Yugoslavia and the attendant constitutions of the republics and provinces as 'clearly charting the roads for the further development and socialist self-management' (Tito, 1974, p. 37). He claimed that

the new Constitution has effected radical changes in the political system—the purpose of these changes is to assure the working class and the working people generally of their dominant position in exercising the functions of power and, in managing social affairs, to develop further the relations between the nation and nationalities of this country. Socialist self-management is exerting itself as *a specific form of dictatorship of the proletariat* . . . [Tito, 1974, p. 45]

Ultimately the set of Constitutional changes that opened the 1970s was 'the introduction of the principle of delegates into all spheres of social decision making' (Tito, 1974, pp. 45–6). Here Tito was referring to Articles 10–243, which set out the definitions and rights of 'self-managing' communities of interest and 'policy of labour and means of social reproduction' (*Constitution of the Socialist Federal Republic of Yugoslavia*, Part 2, Ch. 1). These laid down the law on property relations (Articles 70–84), regulated social planning (Articles 69–74) and the general framework of the socio-economic system. Later articles specified 'the status of working people in the socio-political system' (Articles 88–97); self-management in 'organizations of associated labour' (Articles 114–19); self-management agreements and social compacts (Articles 120–31) and the assembly system described by Articles 132–52 (*Constitution of the Socialist Federal Republic of Yugoslavia*, Part 2, Ch. 2).

From 1974 more and more was heard of 'assemblies of delegates from bodies of associated labour'; already 700,000 workers had been elected, as provided in the new Constitution (Articles 282–312), as delegates for a myriad of organizations of self-management. Workers' councils in factories and offices were supplemented by a delegates' system *from* such councils *to* assemblies at the commune, republican and federal level (Tito, 1974, p. 40). As well, the Constitution *codified* the new system of income distribution (Articles 26, 43, 72), in an attempt both to head off 'reactionary nationalism' (Kardelj, 1974, p. 96) and a way of giving a firm material foundation for the new rights of associated labour. As Kardelj (1974, p. 96) put it,

Our new Constitution . . . assures that the course of income distribution, against the background of integrationalist processes, will move by inverse logic to that which had been imposed on us by the technostructure's monopoly. This means that our new Constitution assures to the maximum possible extent that income based on greater labour productivity does not flow away from the workers, from the people, but rather towards them.

However, Kardelj's comments skated over the big outcry in 1969–71 against the Constitutional amendment which allowed firms complete control over income distribution and the fact that the technocracy fought back strongly by forming 'business committees' in which managerial and technical staff met to discuss tactics, prices and investment strategies without 'blue-collar' involvement.

The Presidency

Under Articles 333–45 of the Constitution, up to Tito's death, the presidency became more and more important. The national leader became the embodiment of state (and Party). The presidency therefore played an important contribution to legitimacy of the Yugoslav Marxist regime. (In the Soviet Union[4] and other Communist states[5] we later saw the same trend.) This need for legitimacy was particularly strong in Yugoslavia and Tito was made president of the League of Communists; 'with no limit on tenure of office' at the 10th Congress of that body[6] in May 1974, six years before his death.

After Tito's death, in accordance with a scheme provided by a series of previous laws amending the Constitution precisely to provide for a post-Tito situation, the Presidency was much reduced in functions to those of ceremonial, representational and chairmanship (Articles 313–45). It consists today of a nine-member collegial body, comprising representatives of each republic and autonomous region, plus the President of the League of Communists' own Presidency appointed *ex officio*. The office of president rotates annually, in a prescribed sequence among the six Republics and two autonomous regions.

Assemblies

The current Constitution establishes a system of indirect election to assemblies at each level of administrative government: commune, republic and federal (Articles 282–312). 'Delegations' are elected to these 'assemblies' from lists circulated by the SSRNJ. The electors are from three separate constituencies: members of work units (i.e., offices, factories); local communities and socio-political organizations. Their elected delegations do not take their seats immediately as 'parliamentarians' or assembly members, but, instead, elect delegates *from their own ranks* to assemblies: the federal (SFRJ) assembly and the 515 assemblies at commune level and eight at the level of republic and autonomous provinces. Details of the numbers involved as voters and as delegates are set out in the statistical publication (*Statistical Pocketbook of Yugoslavia*, 1986, pp. 17–28). The highest legislative body, the SFRJ assembly, is composed of a Federal Chamber and a sort of 'Senate' the Chamber of Republics and Provinces, both elected for a four-year term (Articles 282–97). The Federal Chamber (or 'lower house') comprises 220 delegates elected by commune assemblies from members of the delegation; the Chamber of Republics and Provinces has 88 delegates elected by and from the ranks of delegates to the republic and commune assemblies. As in all federal bodies, the principle of equal representation of all republics, and proportional representation of autonomous provinces, operates.

The SFRJ assembly elects the supreme executive body which is the Federal Executive Council, a Cabinet, whose President, proposed by the SFRJ Presidency is Yugoslavia's Prime Minister. Each republic and autonomous province has its own government apparatus and judiciary. The present holders of these offices are described in the Appendix to Chapter 6.

Courts

Under Article 230 of the Constitution only people with professional expertise and moral–political suitability are eligible for election as judges. Article 219 grants courts independence in the performance of these functions. There are Constitutional Courts, Regular Courts, Military Courts and Courts of Associated Labour at commune, district, republic (and autonomous province) levels as well as federal courts.

The Constitutional Court of Yugoslavia is established with eleven members; as well there are Constitutional Courts for republics with five to eleven members. Articles 375–96 of the Constitution stated the broad function to be protection of constitutionality and legality in society. More specifically, the Court's stipulated role is the interpretation of normative acts, as to whether they conform to all laws as well as to the Constitution; the determination of rights and freedoms of economic units which may be under some pressure from central organs of state administration; intervention where decisions affecting economic units cannot be challenged in other courts for some reason. As well, the Constitutional Court recommends legal changes necessary to protect the operation of 'social self-management', and citizens' freedom and rights as given by the Constitution. From time to time the Constitutional Court has advised the Federal Assembly on whether some aspects of the Constitution of Republics conflict with provisions of the Federal Constitution and whether proposed laws of the assembly on self-management might impinge on the Constitution.

Under Articles 375 and 384 the Federal Government has to obey some but not all the decisions of the Constitutional Court, but mainly it adopts new amendments within six months of a decision of the Constitutional Court; otherwise they may be invalid.

The Court's main business is to rule on procedures to be adopted if self-management rights are under threat: it decides, as well, the order in which cases will be held; it grants affected people and economic units rights of access to government information, interrogates experts and can call for data from government bodies to better inform itself.

The Federal Assembly elected under the 1963 Constitution chose and dismissed judges of the court. Tenure was for eight years and, every four years half the membership has to come up for re-election. Under the current Constitution (Article 381) judges can only be re-elected once.

Only one or two Constitutional legal cases can be discussed in this short chapter. In the period of experimentation (1960-4) both the Serbian and Slovenian Constitutional Courts heard cases about the proposed tax and income obligations to be levied on enterprises before the regulations went into law. As well, a number of communes attempted to take the financial resources of firms from them in an unfair way. In the case of the petroleum industry a series of cases were heard about the right of government to stop it from using monopoly power to increase prices.

Constitutional Guarantees

The Constitution of 1974 guaranteed citizens a number of rights including right to petition (Article 157); freedom of opinion (Article 166); freedom of the press, association and assembly (Article 167); freedom of movement and abode (Article 183); inviolability of the home (Article 184) and confidentiality of mail and other means of communication (Article 185). As well, Article 154 guaranteed citizens equality, before the law, stating that 'they should be equal in their rights and duties regardless of nationality, race, sex, language, religion, education and social status'. Such equality is not guaranteed it may be noted, regarding one's *opinions*, which can be upheld only under Article 166.

The Yugoslav Constitution, like that of the Soviet Union, has protection of the social system written in as one key restriction in the exercise of fundamental rights. The following rather vague formulation has allowed security authorities quite a lot of latitude to imprison: 'no one may use the freedoms and rights established by the present Constitution in order to disrupt the foundations of the socialist self-management democratic order established by the present Constitution' (Article 203). However, the statement that 'the freedom of rights guaranteed by the present Constitution shall enjoy judicial protection' (also in Article 203) perhaps provides some check on police action against dissidents.

While dissent is discussed in a later chapter it should be noted here that the 1974 Constitution gave the citizenry a specific right to draw up petitions. This had already been guaranteed in the 1945 Constitution (Article 45) and in 1974 it was laid down that 'in order to carry out self-management [people] must have the right to address themselves to representative bodies and other organs with petitions and suggestions, and they must get an answer.' (Article 34, para. 7).

This right has since been unevenly exercised and acted upon. In the case of Serbia, the use of petitions became more widespread in the 1980s. Three examples may be given. Some 800,000 Serbians living as the minority in troubled Kosovo signed a petition in 1986 asking the Belgrade government to be more active in their defence against 'machinations' of the 1.5 million Šiptars in the province. Earlier, in October 1985, 2,016 Serbians from the universities, schools and academies (including thirty-four members of the Serbian Academy of Arts and Sciences) addressed a similar petition with 1,500 of them appearing on Belgrade streets in April 1986 and support-demonstrators holding their own meeting in front of the office of the Central Committee of the League of Communists. Another series of petitions was organized by a 'Committee for the Defence of Artistic Freedom' to support leading figures harassed for speaking out, a case in point being the treatment of Zivotić, President of the Philosophy Society of Serbia.

In Kosovo and Croatia the situation developed very differently. Petitions from April 1981 and August 1987 from Šiptars asking for a higher status (that of a republic) for Kosovo brought on police intervention. In the case of the Serbian Kosovans no arrests were made and in Belgrade no demonstrators were harassed. The Šiptars suffered more than 3,000 arrests in the 1980s, while the journal *Komunist* of 7 February 1986 reported that eleven university professors and 511 students had been expelled from their schools in Kosovo.

In Croatia the major row over petitions occurred in the case of a projected atomic power plant in 1985. In 1986 a petition in support of retaining a bust of Dr. Šercer in Zagreb hospital was signed by sixty-three Croatian physicians. However, an earlier petition of 14 November 1986 asking for enactment of an amnesty law was vehemently criticized by the Croatian government. Two of the leaders, D. Paraga and E. Brajder, were allegedly maltreated by the SDS. The former received two years imprisonment and the latter died.

These differential responses partly reflect persons practising regional étatism having different views and partly the uncertainty of the authorities, including the security services, on how to handle petitions once they take on a highly political aspect.

New Constitutional Proposals, 1987

In January 1987, the Presidency of the federation decided to amend the Constitution and sent its suggestions to the Federal Chamber of the Assembly. The Presidency had proceeded under Article 399 of the Constitution in this matter. The main changes sought were (*Yugoslav Survey*, 1987, pp. 3–21):

(a) increased freedom of peasants to own more land;
(b) to 'affirm personal labour' by strengthening the socio-economic status of citizens working and investing in privately-owned small business;
(c) to relax legal restrictions on the setting up of 'new self-managing communities and enterprises';
(d) to relax controls on the *form* of management workers choose to adopt;
(e) to restrict the right of consumers to secure resources from economic organizations;
(f) to expand the force of federal over local law pending decisions of the Constitutional Court;
(g) to repeal the Constitutional right of provinces and republics to pass laws in domains regulated by federal law.

Some factors were said to have prompted the new proposals which were still being debated at the time of writing. First, there was a desire to put some limit on the ability of regional étatism to tie up the central government in the courts. Second, there was the urgent need to stimulate small, private business ventures and to give their vitality a legal protection. This has been prompted by such economic circumstances as a slump in the overall investment rate of the economy in the 1980s and a sharp fall in the level of foreign exchange being put into private bank giro accounts by returning guest workers. Small enterprise was seen as a quick way to expand investments and jobs and as a method of encouraging the returning guestworkers to use any 'nest-egg' by investing in Yugoslavia rather than investing abroad or dissipating the funds earned from working overseas in consumption.

Conclusion

A separate chapter on the Constitution was made necessary by the fact of numerous changes and amendments—certainly more frequently than is usual in Communist states. It has been the aim of this chapter to sketch some of the reasons for the Marxist regime feeling obliged to continually modify the Yugoslav Constitution.

It should be borne in mind that the Yugoslav Constitution does more than codify procedures, set out the balance of power and regulate the rights and duties of parts of a federation. It is also a highly political and ideological document. The whole philosophical basis of 'self-managing socialism' as well as other aspects of Titoism is spelt out,[7] and in the Articles themselves is present—the basis of the concrete powers and rights of individuals, enterprises and political groups. In a way unusual in the Communist states (with the exception of the Chinese Constitution of the 'Gang of Four') such political issues as the role of the state, proletarian internationalism, the character of social property and anti-bureaucratic sentiments are fully on display.[8]

In the new socialist Yugoslavia the formal structure of government was, in the early years, close to that of the Soviet Union, modified for the fact that Yugoslavia was a real working federation of republics and had a Communist Party which was trying to balance its loyalty to the Soviet Union and the strong pressures thrown up by its own revolutionary experience and involvement of different classes and nationalities in a mass liberation struggle.

A feature of the government structure up to 1950 was that at each level, state–Party joint committees controlled political, social and economic affairs. The same personalities were at the apex of power simultaneously in government structure and Party structure. A concentration of political power was the order of the day.

The 1948 Cominform attack on the Yugoslav leaders engineered by Stalin and Mao shook the government structure and changes were quickly made. As a start, KGB representatives in all ministries (especially Trade and Internal Affairs) were removed. Joint-stock companies were closed. The annual plan was scrapped.

A process of debate then began about how the government structure could be made to reflect changes elsewhere in society. It was found difficult to separate politics from economics or from other new proposals concerning social structure. One aspect led on to the other. Forms of economic organization conditioned forms of social organization and political institutions. The commune, for instance, was both the basic social–economic and the administrative unit.

As a result, Yugoslav leaders adopted Lenin's position that Marxist theory offered only a general guide to the development of socialism, the exact path to be taken by socialists and the structure of government would vary according to the different conditions in each country.

Some of the basic presuppositions of the new Yugoslav approach to a social theory that would guide the process of government were: that political rights are dependent on economic rights; the importance of control from below; the importance of the 'withering away of the state'; that democratic socialism means federalism and decentralization.[1] Kardelj illustrated the link between economic and political growth and the need for 'development from below' at this early stage of post-war government in his speech of

7 December 1956 in the People's Assembly. Pointing to the need for sustained economic-advance, Kardelj stated that one cannot speak of a full creative momentum of the Workers' Councils if their material base has been reduced to a minimum:

The political system of socialism must be built up in such a way that the working class and other working people have a direct influence on it, and not only through some ruling party which is susceptible to bureaucratization. New political forms can normally keep emerging and developing solely under conditions when the progressive aspirations of the working masses . . . are growing parallel with the development of the material base of socialism . . . This process is not, nor must it, depend exclusively on conscious action from the top leadership. On the contrary, the political mechanism of socialist society should grow organically from those fundamental social-economic relationships which arise in production on the basis of social ownership of the means of production. In the socialist system man must not become the slave of the prevailing state apparatus under the pretext of some higher interest.

In subsequent years the SKJ in its attitude to government structures attempted, albeit fitfully, to apply some of Kardelj's political positions.

Assemblies

The Constitutional law of January 1953 provided for two Houses of the Federal People's Assembly, the Federal Council elected in the traditional fashion from territorial electorates by universal, equal and direct suffrage, and the Council of Producers, which represented specific economic organizations and working collectives. Professional workers (employees, administrators, bureaucrats, the intelligentsia), individual peasants, and private entrepreneurs were thus not represented in the Council of Producers. As Kardelj pointed out in his address on the Constitutional Law, it followed that 'a worker who is employed in a state agency, let us say an electrician employed in the Assembly, will not vote for the election of members of these Councils (of Producers), but the typist employed in a factory will vote'.

Representation in the Council of Producers as between manufacturing industries, commerce, etc., on the one hand, and agriculture on the other (secondary industry and primary industry), was to be based on the proportionate contribution of each group to the 'Gross National Product'. This aimed to give an effective majority to the industrial workers, even though they were a minority of the population.[2]

Another feature after 1954 was a tendency towards the whittling down of the state apparatus, seen particularly in the abolition of some dozens of ministries at both the federal and state level. Only five federal state secretariats were provided for—Foreign Relations, Defence, Internal Affairs, National Economy, and the less significant one of State Administration. In the six republics the state secretariats were Home Affairs, Economy, Budget, and Administration. The republican governing organs were independent of the federal.

The executive organ was the Federal Executive Council (of thirty to forty-five members), elected by the Federal People's Assembly. Only the heads of the Secretariats of Foreign Affairs and Defence were members of the Federal Executive Council, though the heads of the other three Secretariats were responsible to the Federal Executive Council. This suggests that there was an attempt to arrange more direct control over the Foreign Affairs and Defence Secretariats than over the other three, though in practice Tito's personality was the main operational factor in the work of these secretariats. There was a Republican Executive Council, similar in nature, in each republic.

The Federal Budget, the preserve of the Belgrade Federal Assembly, dealt only with federal matters. Economic independence of the other units of government required this. 'Our country', said Kardelj in his speech on 7 December 1956, 'would be a "federation" in that new sense, as a system founded on social self-government, even if it were not multinational'.

The Federal People's Assembly also dealt with such matters as amendments to the constitution, approval of the annual Economic Plan, approval of the budget, federal financial legislation, and so on. Under the new system the Federal Assembly had more work to do, for decisions were now based on governmental legislation and taken much less through administrative regulations or Party decisions than in the past. This was the key feature that distinguished the Yugoslav system from that of the Soviet Union during 1952–65 and at times it worked in the direction of loosening the influence of federal bodies.[3] While there was some discussion in parliamentary committees, real debate in parliament turned out to be rather rare before 1963: the basic centre of power was still in the Federal Executive Council; and within the Federal Executive Council the influence of the Communist Party was predominant. This remained the case until the decades after 1960.

This system changed in the 1960s and 1970s in a number of ways already sketched in Chapter 5. One different feature was the attempt to divide the Federal Assembly into a number of sub-chambers, such as the Chamber of the Economy, the Chamber of Foreign Affairs. These increasingly played the role, after 1963, of what in the West would be called Parliamentary Standing Committees. Many vigorous debates took place in them, some being televised, and a more 'parliamentary' flavour was given to Communist political deliberations. However, as with the Western assemblies, the locus of decision-making power concerning major policies probably remained in the Federal Chamber as a whole and in the government apparatus. The specialist chambers amended detail and blocked the occasional bill in a welcome change from the usual East European practice; however, only after Tito's death was there a growth in real power of such specialist chambers, or of the republics' chambers and cabinets. Essentially, the structure of government as it emerged through constitutional changes in the 1960s and 1970s and remains today is as follows: the SFRJ assembly is elected for a four-year term and comprises (a) a federal chamber, made up of 220 delegates elected by communal assemblies through members of delegations in turn elected from the work-places, communes and socio-political organizations like the SSRNJ and (b) a Chamber of Republics and Provinces comprising eighty-eight delegates elected by, and from, the ranks of delegates of the republic and two provincial assemblies (Kosovo and Vojvodina).

The Cabinet or Federal Executive Council is elected from the SFRJ assembly. The President of this becomes Prime Minister. The structure is imitated at the level of each republic and autonomous province with 'delegations' from communes and work-places electing assemblies, which appoint republican ministers and government leaders. Each republic and province also has its own governmental apparatus and judiciary.

Role of Communes

The idea of a local government dimension embodied in the communes, as organizations of importance in social affairs, is important in official Yugoslav thinking, and has been from the beginning of the regime. Over time, the notion that there is a coherent 'whole' of government represented by three tiers (government, socio-political organizations, self-managing economic units), has given a special importance to communes which are under the influence of all three tiers.

Perhaps this is best explained chronologically. The first ideas about using the communes as a local 'cell' of government came out of the experiences of People's Liberation Committees during the anti-Fascist war. Building partly on the *opshtina* or traditional village assembly the notion of local communities as something integral to the whole political system took hold.

Next came the period of Stalinism and crash industrialization (1946–50), which greatly modified local government powers in the face of centralized economic planning, and the autonomy that had developed during the Second World War was cut back. Nevertheless *some* formal or machinery aspects of local democracy were applied: workers' meetings were encouraged to send 'inputs' to local government, associations of tenants were a licensed pressure group influencing the Socialist Alliance, etc.

With the coming of formal self-management statutes for factories and offices in 1950, the use of the commune as a basic unit of socialist government was revived. Studies were made of past experience, and, ideologically, of the writings of Marx, Engels and Lenin on the Paris Commune of 1870–1 as well as some workers' control measures of the early Soviets in the Lenin regime. As a result, the 1953–4 Constitutional amendments declaring self-management rights in most work organizations necessitated a totally new legal structure for communes. In 1955 a New Law on Local Communities came into operation to affirm two things: (a) the introduction of a bicameral system in communes, with provisions for both a popularly-elected assembly and a council of producers, made up from delegates from factories and offices in the area of local government (M. Popović, 1961; Đuričić, 1966) and (b) a reduction in the number of communes from 4,000 to 600 to overcome the problem that they had proved to be too small for effective socio-economic administration.[4] It was decided each commune would have a minimum number of industrial units and urban settlements as this would strengthen their economic and financial autonomy.

The communes were now made up of two bodies; (a) a council of producers in which a majority of members had to be manual workers and (b) a 'commune council' which included non-workers. There was a similar division for Republican Committees (the Communal system at the level of local State Government). The functions of the local communes (or 'People's Committees') became those of local government, promoting the economic development of local areas and the welfare of citizens of those areas. Thus workers' councils in the areas managed by the commune consulted with it on the building of workers' flats and amenities from their retained profits. Further, they had to make a contribution to the budget of the local commune. Sitting together, the commune and the workers' council were also responsible for the selection and dismissal of directors of factories and other economic enterprises.

The link between commune and economic enterprises arose because the distribution of net income between wages and funds for amenities is a *social* function. Thus the Workers' Councils submitted statements of accounts and an analysis of the calculation of net income to the Council of Producers of the

Communal 'People's Committee'. The commune had the right to fix a supplementary contribution from firms out of their 'personal income fund', but not exceeding 10 per cent of that personal income.

The members of the People's Committees were, from the start, liable to recall by a one-third vote at a meeting of voters of such a member's electoral unit, while elected members had to present periodical reports on their work to such voters' meetings. In Yugoslavia the 'meeting of voters' had a long tradition and it appeared to represent at least some check on the People's Committees. Usually the People's Committee submitted the more important proposals—changes in fares, rents, rates—to such voter's meetings. As a result of these changes the Commune became self-government in the wider sense of an organ of decentralized power; it was still restricted by the fact of centralized economic plans at both Republican and federal level, although popular participation by 1957 had extended to tens of thousands (Kovačević, 1958). These possibilities of control from above were increasingly lifted after 1963 when self-management principles were extended from enterprises to other social organizations.

With this change made under 1963 Constitutional amendments, the debate as to whether to modify a centralized system or strike out for decentralized decision-making structures ended. The 8th Congress of the SKJ in 1964 also transferred many of its own functions from Party to self-governing organizations reducing its influence to a role of 'education' and 'promotion of the socialist essence' and eschewing direct interference—an idea already raised at the 7th Congress of League of Communists of Yugoslavia in 1958. In the new atmosphere communal assemblies were given a more important place, more taxation rights over firms in local areas and more rights of appeal against interference from 'higher' organs.

Judicial System

In the last chapter the role of federal and republican Constitutional Courts was described. Administrative justice is also carried out by regular courts, military courts and Courts of Associated Labour. The latter hear matters related to self-management and, as with all courts, are organized in an ascending hierarchy at commune, district, republic and federal level. There is a series of Secretariats of Justice structured similarly to Ministries of Justice in other countries, at both republic, province and federal level.

In the case of criminal law, there has been, since 1977, a separate criminal code for each republic and province. There is also a federal code, the

Criminal Code of the SFRJ. In Chapter 15 of this Criminal Code it is laid down that political offences are to be first tried at district court level and then, on appeal, at Republic Supreme Court level. Provision exists for some further appeals to the Federal Court.

The enforcement of law is carried out by two main layers of government.

(a) The Public Prosecutor (similar to the procurator's office in Eastern Europe). The most important of these is the federal Public Prosecutor. Elected by the SFRJ assembly, he can give directives to public prosecutors in Republics and provinces, themselves appointed and terminated by corresponding assemblies;

(b) The militia and the SDS (State Security System), both under the control of the Secretariat of Internal Affairs. SDS is popularly referred to as UDB-a, because of its former name, 'Uprava državane bezbednosti', Department of State Security. (Some instances of the activities of SDS and of political interference in the administration of justice are set out in Chapter 8 below.)

Party Interference with the State Apparatus

The key to East European states of the orthodox kind has been (a) the *de facto* monopoly of power of the Party; (b) leading personalities of the Party doubling as Cabinet Ministers and leading figures of government; (c) interpenetration of government and Party in the administration of social and economic affairs, largely through Party–state joint committees at all levels; and (d) Party dominance of organs controlling military matters and raw materials supplies.

In Yugoslavia, apart from the special position of Tito between 1974 and 1980 described earlier, and some occasional interference with Courts, these features have been severely modified as part of the system of 'self-management socialism'. As a result, the leading personalities in state and Party bodies today are *not* the same people because of the 'rotation' principle enshrined in the Constitution and practised since 1963 and especially since Tito's death.[5]

The 'personality cult' is not the problem it has been in Romania, the Soviet Union or even Hungary. Even Tito was not a Stalin although he gradually allowed a 'cult of personality' to develop after December 1953 (Djilas, 1972, pp. 21–2). The common East European practices of *nomenklatura* (for cadre jobs a list of politically privileged people) and 'democratic centralism' are also rather inoperative. Some ideological lip-service is paid to democratic centralism, but less so since Tito departed and with recognition that there is to be modification in practice especially at the federal level of Party and state. Instead, more reliance is being put on getting the 'faceless' collectives to work largely through the rapid rotation of Party and state 'tops' (Rusinow, 1984, p. 3).

From time to time (as shown in Chapter 8) heavy-handed treatment of political dissenters re-appears; this misleads some observers into assuming Yugoslavia is no different to Eastern Europe. The undeniable presence of a military, still organized federally and with a strong Montenegrin-Serbian element in the leadership of the armed forces and of the political police should not, however, cause us to lose sight of the fact that political institutions are more numerous, more pluralist and more flexible than is the case in other East European states. It is, of course, true that some old habits in style of work die hard. Because self-management and workers' control have not solved the problems of regional imbalance (McFarlane, 1971) or equitable income distribution (Berković, 1969; Wachtel, 1973; McFarlane, 1985) the Party is always under some temptation to go beyond its 'educational-ideological role' as laid down at the 8th and 10th Congresses of the SKJ, and to resort to direct measures of fiscal and monetary policy. This is especially so with provincial Party machines.

This serves to remind us that the major political problem in Yugoslav government is to carry out the careful balancing act needed to achieve two things in the interests of stability: a federal government working with politically ambitious and more autarchical constituent republics and the need to force the technocracy and the Party to abandon not only its economic and political privileges but also its ideological monopoly without causing a great lessening in positive public responses towards 'self-management socialism'.

After Tito's death in May 1980 the collective system came into operation, and the 'chair' (or, more formally, the Presidency of the Federal Executive Committee), was taken by Mrs Milka Planinc. Following the failure of the economy during 1980-4 she was replaced by a Bosnian Communist leader Branko Mikulić who had shown some initiative in fund raising and organization around the Sarajevo Winter Olympics in 1984. He surprised by appointing a set of new ministers recruited from the academic and 'official' economists outside the government as well as practical people from the world of industrial management. However, as shown below in Chapter 12, their success in raising economic performance was extremely limited.

Non-Government Political Bodies

The Socialist Alliance of the Working People is a traditional Communist 'United Front' body. Its 15 million strong membership shows its 'umbrella' role, for only a handful take an active part in its deliberations, which are, in any case, of the 'ventilation of grievances' type. The Alliance is the forum in which the government at each level (federal, republic and commune) 'sells' its policies and attempts to mobilize support. In times of national tension (e.g. 1971 in Croatia; 1987 in Kosovo) it played a useful role in this regard and helped to get some of the more passive citizen-socialists to increase their activity. Traditional overlap in leadership of the Alliance and the League of Communists (e.g., Kardelj for many years doubled in this role) probably prevented the Alliance from playing an effective role in inspiring trust and devotion to the socialist cause.

As an insurance policy against the Socialist Alliance becoming irrelevant, people who join a group, whether a cultural association or a workers' association, automatically become a member of the Alliance. As well, all social mass organizations (youth, women, etc.) collectively belong to the Alliance. Organizations not belonging to the Alliance have to pay taxes and leave their assets to it upon bankruptcy or on ceasing to function.

The Confederation of Trade Unions

The role of the trade unions *vis-à-vis* commune government, factory management and the workers' councils has never been totally clear and has changed with the various alterations made to the economic system: the 1952 Workers' Councils legislation; the 1965 Economic Reform; the 1974 Constitutional changes; the 1980s austerity measures.

After 1952 workers' wages were divided by certain formulae for distribution of enterprise income. The role of the unions was only to ensure that the legal minimum wages were paid and to carry out some educational–cultural activities. During debates on the 1965 Reform the unions played a very vigorous role as they strove to make sure that increased scope for the market did not widen existing inequalities or lead to a neglect of collectivist consumption in the rush of that time to accelerate 'productive' investment. With the 1974 Constitutional changes, the union movement was splintered and seriously weakened, with each republican government now dealing only with a union movement within its borders.

The failure of the unions after 1974 to bargain with government over reforms and packages of economic policies *on behalf of the working class as a whole* was underlined by the way it stood helplessly by when wildcat strikes were staged in Split and other cities in February 1987. 'Democracy in one factory' had led to debilitation of the trade-union bodies as a political force.

The Military and Civil-Military Relations

Civil-military relations in Yugoslavia have been described as 'a function of insufficient political institutionalisation of the YCP', due to 'the rise of potential political competitors in the form of self-managing organs' which 'has seriously undermined the coherence of the SKJ' (Remington, 1978, p. 251). This process can also be traced to the nature of Party control during the partisan war—it had to be diluted, as a 'united front' was involved; much of the Army had to be organized on regional lines due to the terrain and the location of the German forces. The new military hierarchy established after 1945 did not wholly obliterate these experiences. After 1953 the League withdrew from China-style political watchdog functions within the army. The rise of Republican party organizations to government in 1968–70 led to some demand for national (ethnic) regional armies. This Tito blocked, especially after the Croatian Party result of 1971, but the lack of coherence in Party affairs since Tito has spawned fears of demands for territorial/ Republican armies being revived.

The military is the province of the federal central government, which finances it from the federal turnover tax. While relations between government and individual military men have been strained at times (notably at the time that Tito's wife, Jovanka, left the political stage) the present defence minister, Admiral of the Fleet Mamuk, has presided over a cooperative spirit. Fears of Kosovo 'defecting' to Albania or any future *formal* splintering of the federation could lead to a more interventionist role, for the Army in particular.

Government in the Turbulent 1980s

The eight years after Tito saw an early paralysis followed by confusion, as far as government ranks were concerned. This has already been explained. However, the rush of financial/commercial scandals involving a web of issues

from the issuing of uncashable promissory notes to foreign exchange rorting
... and pressure for more government subsidies also draws attention to
something that has been a theme of the book. This is that given the
underlying socialist and state-led economic system *and* given that the
Yugoslav superstructure changes quickly with the economic base, étatism
under post-Tito conditions has become regional étatism. The local 'political'
sphere, local political mafias in Party and government, have become
enmeshed in the behaviour of economic units. The locus of action has shifted
to the Republics.

A few words then, are needed on the views of non-Serbian areas about the
state of the Federal fiscal system and the political economy of the crisis. There
are those who, in 1987, still see the main issue to be anti-Serbian feeling in
general (where Serbian academics and politicians are seen to be dominating
the policy of the federal (Belgrade) banks and governing agents) and, in
particular, being forced to pour funds into the rathole of uneconomic
industrialization of Kosovo–Metohia. This certainly was the key complaint
during the 1964–5 reform debates and in 1970–1. However, the situation is
very different now as the complex provisions of the 1974 Constitutional
amendments have worked their way through the system. The Kosovo
industrial development is *not* now financed mainly by imposts on wealthier
republics. Instead, a federal value-added tax on consumer goods and services
is used for this purpose. Republics now raise their own taxes and loans and
have full power to retain and use all foreign exchange earnings accruing to
economic units in their territories. So the older complaints have been
superseded by the strong trend to regional autarky and étatism in the 1980s.
What then have been the Croatian and Slovenian views about the fiscal crisis
of the state?

The Croatian View

While Croatian politicians and economists in the 1960s were very strong
supporters of a full-fledged market economy, many things changed after the
1971 events and the 1974 Constitutional reforms strengthening (at least on
paper) the role of the republic and communes. Croatian political scientists
however, still complain that

(a) resources of the Federation continue to be 'wasted' on war pensions, army
and non-effective investment in Kosovo;
(b) the federation (i.e. Serbian-influenced Belgrade institutions) operates as a
system of interest-groups in a struggle with the regional interest groups.

While 'socialist pluralism' is strongly defended by Croatians (Bibić, 1986, p. 15), as is the need to broaden civil society as against the state, a restructuring of both spheres is demanded. What sort?

First, that there must be a centre in the federation that can implement decisions agreed to by all the republics and provinces, although each region's rights must be protected. The problem seen here is that of 'traditional mentality' (Balkan) or 'subjective deformations and deviations' in the functioning of the system (Šibek, 1986, p. 107). Regional/local political *mafiosos* have become too strong.

Second, there must be new institutional channels for 'functional' interest-based linkages (Stanovčić, 1986, p. 54). This appears to involve a view that political parties should be revived as a means of institutionalizing political conflict.

The idea of the Croats is to avoid the full market socialism preached by the Serbs by retaining their territorial principle but to put some order into the federal system as a whole.

As part of self-criticism, many leading Croats feel that their own communes and Parliaments have been too preoccupied in discussing an agenda set for them by bureaucrats and too little with the concerns of their constituents of the industrial branches. According to some studies of the behaviour of these bodies, 25 per cent of items are spent on finance and 75 per cent on problems of the commune as such: 'The interests of the delegational base do not figure on the list of the assemblies' priorities *as is required by the Constitutional concept.*' (I. Grdšić, 1986, p. 120).

It remains true, however, that the Croats have less enthusiasm for the 'national market *plus* planning solutions' to Yugoslavia's economic problems that are found in the writings of Serbian academics and politicians. They hope for good decisions to come out of a combination of regionalism and full-blooded application of profitability and productivity criteria in the selection of investment projects. Here the idea is to avoid any haemorrhage of the funds of the country to Kosovo development involved in Serb attempts to placate Šiptar discontent and nationalism there.

The Slovenian View

The Slovenian view on how the federation has been working is slightly different and has changed in the 1980s. In 1982 there had been some eight years to see how the 1974 Constitutional Amendments, which set up new ways of federal budgeting, had worked out. A joint fund for development work had been separated out from the federal budget financing mechanism and was supposed to be financed from 'self-managing interest communities' (communes and republics).

However, the available data (Tiśma, T. 1986) demonstrated that the demands of the federal budget on the 1980s financial affairs of republics increased. This happened because of balance of payments' problems and inefficient financing of non-economic investments (schools, hospitals, etc) and the social services expenditure explosion was largely to blame.

In 1987 the Slovenian view was that while they do have enough foreign exhange earnings and links with Austria and Germany to develop their economy this is only viable if foreign reserves are used rationally, inflation is kept within reasonable bounds and if the Kosovo problem does not lead to the reintroduction of special levies on Slovenia to fund development there.

Slovenian economists are still prone to argue that the authorities have been over-inflating the economy by loose monetary policy, that foreign exchange earnings could be directed more rationally in Belgrade and that the banking system needs to retain its decentralized character. They fear any tightening of monetary policy could be accompanied by a return to the dominance of 'Serbian banks' which they found irksome in the 1960s. There are even some who believe that such a mess has been created it will take years for the Yugoslav economy as a whole to recover.

Serbia, Bosnia and Macedonia

The Serbians reply to the North is that no one is any longer blocking Slovene-Austrian and Croat-Lombardy economic exchange or cultural exchange. In fact, for most Serbian economists the two brotherly republics of the North have virtually broken away from the national Yugoslav market already. The main issue facing the Serbs is what to do about the Kosovo problem in the short term and the long term. The split in the Serbian party between the S. Milusović wing seeking a harsh crackdown on rebellions of Šiptars and the Dr Pavlović faction seeking step-by-step solutions became bitter and was forced into the open during 1987. At the time of writing, Milusović, with the support of the majority of Serbian Communists (though not of the President of Serbia, Petar Stambolić), was conducting a crackdown on 'unruly elements, separatists and rapists' inside Kosovo through use of Serbian paramilitary and police units.

As far as Bosnia is concerned, it will stick to the Serbian line. This is partly a traditional axis, strengthened by the need for the Bosnian SKJ to have allies at a time of its disgrace in the wake of the exposure of a political hand in the excesses and financial collapse of the huge conglomerate and agri-business 'Agro-Commerc' (discussed in Chapter 13 below). Moreover, the resignation of the Bosnian politician Poždarec from his post as Vice-President of Yugoslavia, and the dismissal in October 1987 of the Bosnian state prosecutor and his deputy, while politically damaging, reminds us that Prime Minister Mikulić and other Bosnians remain powerful allies for Serbia (see Chapter 6, Appendix).

As for Macedonia, its fears of the irridentist disputes generated by great Bulgarian chauvinism makes it a very firm supporter of a closer-knit Yugoslav federation and of a governing role for Belgrade.

Fiscal Issues of the Federation

Common to the political conflicts is concern about 'Belgrade' government. What do the statistics actually show about the working of the federation's finances?

First, there is the share of the federation in the total national product (i.e., the role of the central, Belgrade, government which conducts defence, war pension allotment and foreign affairs). This is indicated in Table 6.1 and shows the substantial decline in the decade after 1975.

Table 6.1 Share of the federal government budget in gross social product, 1972–84

	Total federal governmental outlay as % of GSP	National defence as % of GSP	State admin. expenses as % of GSP	General services as % of GSP
1972	7.74	4.14	0.53	1.28
1974	9.20	5.10	0.74	2.00
1976	10.01	5.50	0.69	2.00
1978	9.40	4.70	0.80	1.82
1980	8.50	4.90	0.66	1.59
1981	7.50	4.50	0.55	1.43
1982	6.70	4.02	0.38	1.33
1983	6.40	3.78	0.37	1.35
1984	6.17	3.90	0.37	1.16

Source: *SG*, 1985, various sections.

Table 6.2 Share of federal government in total loans and credits, 1976–85 (million dinars; values at current level of the year)

	1976	1979	1980	1981	1982	1983	1984	1985
Total loans at end of year (republic and federation)	42,114	114,463	130,685	192,965	256,037	284,664	329,152	355,801
of which								
Federation and federal bodies	13,385 (32%)	12,820 (11%)	11,446 (9%)	33,628 (17%)	33,628 (13%)	33,628 (12%)	33,628 (10%)	33,628 (9%)
plus								
Federation fund for underdeveloped areas*	24,167	53,785	96,709	133,920	194,663	236,212	256,627	310,497
Federation share of total loans issued	32%	11.0%	9.0%	17.0%	13.0%	12.0%	10.0%	9.0%

* To be used for federation's own purposes, but shows redistributive action of federation.
Source: SG, 1986, p. 213.

A similar picture can be seen from the next table which looks at the share of the federal budget in total loans and credits, which has fallen from 32 per cent in 1976 to 9 per cent in 1985. There has been a freeze on the central government's right to raise new loans as shown clearly in the table. Nevertheless funds for Kosovo have increased. The figures from the 1986 yearbook show that the federation fund, the one which taps credits from the national bank (as well as the turnover tax) for the use of underdeveloped areas, has changed as shown in Table 6.3. However, when one looks at the figures for Kosovo, relative unemployment rate and its relative position in relation to production per inhabitant, the reasons for increase seem self-explanatory (see Table 6.4). With figures like this bringing out the extreme

Table 6.3 Increase in Federation fund, allocated in 1976–85

	Million dinars (value of current year)
1976	24,167
1977	43,983
1978	55,728
1979	83,705
1980	96,709
1982	194,633
1983	236,212
1984	255,629
1985	310,479

Source: SG, 1986.

Table 6.4 Kosovo and Yugoslavia: unemployment rate and relative position concerning social product per inhabitant

	Unemployment rate (%)	Social product index with Yugoslav average = 100
Yugoslavia (1980)	12.6	100.0
Kosovo (1980)	27.3	26.8
Slovenia (1980)	1.3	205.8
Croatia (1980)	5.2	126.4

Source: SG, 1981, pp. 405, 431.

disparity between Kosovo and the rest of Yugoslavia, especially the north, Belgrade's interventionism to help Kosovo becomes more explicable, even if this does not remove the source of Slovene and Croatian tensions surrounding the whole issue, which, in the 1980s, has come almost as close to splitting the federation as Croatia's own breakaway moves in 1971.

Appendix: The Government Leadership Team

In April 1986, new elections to leading bodies of the SKJ and the Yugoslav government apparatus were held. The new Presidency of the Yugoslav federation was assumed by S. Hasani with L. Mojsov as new Vice-President. In 1987, Mojsov took his turn as President. The Cabinet (FEC) was formed by the New Prime Minister Branko Mikulić, who replaced Mme Milka Planinc. The full cabinet was formed on 16 May 1986 after a new Parliament was elected. The full membership of the Cabinet was:

Branko Mikulić (Prime Minister or President of the FEC)

Janez Zemljarić (Vice-President of FEC)

Miloš Milosavljeć (Vice-President of FEC)

Branko Mamula (Admiral of the Fleet and Defence Minister)

Svetozar Durutović (Federal Secretary for Information)

Raif Dizdarević (Federal Secretary for Foreign Affairs)

Dobroslav Čulafić (Federal Secretary for Internal Affairs)

Svetozar Rikanović (Federal Secretary for Information)

Petar Vajović (Federal Secretary of the Judiciary and Federal Administrative Secretary)

Aleksandar Donev (Federal Secretary for General Economic Affairs)

Andrej Ocvirk (President Federal Committee for Industry and Energy)

Vucinic Momčilo (Member of FEC)

Herga Franciska (Member of FEC)

Nevenka Neralić-Milivojević (Member of FEC)

Mustafa Pljakić (President Federal Committee for Transport)

Ilija Vakić (President of War Veterans)

Janko Obočki (President of Federal Committee for Labour, Health, Social Welfare)

Bozidar Matić (President of Federal Committee for Science and Technology)

Miodrag Mirović (President, Federal Tourist Commission)

Lojze Ude (President Federal Committee for Legislation)

Radovan Makić (Member of FEC)

Oskar Kovač (Member of FEC)

Radoje Kontić (Member of FEC)

Pejovski Mito (Member of FEC)

Danev Dragi (Member of FEC)

Ibrahim Tabaković (Member of FEC)

Salma Tibor (Member of FEC)

Egon Padovan (Member of FEC)

Mustafa Muhamed (Member of FEC)

This 'Cabinet' of 'Ministers' (members of FEC) was elected partly from the parliament (Federal Assembly) of the SFRY. The new leading office-bearers of the Federal Assembly elected in April/May 1986 were:

Ivo Vrandečić (President of the Federal Assembly of SFRJ)
Nedo Borković (Vice-President of the Assembly of SFRJ)
Milka Gligorijević-Takeva (President of Federal Chamber of the Assembly of the SFRJ)

Milenko Bojanović (President, Chamber of the Republics of the Assembly of the SFRJ)
Nikola Filipović (Vice-President of the Chamber of the Republics of the SFRJ)
Ljubomir Bulatović (Secretary General of the Assembly of the SFRJ)

Biographical Notes

A short sketch of the 'leading personalities' follows. The shift to Bosnians, Montenegrins and leaders from other 'underdeveloped' republics is quite marked compared to the 'Tito era' situation of Serbo–Croat dominance.

Leaders of the Presidency

Sinan Hasini (President, 1986), born 1922, is a Šiptar from Kosovo Autonomous Province and a veteran partisan. Graduate of the 'Djuro Djaković' Higher Party School in Belgrade and later active in the leadership of the Socialist Alliance of the Working People of Yugoslavia. Elected to CC of the LCY at the XI Congress of SKJ.

Lazar Mojsov (President, 1987), born 1920, former partisan, is a Macedonian and a graduate of the Faculty of Law in Belgrade. Was a judge of the Supreme Court of Macedonia and later Ambassador to the International Atomic Energy Agency in Vienna, and Federal Secretary of Foreign Affairs from May 1982–May 1984

Hamdija Pozderac (Vice-President, 1986-7, resigned August 1987). Party functionary from Bosnia. Forced to resign Vice-Presidency in 1987 because of complicity in the financial management of giant agri-business conglomerate 'Agro-Commerc'.

Leaders of the Federal Assembly

Ivo Vrandečić (President of the Assembly), born 1927, is a Croat from Split who is a graduate of the Engineering Faculty, Zagreb University and a boat-builder by trade. He was a member of the CC of the SKJ of Croatia for many years and is a representative from Croatia's delegation in the Chamber of Republics of the federal assembly.

Nedo Borković (Vice-President of the Assembly), born 1926, is a Serb who joined the YCP in 1945 and is a graduate of the Higher School of Political Sciences. He was a

Secretary for some time of the Communist Youth in Kosovo–Metohia and later on the Executive Council of the Assembly of that region. He was a delegate to the Congresses of the SKJ at the 7th, 9th and 10th Congresses.

Mme Milka Gligorijević-Takeva (President of the 'Federal Chamber' of the Federal Assembly), born 1935, is a Macedonian and graduate of the Higher School of Political Sciences, who joined the SKJ in 1952. She was active in parliamentary bodies in Skopje, developing a specialist interest in health and labour policy.

Milenko Bojanić (President of the 'Chamber of Republics' of the Federal Assembly), born 1924, is a Serb who joined the SKJ and the partisans in 1943. He is a graduate of the Law Faculty, Belgrade, and a former Professor at the Faculty of Economics. A deputy of the Assembly of Vojvodina he was for a time director of the 'Red Flag' motor vehicle production factory in Kragujevac (Serbia) and also Federal Secretary for Foreign Trade.

Wilmoš Molnar, born 1930, is a member of the Hungarian national minority from Vojvodina. He is an electrical engineer who joined the SKJ in 1963. He was active in both the Alliance of Working People of Yugoslavia and in Chambers of Commerce before becoming a deputy and the President of the Assembly of Vojvodina, an 'autonomous province'. Since 1982 a deputy of the Federal Assembly (Federal Chamber) from the delegation of Vojvodina.

Nikola Filipović (Vice-President of the 'Chamber of Republics' of the Federal Assembly) was born in 1928 in Sarajevo and is a Serb by nationality. He is a graduate of the School of Economics and joined the SKJ in 1949. He was active in work with agricultural cooperatives and prices before becoming Director of Yugoslav Railways. His Party background was as an organizer of the Communist youth bodies in Sarajevo, and in that category he developed a specialist interest in the administration of sport.

Ljubomir Bulatović, born 1936, is a Montenegrin. He is a graduate of the Faculty of Law and joined the SKJ in 1954. He has experience as secretary to an enterprise, and, later, was a judge of the District Court of Pristina in Kosovo. He specialized in legislative work in its legal aspects. He is now secretary-general of the Federal Assembly.

Leaders of the Cabinet (or the Federal Executive Council)

Branko Mikulić (Prime Minister or President of the FEC), born 1928, is from Bosnia-Hercegovina and a graduate in economics. After being a member of the Sarajevo assembly he was elected in 1965 as secretary of the SKJ of the province of Bosnia-Hercegovina. Chairman of the organizing committee of the successful Winter Olympic Games in 1984 he became a member of the Presidency of the SFRJ. While holding that office he was designated Prime Minister (President of the FEC).

Janez Zemljarić (Vice-President of the FEC), born 1928, is from Slovenia and was active in the city of Ljubljana in the leadership of the Socialist Alliance. Later was responsible for 'Internal Affairs' in Slovenia.

Miloš Milosavljević (Vice-President of the FEC), born 1932, is a law graduate from Serbia. A former director of the Business Bank in Čačak he became Secretary for finance for Serbia.

Branko Mamula, born 1921, is from the northern Adriatic coast and is Admiral of the Fleet and Minister ('Secretary') for Defence. He is a member of the CC of the SKJ.

Raif Dizdarević, born 1926, is from Bosnia-Hercegovina. He is the Foreign Affairs Minister ('Secretary') and a member of the CC of the SKJ.

Dobroslav Čulafić, born 1926, is from Montenegro and is a Minister ('Secretary') for Internal Affairs. He has had a career in the youth movement in Montenegro and in SKJ of Montenegro.

Svetzar Rikanović, born 1938, is from Serbia. An economics graduate he has been a director of the Belgrade Bank and active in the City Committee of the SKJ of Belgrade.

Svetozar Durutović, born 1935, is a law graduate and is from Montenegro. He has edited a number of magazines and was active in Titograd communal politics. He is now federal secretary for information.

Petar Vajović, born 1930, is from Serbia. A doctor of laws he is federal secretary for the Judiciary.

Aleksandar Donev, born 1931, is from Macedonia and is 'Federal Secretary for Market and General Economic Affairs'. His political experience has been in the Federation of Trade Unions of Macedonia.

Nenad Krekić, born 1942, is federal secretary for Foreign Trade and comes from Croatia. He is a technology graduate who was a leading figure in the Vukovar SKJ.

Savo Vujkov, born 1936, is an economics graduate and comes from Vojvodina. Formerly director of the 'Vrbas' Industrial and Agricultural Combine, he is now President of the Federal Committee for Agriculture.

Mustafa Pljakić, born 1934, is from Kosovo, and was an activist in the Socialist Alliance of the Working People in Pristina. He is President of the Federal Committee for Transport and Communication.

Ilija Vakić, born 1932, is from Kosovo and comes from Vucitrn. He was a member of the Presidency of the SKJ and is now President of the Federal Committee for War Veterans.

Janko Oboćki, born 1935, is a medical doctor from Macedonia, who is President of the Federal Committee for Labour, Health and Social Welfare.

Bozidar Matić, born 1937, is from Bosnia-Hercegovina, and is President of the Federal Committee for Scientific and Technological Development. He was formerly a director of the 'Energoinvest' organization.

Miodrag Mirović, born 1934, is from Montenegro, and President of the Federal Committee for Tourism. He was a former Director-General of the 'Ulcinj' hotel chain.

Lojze Ude, born 1936, is a Doctor of Laws from Slovenia. He was a judge of the Slovene Supreme Court.

Andrej Ocvirk, born 1942, is from the Socialist Republic of Slovenia and is President of the Federal Committee for Industry. He was a former director of the 'Julon' enterprise, a textile firm.

Vucinic Momčilo, born 1929, a law graduate is from Montenegro and was a judge of the District Court of Titograd and President of the Constitutional Court of Montenegro.

Mme Nevenka Neralić-Milivojević, born 1939, was President of the Business Managing Board of the 'Karlovac' Medical Centre.

Radovan Makić, born 1924, was Governor of the National Bank of Yugoslavia before election to Cabinet.

Herga Frančiska, born 1944, was Vice-Chairperson of the Confederation of Trade Unions of Yugoslavia.

Radoje Kontić, born 1937, was formerly vice-president of the Executive Council of the Assembly of Montenegro.

Pejovski Meto, born 1932, is an economics graduate.

Danev Dragi, born 1942, was full Professor of the Faculty of Mechanical Engineering in Skopje.

Salma Tibor, born 1930, is a former member of the Executive Council for the Assembly of the 'semi-autonomous republic' of Vojvodina.

Ibrahim Tabaković, born 1942, is a Serb from Banja Luka, where he held the post of Professor of the Faculty of Technology.

Egon Padavan, born 1941, is an economics graduate who was formerly Under-Secretary in the Ministry of Finance.

Mustafa Muhamed, born 1950, is an economics graduate and was formerly an economic planner and member of the Assembly of the 'autonomous province of Kosovo'.

Comment

Two features of the 1986 election to the leading posts are: (a) the big rise in the proportion of leaders, including FEC (Cabinet) office-holders, from the more underdeveloped regions of Yugoslavia: Montenegro, Kosovo, Macedonia; (b) the rise in people taken from 'practical' posts in the economy: directors of firms, investment companies, bankers, engineers and health workers by comparison with earlier periods when 'professionals' in the art of active politics were more to the fore.

Official Marxism

Tito and Kardelj, amongst the leadership, became the main spokesmen for
theoretical and ideological positions in the Party after Djilas's departure in
March 1954. They were supported, in economic matters, by Svetozar
Vukmanović-Tempo, while earlier Boris Kidrič had written a number of
works on the role of commodity production in markets under socialism
(Kidrič, 1950), as well as questions of Marxist economic theory such as
differential rent. The 'theory' and practice of *foreign* economic relations were
handled by Milenteje Popović (M. Popović, 1949; 1961) and by foreign
minister Koča Popović, although Tito had a great say in this area, especially
on China. Social factors (argued the 1958 Party programme) had led to
deterioration in working-class ideology and to an inability to develop
Marxist thought so as to explain current developments. According to
Yugoslav Party theory:

> Marxist thought in the course of the last few decades has not kept in step with the
> advance of contemporary society, and its subsequent development has not always
> proceeded consistently from the basic postulates and results of Marxism. . . . Many
> contemporary social problems have not been fully explained from a scientific
> Marxist point of view, nor have the laws and contradictions of the period of
> transition from capitalism to socialism been sufficiently illuminated, thereby leaving
> gaps in the interpretation of contemporary social phenomena. [League of
> Communists of Yugoslavia, 1958]

After this homily the 1958 SKJ programme argued that: (i) in some cases it
might be possible for underdeveloped countries to by-pass some of the stages
of capitalism; (ii) the growth of wider state control and administration of the
economy in capitalist countries raised the issue of extending bourgeois
democracy to include economic democracy, i.e. working-class participation
in nationalized industries; (iii) in some cases there is the possibility of a
comparatively peaceful transition to socialism; (iv) the working class should
not renounce 'revolutionary means of struggle for power'; (v) state-socialism
and centralized planning as practised in eastern Europe and previously in
Yugoslavia itself had become ossified. One way of restoring a 'scientific
Marxism' and overcoming those practices was to abandon Soviet ideology

and to reap the benefit of a plurality of experiments in the various socialist countries. From this point of view, Yugoslavia's own contribution was 'self-management by the direct producers'.

Tito's position on *self-management* was that, despite critics abroad and internally (like Djilas), Yugoslavia's version of self-management was working in practice. In an important address to the First Congress of Workers' Councils (Tito, 1960) he said:

> It is necessary that critics come to our factories and talk to our workers and try to understand where the foundations of a true democracy lie; whether in a multiple-party political rivalry which stubbornly proclaims itself for perfect democracy or in a system where the producers themselves manage the means of production and participate in the management of the economy.

This shows that Tito regarded multi-party systems as reflecting multi-class antagonisms of non-socialist society. If the Yugoslav working class self-managed social property on behalf of all society why did it need many parties?[1]

Kardelj, too, had long proclaimed that self-management in factories combined with a lenient policy towards the peasants (Kardelj, 1960) could transform 'social relations of production' in Yugoslavia from those prevailing in a 'state-bureaucratic system' (Kardelj, 1961a; 1961b; Tito, 1956, 1960). These views had been officially codified in the 1958 programme of the League of Communists (League of Communists of Yugoslavia, 1958) in which the validity of nationalization of enterprises in Western countries, of a non-aligned foreign policy and self-management socialism had all been defended against attacks from *Pravda* and the East European party intellectuals.

Self-management in the 1950s meant workers' councils being elected and gradually taking more control over the business affairs of enterprises. It meant, by the late 1950s, that government regulations on how workers' councils should allocate 'net income' of enterprises between wages, depreciation funds, welfare and ploughed-back profits were relaxed and then abolished.

In the mid-1960s, however, the Yugoslav theorists began to talk about *associated labour* (Djordjević, 1966) and 'economic units' (Confederation of Trade Unions, 1964). Gradually, then, a series of new ideological positions arose from attaching to self-management the powerful motor of a market system.

The Djilas assault on Yugoslav Marxism had included a very important revelation as to the origin of the post-1948 Titoist ideology on free markets and self-management by workers' councils (later, 'associated labour' groups). It happened in a way that is worth quoting in full (Djilas, 1972, p. 158). In 1949 after a half-hour discussion with Kardelj and Kidrič about changing the whole economic system on principles found in Lenin on the withering away of the state and Marx on the concept of a future socialist society in which the immediate producers, through free association, would themselves make the decisions regarding production and distribution, it was decided to approach Tito:

His first reaction was: our workers are not ready for that yet! But Kardelj and I, concerned this was an important step, pressed him hard and he began to unbend . . . Suddenly he stopped and exclaimed: factories belonging to the workers—something that has never been achieved . . . a few months later Tito explained the Workers' Self-Management Bill to the National Assembly. [Djilas, 1972, p. 158]

Two other things are clear from Djilas's account. First that Kidrič was the one who forged the link between *self-management* and a *market* system by saying that you could not have self-management in a situation of continuing blockade where central planning was making things worse and not better. A market would help the workers' councils. Second, we are given a glimpse into the extreme pinnacle of power held by the three or four main Communist leaders.

This harmony did not last. The 1954 split with Djilas widened when, in his *The New Class* (1957) Djilas made the following points about Yugoslav Marxism in the context of ideological struggle:

(a) That it had not truly broken from Stalinism because the Party still sought in practice a monopoly control of the mass media.
(b) Those with connections to the Party bureaucracy and the leadership themselves constituted a new class of rulers emerging in the special conditions of an underdeveloped country undergoing forced-draft industrialization from the top at the behest of the Party. The Party was substituting itself for the middle-class entrepreneurs who undertook industrialization in Western Europe.
(c) Despite the use of market forces to allocate resources and some anti-bureaucratic rhetoric from Communist leaders like Tito and Kardelj, the economy was an 'ideological' one. Party political priorities determined planning goals and strategies, while controls of all sorts (as well as construction of 'political' factories) proliferated.
(d) Marxism had become, even in its Yugoslav, pro-'Paris Commune' version, a sort of state religion and no longer functioned as a critique of reality; it had become non-dialectical.

However, there were a number of curious aspects in Djilas's criticism. First, as he himself acknowledged (Djilas, 1957), he used the Marxist method of criticism and the dialectic on his objects—Yugoslav and Soviet Communist society. As he later put it, he had 'a desire to expose the Communist social system by means of a theory on which it relies spiritually' (Djilas, 1972, p. 5). Second, in his book, *The Unperfect Society*, significantly sub-titled 'Beyond the New Class', Djilas admitted to respect for a number of achievements of Marxism, which he nominated as 'the possibility of change in social patterns, the inevitability of internal contradictions in every society, the importance of economic factors in society and human life, the treatment of society as an object of scientific research'. Clearly this is a pretty wide ambit for one 'rejecting Marxist dogmatism'.

There was a pause before the theoreticians replied to Djilas. Then a new ideological campaign began among Yugoslav ideologists in 1961 over the distribution of income issue and its significance for 'self-managing socialism'. Milentije Popović, a Cabinet Minister, argued that the changes in laws and regulations allowing workers' councils to distribute enterprise net income represented 'a negation of the older socio-economic categories wages and profits as they had appeared in capitalism' and those which, 'owing to various deformations of a monopolistic or bureaucratic character remained the fundamental social contradiction in socialist Yugoslavia to date' (M. Popović, 1961, p. 5). The new laws, by reducing state interference in income formation would go a long way to democratizing the state, with self-governing bodies neutralizing the tendency of the state to become a force above society. Those intellectuals closest to the Party and government tried to meet the Djilas challenge by distinguishing sharply 'Stalinism' and 'Yugoslav self-governing socialism' and emphasizing the willingness of the Yugoslav Marxist regime to experiment and to change. They also drew attention to real achievements since 1945 and to the sharp differences that had emerged in Yugoslav mechanisms from the 'model' of Soviet planning and Eastern European practice (Predag Vranički, quoted in Djilas, 1972, p. 83).

From the late 1950s, the obstacles to a positive and humane development of self-management were further identified by dissidents and some reforming Communists as 'bureaucratism' and, by deduction, Party monopolistic controls in socio-economic affairs (Djordević, 1962). Where Djilas had concentrated on the complaint that Titoism had not really broken from the Stalinist way of looking at politics, other critics saw the roots of 'bureaucratism' in the divorce of the worker from the fruits of his labour under conditions where the state needed ever-replenished sources of accumulation for its own needs and functions. These critics (Djordjević,

1962) felt that the new Yugoslav system had only partly countered the powerful 'statist' tendencies at the base of the system. Apart from re-arrangement in the economic sphere, a whole new spirit was needed in the administrative apparatus.

The limited changes in bureaucratic spirit would also need to be countered by the spirit of a new humanism, of more planning for needs, and a widening influence of a practice of democracy. A reply from Kardelj (Kardelj, 1961, p. 97) expressed the reaction of official Marxism to the developing scepticism about claims to have pushed Yugoslavia to new, freer social relations of production: 'Their criticism is of two varieties. One is based on the postulates of political economy and the other on humanism and democracy'. In answer to 'political economists' he said:

The common objection, voiced abroad and at home, is this: You speak of some kind of economic freedom but actually you want to establish some sort of *neo-liberalism in the economy*. But liberalism has long since been transcended. Planning, the guided economy, is gaining ever greater prominence even in capitalist countries; in a socialist economy it is all the more indispensable . . .

Such critics overlook vital facts. First, that we do not refer to freedom of the private capitalist. When we speak of the *free economy* we mean giving full scope to emancipated labourers, i.e. assuring an adequate living to every individual *from income earned by labour performed* and to enable him to influence his living and working conditions.

Second, we do not refer to an anarchistic, free economy; ours remains a planned economy but is free of remains of state-monopolist forms and centralised economic management. There are still many weaknesses but we will implement definite changes in the methodology of planning so as to adjust plans to our new system of income distribution.

Turning to the 'humanist-democratic' school of critics, Kardelj noted that it was 'founded on a certain philosophy which was based on a particular reading of the young Marx, the alleged dehumanization of labour, fetishism of the dinar, the commercialization of spiritual life, etc.'

These ideas, said Kardelj (Kardelj, 1961, p. 98) did not apply to the sort of market-socialism developing in Yugoslavia except that, like all societies, Yugoslavia was influenced by certain unchanged aspects of human nature. On the contrary (Kardelj, 1961, p. 98), 'the Yugoslav system of income distribution actually represents a supreme achievement of "humanism" and "genuine democracy" and there is no reason why we should not oppose such attempts to minimize this achievement in the name of bogus humanism and pseudo-democracy'. Kardelj's difficulty in the Yugoslav debate had always been that, in practice (Ward, 1957), workers' councils were pressurized by management and by the white-collar coteries that management could constrain and that there was a rising degree of monopoly and *integracija* in the 'free economy'. This meant collusion by managers with attendant problems of not 'consulting' workers about movements in the firm's revenues.

The 'Praxis' Group

Nor could Kardelj solve the dilemma that under these conditions there was an inbuilt tendency for the freer economy to produce instability and encourage tighter political control. After 1968 it was the group of sociologists and philosophers around the journal *Praxis* which took up criticism of Yugoslav official theory and practice from this point of view. Their influence had grown as a result of disappointment in academic and student circles with the aftermath of the student revolt in Belgrade of June 1968. These groups considered that important circles of Yugoslav bureaucracy and 'technocracy' had been left largely intact.

Building on early writings in Poland by Adam Schaff and Leszek Kolakowski, *Praxis* writers used the insights of the young Marx (of *Critique of Hegel's Philosophy of Right*, and of the *Philosophical Manuscripts of 1844*) to attack censorship and the overwhelming role of the bureaucracy. Their targets became 'étatism' and *birocratizam'*:

The term étatism denotes a system based on state ownership of the means of production and state management of production and other social activities. The state apparatus represents a new ruling class. As a collective owner of means of production it employs and exploits labour. The personal share of the members of the ruling class in the distribution of surplus value is proportional to their position in the state hierarchy. [Stojanović, S. 1967, pp. 35 ff.]

The implications of this particular ideological position were clear enough: either there had to be a thoroughgoing transformation of the whole Yugoslav system to a self-managed economy or the existing system had at least to be modified by steps towards pluralism and a concerted attack on the Party's monopoly of influence.

Many of *Praxis*'s views were couched in the language and methods of Marxist analysis; its project was, in large part, an exercise in 'boring from within', similar to the attempts in Hungary (Fehrer, Heller & Markus, 1983) to bring down 'Party' Marxism and to return to a version of Marx based on human needs and combating the danger of bureaucracy, an approach that might eventually lead to acceptance of the inevitability of more humanism and extended democracy. *Praxis* continued, with the aid of Belgrade and Zagreb-based philosophers and sociologists, to criticize the economic reforms and experiments from the mixed viewpoint of humanism and democracy on the one hand, and the need for more planning for human needs on the other. It *criticized both the fetishism of commodities and the fetishism of the plan*, suggesting that Yugoslavia was getting the worst of both worlds—the ardent and excessive commercialization of life under capitalism, and the political monopoly of Communists so much the feature of Eastern Europe.

The 1970s Debates

If one theme dominated ideological discussion in the 1970s, it was whether associated labour groups (economic units in factories, for example) amounted to a form of syndicalism.[2] This was the view of researchers at the Institute of Economic Investments, who said that despite the claim that the law preserved state ownership of social property, in practice there was group ownership and unit ownership.[3] Given this, there was little point in treating capital and labour markets as an essential part of socialism. Others, led by Horvart (Horvart, 1971a) held that labour and capital have their existence and price on the market, and any other arrangements represented a danger to the existing social–economic relations of Yugoslavia.

Two related issues were (a) whether productive units 'integrating' would curb self-management as centralized decision-making would be inevitable and (b) whether the by-products of market socialism in the form of pollution and urban blight should be corrected by Party or state intervention or whether it would be more consistent with self-management to allow tenants and consumer organizations to develop into political organizations. In this matter it was noted that deterioration in social hygiene had been most marked after the 1965 Reform. Among reasons given by the critics (in a number of articles in *Praxis* Nos. 3–4, 1971) were that this trend reflected a re-organized evolution of power to the point where garbage collection and urban decay were no one's legal responsibility; that it was a result of the squeeze on all funds for 'social' needs in a very weak economy. Even more disturbingly for the Yugoslav Marxist regime, it reflected declining social consciousness (due to ineffective propaganda work by the Communists), concerning the importance of collectivist consumption.

During the 1970s, 'capitalist tails' were discussed again. The issue of the *kulaks* in agriculture was raised anew, as they became more visible in the cities. It was noted that in Vojvodina especially, no attempt had been made either to enforce the ten-hectare ownership limit or to prevent Bosnian labourers going to Vojvodina to work as an agricultural proletariat.[4]

Finally, various bans on journals were lifted after mid-1971; courts reversed some verdicts under ideological pressure of party officials and demagogy about 'our Yugoslav democracy'. However, this only fanned a plethora of small journals wanting to discuss 'Marxism and Democracy', while most critics[5] complained that the technocratic-managerial strata continued to frustrate self-management in practice, producing a gap between idealism on worker-management and the reality of enterprise life. By the end of the 1970s these debates had not been resolved and represented a continuing problem for official Marxist ideology. The Croatian revolt of 1971, coming on top of the student revolt (in which Maoism and Utopian socialism were raised), ensured that the more orthodox Serbian Party intellectuals kept vigilant, and the 'fear of disunity' which they fanned, enabled them to continue to push for a unitary system.[6] The regime as a whole, however, found itself, on the ideological level, having to convince the outside sceptics that market-socialism, self-management and non-alignment were not synonymous with creeping capitalism, anarchy and opportunism.

The 1980s

Any review of the ideological debates would note that a number of heated ideological debates continued in the 1970s and 1980s. Among the most important were the role of state violence; the respective place of private and social property in a socialist system; the respective weight to be given to individual and collective rights under socialism; the legal basis and the operation *in practice* of social management of collective assets under conditions of 'self-management socialism'.

However, such debates did not change the specific features of Yugoslav ideology earlier outlined by Kardelj or, semi-officially by Horvart (Horvart, 1964, 1969). This ideology supports a market-communist ideal. Commodity production itself will be part of socialism and then of communism. Socialism, Yugoslav style, will be a unique combination of workers' self-management and extensive use of market mechanisms. The problems listed in the penultimate paragraph are brushed aside in official ideology, as is the fact that those problems arise from the still present monopoly of behind-the-scenes decision-making by an admittedly less purposeful and interventionist League of Communists.

The Marxist regime would have been gratified by the anti-bureaucratic ideology which began to develop in the Soviet Union in the 1980s, although it was not until 1986 that the Kardelj-Tito line came to be openly propounded in the Soviet Union. As an example take the 1986 article 'The Shadow of Bureaucracy' by Professor Vladimir Shubkin which said:

> The key advantages of organizations—competence and efficiency—often turn into their exact opposites. The decisions taken only serve to camouflage personal ambitions. Executives, in the hope of keeping everything under control, try to place all decision-making in the hands of the higher echelons. Bureaucracy breeds bureaucracy. Those who possess a greater amount of information have greater power within the organization. Information takes on an hierarchical nature, gets distorted, withheld, or moulded into stereotypes.
>
> In sociology, bureaucracy is analysed from the point of view of the theory of organization (there is much in common here from country to country) and from the point of view of specific cultural and historical conditions. In other words, the shadow (of bureaucracy) is present everywhere—only its size, intricate shape and tendencies vary. *Bureaucracy tolerates no self-management, no self-government* . . . Not surprisingly, bureaucracy is the chief opponent of putting to use self-adjusting mechanisms, or implementing a radical economic reform.[7]

In Yugoslavia itself these themes have been a source of renewed debate among Marxists, especially in the period 1983-7, coinciding with social and economic crisis as expressed in urban decay, bank scandals and hyper-inflation. One Yugoslav author[8] has gone into detail about the difficulties of achieving self-management in the face of break up of a national market and sustained economic growth, concluding that 'without progress on the economic front there can be no humanist ways of living or liberation of the personality'. Without an efficiently operating economy, the rhetoric of official ideology will remain just that—rhetoric. In books and articles he has stated a number of things that have become widely acknowledged in official Marxism—at least in the Serbian Communist League. This chapter will close with one of these statements which I believe to be widely shared within the Serbian and Croatian Academies of Social Sciences and hence pose a challenge for Party theory to deal with.

The author, Radisav Marinković, wrote:

> To demand self-management without economic restraints is to relapse into Utopianism and to end in *birokratizam*. Democratic norms are obtainable only by real forms of decision-making and not on the basis of Utopianism towards real needs. It cannot be built without a market and market competition.

At first sight this seems to sit quite easily with the ideas of Tito and Kardelj. Yet it operates in the mid-1980s as a reproach to a great deal of official policy and practice of Yugoslav Marxism. For the criticism of policy without economic restraints is an attack on regional autarky, regional étatism and the dominance of the political realm over the economic. It is, at the same time a warning that in many 'self-managing' enterprises, workers and managers have voted themselves higher personal incomes to the detriment of re-investment in the expansion of the firm. And it is a criticism of the Yugoslav official sociologists who preach the 'liberation of man' without reference to the economic foundations of society.

Intellectual Opponents

The Government, along with the Courts, implements any crackdown on the rights of political, religious or cultural dissidents. Among the political dissidents, we might begin with the case of former Vice-President Djilas. This affair has been discussed as part of a Party split in Chapter 5 and of an ideological controversy in Chapter 7. Here we will merely note that after Djilas was forced (by moral pressure and insults) out of the Party in 1954, administrative action was taken by the Procurator's Office three years later, with the claim that only Djilas's deeds (the publication of a book and articles in the United States) were being punished, not his dissident thoughts *as such*. The procurator said:

The statements of the accused that he only wished to make an objective criticism of the situation in our country, without any desire to act in a destructive way, has no foundation. On the contrary, the book clearly reveals not only the writer's hostile attitude towards Socialism and the present constitutional order in Yugoslavia, but also his intention to mobilize all the enemies of the social order at home and abroad for action against the Socialist system and against Yugoslavia's political interests abroad.

The authorities feared that if Djilas were given free speech opposition groups might gather round him.[1] The still-strained economic situation of the 1950s made this a possibility, but one which, in retrospect, the regime might have risked in the interests of socialist plurality and avoiding trouble. In any case, this was little reason for its objections to Djilas arranging overseas publication, for their trial of Djilas probably did more than his writings to 'harm Yugoslavia's political interests abroad'. How ironic, too, that Edward Kardelj who condemned Djilas's statements in 1954 and 1956, especially those about the overall trend in Communist societies, should, in his last major work, advocate a system which he nominates as 'a pluralism of self-managed socialist interests' (Rusinow, 1984, p. 2).

Writers

Apart from Djilas and Dedijer the main political dissent has come from academic staff and students, especially those located in sociology, law and philosophy. In 1963-4 action was taken in Lljublana against a group who formed around a journal called 'Perspektiva'. The activists were a mixture of economists dissatisfied with the 'deal' the Slovenian economy was getting out of its membership of the federation,[2] a number of clerics and catholic militants, one of two former collaborators (i.e. followers of Ante Pavelić and his Croatian state of 1941-44) and younger teachers of Ljubljana University challenging the Party authority on a whole number of fronts.

In 1965 writer Mihajlo Mihajlov was tried for articles he wrote in a Belgrade literary journal criticizing Soviet cultural policy and lack of freedom. He was given a suspended sentence. A year later he was imprisoned for a public statement that he was about to found an 'oppositionist' journal.

About the same time (1963-5) some Law Faculty members of Belgrade, Lukić and Marković, were discussing multiparty systems and playing an *enfant terrible* role in relation to orthodox Party intellectuals. After the student revolt of 1968, some of these professors lost their jobs. Another journal *Praxis*, then became a focus for dissidents and had intermittent problems with the authorities.[3] Further numbers of Belgrade intellectuals and dissidents were sentenced in 1971-3: Vladimir Mijanović, Milan Nikolić and P. Imsirović (Amnesty International, 1985, p. 10), while Mihajlo Mihajlov was again arrested, this time for 'hostile' propaganda and given seven years' jail. He received a presidential pardon in 1977 probably because of embarrassment arising from Tito's public criticism of him on 25 February 1975, while he was still on trial.

In the 1980s, two significant groups of trials of dissidents took place. During the first (1980) writers Momčilo Selič and Gojko Djogo were jailed. The former received seven years' imprisonment for writing and distributing a ten-page document critical of the SKJ's history and policies. He was later pardoned by the SFRJ Presidency and released in May 1982 (Amnesty International, 1985, p. 16). In September 1981 Djogo received two years' imprisonment for publishing a collection of poems satirizing Tito and depicting the socio-political situation in Yugoslavia 'maliciously and untruthfully'. He was released after seven weeks, due to ill health.

Six Belgrade intellectuals including Mijanović, Nikolić, Imsirović (mentioned above), as well as Miodrag Milić, D. Olvjić and G. Jovanović were arrested as a result of a serious police provocation occurring in April 1984.

Police raided a private apartment where twenty-eight people had assembled to hear a talk by Milovan Djilas. This was a Polish-style 'rotating Open University', an unofficial dicussion group, which had been meeting (with official knowledge) for seven years without previous harassment. World press coverage and internal support (including eighteen petitions) led to Imsirović, Mijanović and Jovanović having charges dropped, due to their illness; the others were found guilty of the least serious offence of hostile propaganda and allowed to go free pending appeals.

Religious Liberty: Church and State

At the census of 1953 the 16,000,000 people of Yugoslavia were grouped in the following main affiliations: Orthodox 41 per cent; Roman Catholic 32 per cent; Moslem 12 per cent; No Religion 12 per cent; Others 3 per cent. The main clash between state and church has occurred with the Roman Catholic hierarchy, while the Moslems have no strong religious organization. The Orthodox Church has always had a long tradition of cooperation with governments.

In the immediate post-war period state–Church relations were influenced by the wartime behaviour of the clergy. Some of the Orthodox Church hierarchy had supported General Nedić, the Serb quisling, and a number of them were punished with imprisonment. The Catholic hierarchy who collaborated with the Germans and Italians were also punished, particularly Archbishop Stepinac, who was sentenced to sixteen years' imprisonment in 1946.

During the 'second revolution' a change occurred also in relations between Church and state. In 1953 the government removed the theological faculties from the universities and stopped its subsidies to Church schools. Associations of Orthodox Priests, Moslem Priests, and Catholic Priests were set up, in an attempt to strike at the hierarchical nature of the churches. There was no trouble from the Moslem priests, and only a limited amount of disapproval from the Orthodox bishops.

In the 1960s the Orthodox Church grew closer to the Serbian government (e.g. it subscribed to loans for the building of the Belgrade to Bar railway) but the relationship between the SKJ and the Catholic clergy remained uneasy.

There was less support from the Catholic priests for any new form of organization, particularly in Croatia. The pattern of relations may perhaps be seen from the number of priests in the Association in March 1954: thirty-two Orthodox, two Protestant, and twelve Catholic.

In December 1952 Archbishop Stepinac was released after serving five of his sixteen years in prison, partly as a gesture to public opinion in the United States, whose aid Yugoslavia then needed, and partly as a new liberalization step. But the Vatican then named Stepinac a cardinal; as a result, on 17 December 1953 Yugoslavia broke off relations with the Holy See. In April 1954 there was some attempt to reach an agreement by negotiation with the Catholic Church in Yugoslavia, but little eventuated.

In May 1954 a new law was passed guaranteeing freedom of religion, but placing the churches under control by the state. After that date there was for fifteen years a quietening down of religious problems in Yugoslavia. The state after the 1950s supplied financial aid to the religious groups, though aid to the Catholic Church became less regular than to the other groups depending on the state of relations with the regime. Monastries of the Orthodox Church were renovated vigorously (partly for tourist reasons) in Vojvodina, Macedonia and Eastern Serbia during 1956–71. However, Party propaganda against religion continued in 'workers' universities', assemblies of the socialist alliance, etc., which may have deterred some from open practice of religious beliefs.

The events in Croatia in 1969–71, with an upsurge of Croatian nationalism, created new problems. Professors like Dr Marjo Veselica who demanded more autonomy for Croatia on economic grounds were strongly supported by nationalists grouped around the Catholic-Croatian traditional cultural organization Hrvatska Matica. As well, a tradition started that on 10 February each year a Mass was held in the Catholic Cathedral in Zagreb to celebrate the anniversary of the death of Cardinal Stepinac with the Savka Dabčević wing of the Croatian Communist Party tolerating the upsurge in nationalism. The church expanded its influence but had to go quietly after the Tito crackdown on Croatia at the end of 1971.

During 1971–2 a number of Catholic priests were cautioned and sentenced for saying that Croatians in Bosnia and Hercegovina were discriminated against. Some laymen like Veselica, Dr Tudjman (ex-general) and writer V. Gotovac were jailed (Amnesty International, 1985, p. 14) while on 8 April 1986, fifteen years later, Filip Lukenda, a Catholic priest from Banja Luka (Bosnia) was sentenced to four years' jail for the same offence.

School students taking pilgrimages to Rome developed as a new phenomenon in the 1980s to the irritation of the authorities. In 1986 there were reports of a crackdown on this with militant youth adhering to the Catholic ideology in Croatia being threatened with loss of job and school places.

Croats, Serbians and Bosnians: Acute Nationalist Dissent, 1970-1

In 1970-1 a debate took place about a new federal constitution and also new constitutions for each republic. As explained in Chapter 4, the leadership of the Croatian Communist Party was eventually dismissed for failure to 'contain' politically, educationally and administratively the explosion of nationalism and the rising tension between Serbs (in Serbia) and Croats, and Serbs (in Croatia) with Croats.

As the issues affected the federal government via the demand to alter the 'Belgrade-based' banking system and the shape of the new Constitution—as well as affecting Yugoslavia's foreign relations[4]—the events and what changes in Government they led to are set out here in more detail.

The Student Movement and the Nationalist Question

The stranglehold of the SKJ on the Croatian student movement was fatally loosened by the student revolt of 1968. Although centred in Belgrade the ripples of that event led to wide questioning of the system of politics, police, University administration and eventually of the leading role of the party on the part of many students (Perlman, 1973).

Into the vacuum of firm leadership stepped new student leaders, some anti-Communist, most vociferous about a better deal for Croatia—within or outside the Yugoslav federation.

In October 1971 a caravan of Croat students led by Budiša and Bušić caused an incident in Vukovar, Croatia, by marching and singing 'patriotic' songs in the city café and chanting 'Djordan—Veselica' (the names of two leading Croatian activists in favour of separatism for Croatia). This created tension in the Serbian community and brought condemnation from commune leaders (*Borba*, 27 October 1971, p. 5).

A conference of University students of Zagreb University's Philosophy Faculty on 29 October argued for an autarchic Croatia with its own economic policy and control over its own international economic relations. At the discussion a leading role was taken by Dr. Hrvojé Šosić and student prorector Čičak, who criticized the assembly of the SR of Croatia and the League of Communists of Croatia (*Borba*, 4 November 1971, p. 7). These people were later removed from their posts and a number of professors were expelled from Communist ranks, and from the University, for advocating 'separatism' after being condemned by Party-organized meetings of 3,000 workers at the Šišak metallurgical combine (*Borba*, 5 November 1971, p. 5). Earlier, Bosnia–Hercegovina students had walked out of a conference of the all-Yugoslav Students' Federation in protest at a Croatian–nationalist article in the Croatian Student Paper *Naši Dani* (*Borba*, 20 October 1971) indicating that the student political groups were lining up to defend the federation and the Tito line or, on the other side, to press in a militant way, Croatian sentiment.

The Professors

A major issue for the professoriat was how to respond to the upsurge among Croatian students, but more generally they had to deal with the implication of a mass revival of interest in Croatian language, culture and history and how this could be accommodated in their pedagogical practice, at least to the point that it did not provoke Party measures against Faculties or Cultural societies. In October 1971 the issue of inter-Republican recognition of each others' diplomas was under discussion. Professor Ljubiša Rakić, editor of *University Today*, was forced to make known his opinion (*Borba*, 9 October 1971, p. 5). He said that 'within our borders the problem should not be raised: most of our Faculties have already adjusted instruction. Demands for local nostrification of diplomas can only be of a bogus political character'. But this defence of the status quo came only after demands that Serbian students be instructed in Cyrillic if living in Croatia and that more cultural content be inserted in Croatian courses. In particular, the setting up of a branch of the Croatian cultural organization Matica Hrvatska[5] in new areas (such as the island Brač) forced academics to declare where they stood, especially when (as in the Brač case), it was revealed that supporters of the old Maček Croatian Peasant Party and militant priests were on founding committees (*Politika*, 14 October 1971, p. 6). One method to avoid such embarrassment for academics loyal to the Party and supportive of its Constitutional amendments program aimed to quieten nationalist dissidence was to set up or revive new pedagogical-literary societies; those in Zagreb who wished to do this and avoid being associated with disgraced professors reformed older groups like the Croatian Pedagogical Society, Zbor (*Politika*, 28 October 1971, p. 7) but clearly Hrvatska Matica was the more dynamic force there at this time.

War Veterans

Discussion and debate at war veterans' meetings was sharp, nationality-focused and tough. Clarity and dissent rather than Party obscurantism were the order of the day. In Podravška Slatina, a motorcade of veterans was decorated with older Croat flags without the socialist insignia (*Politika*, 13 October 1971, p. 7). A Croatian veteran and nationalist, Mate Matković from Split, said at the plenum of Croatian War Veterans that Belgrade newspapers were smearing the Croatian political interest, notably the newspaper *Večerni Novosti* by discussing whether Serbs in the Croatian part of Split were in danger. He attacked the journal *Jez* for saying that events in Croatia contained the danger of 'the awakening' of the 'sinister Ustashi spirit',[6] and *Ekonomska Politika* for a cartoon showing Croatia as a chicken abandoning the hen (*Politika*, 13 October, 1971, p. 7). Ivan Sibl, the President of the Croatian War veterans, attacked 'some people' who 'attempt to give the impression that the Ustashi are on the threshold of seizing power' (*Politika*, 12 October 1971, p. 5). The strong support for nationalist academics and sympathetic Communist politicians from war veterans did not, however, prevent the removal of all such people from their posts during 1972.

The Church

Although, as noted earlier in this chapter, it was mostly Catholic priests who were harassed for the events of 1970-1, Serbian orthodox religious leaders were sometimes accused of fanning Serb nationalism in reply to the Croatian events. The most discussed case (*Politika*, 15 October 1971, p. 7 and *Nin*, 24 October 1971, p. 20) was that of the Bishop of Zica who had referred to ancient Serbian cultural values and religious hymns as weapons in the struggle to defend Serbs in Croatia and other republics. The Bishop was ferociously attacked in the official press. The fate of Croatian priests was outlined in the previous section, but some Moslem religious leaders were also harassed by policemen, one of whom K. Tanaskovic, head of SDS in Prizren, was transferred from his post for such actions (*Borba*, 31 October 1971, p. 5).

The Party Response

While the year 1971 lasted, Party leaders wanting to curb Croatian revivalist sentiment contented themselves with holding rallies and giving parliamentary speeches deploring chauvinist revivals and appealing to people to support Tito's Constitutional amendments as the main way of satisfying Croatian aspirations and blunting complaints about treatment of the republic in federal economic arrangements. The President of the Croatian Executive Council, D. Haramija, addressed public meetings on these lines at Dvor and M. Gruic of Zagreb City Conference spoke to political activists on the 'neglect of Marxist political theory', while also criticizing 'unitarianist forces' for exaggerating the events in Croatia (*Borba*, 23 October 1971, p. 7). He also noted that the nationalistic Croatian newspaper *Tjednik* was selling 100,000 copies per issue. In perhaps the final warning by the party, M. Todorović, a senior SKJ leader made a major speech on the issue of the lack of flexibility in the political system and the Croatian events. That, however, was the end of the 'gloves off' period. By May 1972 Tito and the leaders of the SKJ had engineered the dismissal of most of the leaders of the League of Communists of Croatia, dissident academics, militant war veterans and student leaders and had curbed Hrvatska Matica and the paper *Tjednik* (Cviic, 1974).

Cultural Freedom

There is insufficient space here to do more than merely suggest some of the issues involved in the question of cultural freedom in Yugoslavia. Undoubtedly there has been an increase in such freedom since the 1950s. The very requirement that economic enterprises become self-sustaining economically meant, for instance, that cinemas had to cater to the interests of their customers. Hence there came a change in the nature of films shown, (e.g., the massive importation of 'westerns' from America). On the other hand, there have been clear limits to this freedom, as one film company found when it produced a film attacking bureaucracy somewhat too vigorously. The film, *Ciguli Miguli*, made in late 1952, was withdrawn from Zagreb cinemas after two days of screening. It had cost, 8,000,000 dinars to make. In 1972 a film about the superiority of the ideas of the ex-Marxist Willhelm Reich over those of Marx and Lenin entitled *Mysteries of the Organism* was banned. In the 1980s both film and art have been given virtually free rein. Belgrade is full of smart art galleries displaying promising individual artists. The new National

Art Gallery on the north side of the Sava River contains modernists, abstract art and a range of styles unthinkable in the Soviet Union and Eastern Europe.

Irridentist Dissent in Kosovo

The 'Muslim' cultural issue began to develop strongly from the late 1970s. At the heart of the problem was a fear that the very high birth rates of Muslims in the Southern republics would somehow 'swamp' the Croats, Serbs and Montenegrins: atavistic demographic terror ensued, including the killing of 300 Šiptars in March–April 1981. Also many of the young conscripts with the army from the 'Šiptar' (Albanian) minority in Bosnia, Montenegro and Kosovo–Metohia resist Marxism and even fighting for Yugoslavia.

Serious riots erupted in the 1980s and mass arrests followed: some 6,000 of the 2 million Šiptars became political prisoners between 1981 and 1986. Over the same period only a handful of political sentences were handed out to the Serbs, the most controversial being the sentencing of a Serbian soldier, son of a high official in the Serbian Orthodox Church, for saying that Serbs were being discriminated against by Muslims and Roman Catholics in Bosnia (Amnesty International, 1985, p. 26).

While the arts and film have experienced 'liberalism' in the implementation of government attitudes and expenditures, those who develop their cultural aspirations into volatile, even virulent political dissent—the Croats in the 1970s and the Albanian minority in the 1980s—have felt the heavy hand of a government clamp-down. Estimates of 'prisoners of conscience' (as Amnesty calls them) or 'persons committing offences against the people and the state' (Section 10 of the federal criminal code first adopted in 1951) are available to give guidance on the significance and on the trends as to crackdown (*Statistical Yearbook of the SFJR* , 1986).

The period 1971–8 saw 3,778 persons convicted under section 10, of which 2,767 were 'light' (under one year in prison) and 33 more than ten years while some 398 were acquitted. As explained earlier, the highest incidence of convictions for political offences between 1971 and 1978 occurred in Croatia and Bosnia–Hercevogina and were related to Croat–Serb tensions in both areas.

In the period of the 1980s there was a drop in the number *charged* with political offences from 1311 in 1976 to 553 in 1980, 594 in 1981, 516 in 1982 and 545 in 1983 (Amnesty International, 1985, p. 72) despite the wide police action against the Šiptar students' revolt during 1981 in Kosovo–Metohia.

Underlying a very large number of these trials has been a very sensitive official reaction to the challenge made to a very deeply-held sentiment amongst Communists: that consciousness of the benefits of self-management socialism reinforces national unity. It may be noted, for example, that at the trial of the six Belgrade intellectuals arrested at the semi-legal 'Open University' seminar to hear Djilas, it was alleged by the prosecution that they had attacked 'the heritage of the liberation struggle, the building of socialism and the character and acts of Tito' (Amnesty International, 1985, p. 54).

The death of Tito and the carrying out of state authority by a collegiate body, the 'Presidency' of SFRJ, has not altered this situation. On the contrary, the need to claim some residual legitimacy by upholding Tito's reputation has increased, while weaknesses in the self-management system, exposed under the glare of publicity around the 1980s economic crisis, have had to be shielded from withering political criticism to uphold the status of a leadership that delayed taking strong action to save the economy for some two years after Tito departed the scene.

Overview on Political Dissent in Yugoslavia

In this chapter the cases of 'dissent' discussed were not taken *in abstracto*. Rather it was asked whether each case was outside the socialist framework or within it, and if there was a connection with the uneven economic development of republics. The problems of the Marxist regime were various—having to deal with leading regime figures like Djilas and with intellectual circles like *Praxis*, Yugoslavia's Petofi Club.[7] As well, it had on its hands larger movements like the Croatian cultural upsurge of 1970-1 leading to mass 'separatist' sentiment, and the later Kosovo pro-Albanian demonstrations. To make sense of the motivation of the actors involved, it was important to link their activities with *politics*, with moves taken to counter real or imagined wrongs imposed by the structure of the Party, of the Yugoslav Constitution, of the Federation. As well, the counter-measures of the regime have been outlined and some reasons for the level of repression used were suggested.

Part III
The Economic System

9 The Shape of the Yugoslav Economic System

The course of changes in economic institutions and economic policies in Yugoslavia is outlined in Chapters 10–12 below. Here the major contours of the economy are given as background.

Price Formation

A good deal of the fascination about Yugoslavia stems from its nature as a market-socialist system. Although there are no capitalist stock exchanges or large private owners of the means of production, Yugoslavia is not as the Eastern European state emerged: a system of centralized socialist planning. Rather, the worker-managed firms compete with each other in a market system recycling earned profits for their own needs and expansion or else, via the taxes they pay, into collective funds for social consumption.

Groups of citizens who can convince the authorities and the banking system of the viability of setting up an enterprise can do so (Djordjević, 1966, p. 5). In this way, they manage social property on behalf of society. As with all market systems, enterprises not only compete via price reductions but by 'integrating', by improving output, quality, advertising and other non-price competitive techniques. Enterprises are quite sufficiently motivated to make the profits they receive and the wages they pay a function of capital intensity, technological rent and institutional monopoly.[1]

Notwithstanding the blinkers of some economists, market prices or prices determined primarily by supply and demand are *not* the only operational prices; nor does the price system have only *one* function—the economists' favourite of 'allocating resources optimally'. This was recognized early in the regime's evolving attitude to market socialism (Kidrič, 1950, p. 106).

Until the 1961 economic reforms, prices set fundamentally by 'supply and demand' were those at particular points of the chain of production. As an example, take animals which become first hides, then leather, then shoes at the factory gate, then shoes at the retail stores. The older system was that price controls were set at the initial stage (price of animal) and price control (or sales taxes) at the retail end. The intermediate phases were ones in which market forces set the price (hides, leather, wholesale shoe price). This combined system worked well and produced only a moderate rate of inflation.

However, after a conference of the SKJ in 1964 this system was abandoned and a large number of price controls were removed at all those levels and phases of production where they had played a useful moderating role. 'Market price' became the new dogma not only of the economists (Round-table, 1968; Uvalić, 1960; Vuković, 1968) from whom such an attitude might have been expected, but of the politicians (Broekmeyer, 1977).

Over the last twenty-three years, although there has been sporadic re-introduction of some price controls at the time of crisis (most recently in 1983-4), the trend is towards freer and freer prices—indeed many warned that this was the heart of Yugoslavia's problem with inflation and dis-appointing exports, as it was unaccompanied by sustained rises in real product per man hour in most sectors.

Two other developments in price formation have affected the economy. First, the terms of trade between agriculture and industry have altered in favour of the former. This was done partly to recompense peasants for the way surplus was screwed out of them to finance rapid industrialization in the first sixteen years of the regime, partly to encourage the growth of markets in land. Second, tariff protection has been lowered in an attempt to give the more ramshackle parts of Yugoslav industry a 'whiff of competition' from oversea competitors. Finally, world prices, apart from affecting exports, have increasingly influenced the structure of domestic prices as well. Whether these trends have gone far enough has been a matter of lively controversy in the 1980s (CC of Serbia Communist League, 1985).

The extensive use of market mechanisms is strongly defended by Yugoslavia's leading economists (Sirotković, 1966; Horvart, 1964, 1971a); although there have been critics of its impact on social opportunity and inequality by both at home (Berković, 1969; Samardžija 1968) and abroad (McFarlane, 1966, p. 123; Mandel, 1967, pp. 40-6). In the 1980s, with the decline of the economic unity given by a national market, these pro-market views (Pjanić, 1986) have been forcefully restated.

Ideological objections to the price-mechanism were overcome in the way described in Chapter 7—the main problem having been Engels' view that the building of a socialist economy takes place simultaneously with the 'withering away' of commodity production of market mechanism after a brief first stage of socialism; and Lenin's oft-repeated statement that simple commodity production inevitably reproduces primitive capital accumulation and bourgeois ideology—seedbeds of potential capitalism. The Chinese in 1978–83 had the same debate,[2] but in Yugoslavia the perceived inefficiency of central planning and its association with the disliked Soviet bureaucracy has cleared the way for the Yugoslavs to enshrine 'market forces' as a permanent feature of present-day Yugoslav society (Horvart, 1964, p. 132, p. 225).

Some rather remarkable policy conclusions have been drawn by Yugoslav economists after discussion on price formation. The first is that the 'marginal cost' pricing favoured by most Western writers on welfare economics[3] has been rejected as being more relevant to public utilities and a planned economy. Instead, full-cost pricing, associated with Hall and Hitch and P. W. S. Andrews in Western economics is favoured.[4] These prices, in actual operation, are linked to a process of profit-maximization in Western theory dealing with capitalist firms, but Horvart and other economists in high positions in Yugoslavia (Sirotković, 1966) saw no problem with this: they believed that 'provided the institutional set up ensures an identity of interests between the firm and the community, profit becomes a device for a continual correcting of productive choices in the direction of achieving national economic efficiency' (Horvart, 1964, p. 30).

Moreover, a very big step is then taken in these theories as regards policy conclusions. This is the assumption that firms, which offer *ex-ante* the highest rates of return on credits they apply for, will also produce *ex-post* the highest accretions to national output and income. In practice, this has not happened. From the beginning, many 'bidders' at investment auctions were promising highest productivity without being able to deliver (Neuberger, 1959). More important, perhaps, is the practical situation that the sum total of each enterprise's attempts at individual output and profit maximization do not *maximize* output of the whole economy. Such a maximization requires that some firms incur losses and subsidies—a point familiar in theories of optimization.

The Yugoslav economists tend to ignore two other practical issues. The first is that as stability on the market is achieved profits and losses will depend on the initial relative productivity of the firms (Mandel, 1967, p. 47) as well as on the efforts put in by the workers' collectives. Those with higher quality of capital equipment and better plant will obtain a sort of 'rent' from the start—unearned incomes, unrelated to effort will go to some and losses go to others. The Yugoslav tax system has been very slow to respond to this, the only serious attempts being made in 1957–9. The second point is the curious blindspot represented by the belief in automatic checks to bureaucracy.

Market mechanisms, while they do counter the power of 'vertical' bureaucracies, do not operate as an *automatic* check on bureaucracy at plant and commune level—'horizontal' bureaucracy is present and powerful, a lesson that was being rapidly learnt in Yugoslavia in the 1980s as a social and economic crisis unfolded.

Wages and Industrial Relations

There are labour markets of a peculiar kind in Yugoslavia, the 'employers' being collectives of *other* workers. The notion of 'wages' is not clear-cut in a system where collectives hire capital for rental and workers' earnings are distributed as a share of a firm's 'net income' and take on the character of 'personal income'.

What about pay disputes and the use of industrial muscle in Yugoslavia? Strikes do occur in Yugoslavia and there was a rising incidence of them from 1982 to 1986, including two serious ones, at Niksik among steelworkers and by dockers and bus drivers in the town of ('Red') Split on the Dalmatian coast.[5] Strikes were fanned by the general reduction in real wages of about 25 per cent during 1980-4 and more particularly by a new law, promulgated in the first months of 1984, which forbade enterprises which had made losses from paying enterprise work-forces above the (low) legal minimum wage. Yugoslav ideologists have great difficulty with strikes since, in the absence of private ownership of major means of production, it is not clear (to them) why workers need to strike against 'their own' property. Here Marxist theory ignores the 'alienation' of 'man' from the *state* which Hegel and the young Marx noted[6] but on which 'Marxism-Leninism', Yugoslav style, has little of substance to say.

Money and Banking

Yugoslavia, as the new FPRJ, inherited the Serbian National Bank (created 1882), the State Mortgage Bank (1862) and the Agricultural Bank started in 1929. By 1946 there were also six regional banks. So a process of consolidation began in 1946 under which all existing banks were merged into two: (a) the National Bank entrusted with currency, government banking and short-term credit control and (b) the Investment Bank, given control over investments and foreign loans. By the 1950s, complaints about over-centralization had resulted in the creation of six regional State Banks (mainly to serve agriculture) and ninety communal banks, which serviced communal budgets, collected savings and checked on plan-fulfilment of local enterprises (Vučković, 1956, pp. 10–50). Communal banks ceased in 1952.

Until the mid-1950s the banking system worked within the framework, pioneered in the Soviet Union, of a government credit plan, a cash plan and automatic collection of invoices (Davies, 1958, pp. 157–79, 271). After that date, banks themselves drew up credit balances (Vučković, 1963, p. 366). Enterprises were not allowed to give credits or conduct debt cancellation with each other. This reflected the desire for very tight financial discipline, but the automatic crediting of sellers' accounts when goods were shipped, and automatic credit pipelines to buyers' account, strained the credit plan as the volume of credit depended on the behaviour of debtors rather than on bank policy. By 1951 the system had to be replaced by one of free contracts among trading partners. In 1953 the amount of credit extended was related to the maximum credit used by the enterprise in the previous year; yet this was seen to favour the spendthrift and to penalize the thrifty firm.

The idea of investment auctions, thought to be more suitable to market socialism, was proposed and implemented in 1954 (Neuberger, 1959). A 'socialist credit market' with licensed bidders developed. Those seeking credits competed by rival 'bids' in terms of interest rate and period of repayment. This was in part successful, but only increased the pressure for a thorough-going decentralization of the whole banking system and for 'social self-government' in place of bureaucratic monetary management exercising the main influence over credit functions. The mood in politics in 1954–7 was such that the National Bank could not continue to monopolize all aspects of banking. As a result, foreign credit business was taken on by a new Foreign Trade Bank, and other operations by an Agricultural Bank and an Investment Bank. Interest rates of 6 per cent were introduced for all working capital issued to the industrial and agricultural enterprises.

It was not until 1961 that a series of new banking reforms started up again, beginning with the re-introduction of communal banks as 'basic and universal credit institutions'. Puzzling at the time, the move is now seen by historians as part of the reformers' plan to eliminate centrally-based political interference with the bank: a two-thirds majority of bank management boards were to be nominated by workers' councils located in the territory of the bank (Horvart, 1971a, p. 134). Banks asked foreign firms to consolidate fixed capital (formerly cheap) and working capital funds into a single business fund. The financial autonomy of enterprises was to be strengthened under the 1961 reform of financing from their own ploughed-back profits, a larger proportion of their constant overheads. However, the system was, in a sense, hostage to frequent institutional changes elsewhere in the economy (Basaraba, 1967).

So it proved. The inflationary trend of the 1960s finally made it clear that credit policy must, in a modern economy, be part of overall monetary policy, which is inevitably linked to policies about foreign exchange rates, government budgetary policy and wages policy. To this end, the National Bank discontinued commercial links with firms and reverted to traditional Central Bank role. The space left was taken up by a newer network of commercial banks (Neuberger, 1959). As well, the notion of semi-autonomous banking systems in each republic was overtaken by the idea of establishing banks with enterprises and socio-political communities as equal partners (Jovanović, 1965; Pertot, 1966).

Yet the strong feelings of Croatian and Slovenian politicians in 1971 against 'Serbia-influenced banks'[7] constantly brought the issue of diminishing republican and commercial funds in a federation back to the centre of discussion, and with it, the need for stronger republican-based and commune-based banks (Dmitrijević & Mačesić, 1973). This pattern has continued up to the present time.

Ultimately, the shape of the banking system depends not only on institutional changes and regional-political conflict resolution but also on the type and virulence of the inflation being experienced.[8] Excess demand inflation will be the result of mis-use of short-term credit for longer-term investments and for covering losses on goods that cannot be sold. To solve this required tougher central controls but both nationalism and the desire of Republican/commune leaders to protect uneconomic enterprises ('political factories') worked against this and *for* a regional banking system. The desire of all levels of government to coax the banking system into financing budget deficits also pulls in this direction, exacerbating excess-demand inflationary pressures. Where inflation was of the wage-push variety, as claimed by the Institute of Economic Research in Belgrade for the 1960s, wage increases could only be controlled either by wage moderation exercised by the worker-managers or by means of the banking system refusing to supply increased working-capital funds from which wage rises in enterprises were to be paid. This second alternative, however, ran the risk of causing illiquidity in firms that had fixed taxes to pay and no chance of raising their prices. Incredibly, this sort of consideration was unknown at the time monetary and banking reforms were put through in 1962 (Horvart, 1971a, p. 142).

Once the notion that Yugoslavia had a permanent cost-push inflationary pressure gained ground in official circles, monetary and banking policy altered. The commercial banks had to hold blocked accounts in the National

Bank as a limit on their credit operations; the notion that the banks must play a role in depressing costs to assist in export drives came to be accepted as part of monetary management, although many question whether it remains so today (Pjanić, 1987, ch. 3).

The contemporary Yugoslav banking sytem bears no resemblance as to function, structure or management to the system in the Soviet Union, as espoused in textbooks on Soviet banks (originally, in State Bank of the USSR, 1927, pp. 15–48) or banks of other East European countries (Sulyok, 1966, pp. 24–38). Rather, it is a system that has adjusted first to the new ways enterprises relate to each other on the market, second to the decisions emanating from assemblies of political delegates, and third to changing diagnoses of inflation and consequent re-assessments of the nature and scope of monetary policy. A graphic, if bizarre, example of what I mean here was the decision of the Mikulić cabinet in 1986 to lower the real rate of interest for new bank loans dramatically at a time when Yugoslav enterprises, 40 per cent of them insolvent, were putting pressure on resources via optimistic investment plans.

Foreign Trade

Yugoslavia's rapid economic development in the first sixteen years of socialism altered the sectoral structure of the economy in that the rapid development of producer goods industries in the earlier period set up a spiral of heavy import demands for equipment and some raw materials. Incentive problems in the rural sector robbed Yugoslavia of the status as a successful food exporter, forcing decollectivization of agriculture. Ever since 1961 the growing international trade account deficit has periodically forced tariff cuts (Domandžić, 1966), internal deflation and cuts in living standards (OECD, 1986). These events forced, as early as 18 January 1961, a totally new foreign exchange and foreign trade system based on liberalization and decentralization (Yugoslav Bank for Foreign Trade, 1960, p. 27). This system was again liberalized in 1986 with the introduction of a single foreign exchange rate.

So trade with foreigners is a key weak spot in the whole Yugoslav economy—there is still a problem of low quality goods exported and relatively high costs of production. A lesser, though still significant, issue is severe competition for markets in Western Europe while the political dimensions of Yugoslavia's economic relations with COMECON and Eastern Europe are of no help to rapid improvement in this sphere of operations.

As the 1970s opened, there was a short-lived attempt to reintroduce a form of foreign trade monopoly,[9] to prevent individual firms freely making contracts with foreign firms. The aim was to tighten controls to reduce the balance of payments deficit. However, this policy was short-lived and no general foreign exchange control reappeared until 1983, being soon abandoned. During the rest of the 1970s, the Common Market countries increased their imports from Yugoslavia by 200 per cent, which was much less than the accelerated EEC imports from other countries of 300 per cent. Worse was to follow: between 1980 and 1985 trade between Yugoslavia and the Common Market fell by 15 per cent.

Because of such trade patterns and the fact that Western Europe is the largest lender to the SFRJ, Yugoslavia's economic relations with Common Market countries became a matter of grave importance, as early as the 1960s (Amacher, 1972). However, some of its trade connections are fragile: Yugoslavia is not a member of the Common Market but has made a number of 'special agreements' with the European Union. Moreover, as former colonies of France and Britain, as well as Spain and Portugal, have entered the EEC, Yugoslavia's products face more and more competition so that the 1981 agreement with the Common Market under which the SFRJ can export 70 per cent of her industrial products without duties to Western Europe, may not be enough to head off this competition. As a result Yugoslavia panicked in the 1980s: it adopted a slogan, 'export by any means', involving accelerated exports at low prices of products that the EEC regards as 'sensitive goods'. The unpopularity of Yugoslavia as a result was muted by one bit of luck—the Federal Republic of Germany has Yugoslavia as its twentieth ranking trade partner. As a result it has supported Yugoslavia exporting produce to Western Europe against protests of Southern European states although only 1 per cent of industrial exports from Germany go to Yugoslavia.

The Yugoslav trade deficit with the Common Market under the influence of an intense export drive by Yugoslavia dropped from US$4 billion to US$1 billion in 1980–6 (*Statistical Pocketbook of Yugoslavia*, 1986). Nevertheless, a worry remained for SFRJ; the drop in deficit was more a result of cuts in imports caused by the Yugoslav economic decline of the 1980s than better export performance, and, as noted above, trade between Yugoslavia and members of the Common Market declined by 15 per cent from 1980 to 1985. Overall, receipts on Yugoslavia's total balance with all traders were US$2.166 billion in 1984, while its expenditures for that year were US$2.10 billion. The purely physical trade gap was plugged, therefore, by remittances of Yugoslavs working abroad (US$0.4 billion) and credits. But debt rises offset this contribution as a solution to overall balance of payments' problems.

In the 1980s credits from European investment banks were smaller than expected on the Yugoslav side. By 1980 Yugoslavia already owed a huge US$14 billion to creditors and had promised to pay off US$3 billion each year as various loan repayments fell due.

With IMF help all this had to be rescheduled when new Prime Minister Branko Mikulić replaced Mrs Planinc in 1985 and a deal was made to attack the problem of re-paying an accumulated debt of US$22 billion. Yugoslavia agreed to begin serious repayments in 1988 but to limit the yearly sum to 25 per cent of total hard currency foreign exchange receipts in any one year. This made the whole problem of shifting the debt very much dependent on a rise in exports to countries with convertible currencies. As total exports in 1985-6 were about US$9 billion (and half of this only with convertible-currency countries) it was hard to see how a projected US$6 billion in interest *and* debt repayments could begin even by 1988. The fall in trade deficit with the Common Market was insufficient to offset the destabilizing effects of an overall high level of deficit during 1980-5.

After each balance of payments crisis the inevitable 'stabilization package' has inexorably followed—one familiar to students of IMF–World Bank economic attitudes: (a) contraction of money supply, credit, government budget deficit; (b) devaluation of the currency and relaxation of controls on profit remittances by foreigners;[10] (c) encouragement of new foreign investment by tax benefits and other means.[11]

CMEA, the Communist bloc's common market, is an important influence on Yugoslavia's trade and before 1948 had been totally dominant. Today the Soviet Union remains Yugoslavia's largest trading partner, while Yugoslavia has been an observer at meetings of CMEA since 1964 and at its specialized committees, some of which have been held in Yugoslavia itself. How much technical aid SFRJ gets from the Soviet Union and members of Comecon, however, is not publicly canvassed.

Trade with the Soviet Union is based largely on Yugoslavia paying for Soviet oil with exports which amounted to 623 billion dinars in 1985 compared to imports of 367 billion dinars. This compares to about 170 billion dinars of exports to Italy and 167 billion dinars to Germany, Yugoslavia's biggest Western market. Soviet oil in the 1980s was increased in price and then, when this was not possible due to world oil price trends, the Soviet Union cut back its imports of Yugoslav food, shoes, textiles and furniture.

Here we see that Yugoslavia's non-bloc, pro-Third World stance, a cornerstone of its foreign policy moves imposes costs on the economy.[12] A 'non-aligned' policy hardly allows declining trade with one bloc to be offset by improvements with the other, while it has not proved possible for Yugoslavia to offset trade problems with the various 'blocs' by developing economic relations with the Third World. Few of the 'Group of 77' countries have sizeable trade with Yugoslavia: for example in 1985 exports to the whole of Asia were only worth 1 billion dinars, to Africa 1.92 billion dinars and to South America 1.2 billion dinars compared to 15 billion dinars of exports to Europe (*Statistical Pocketbook of Yugoslavia, 1986*, pp. 105–6).

These exports to 'developing countries', while useful, are too small for a country which stresses the potential of integration with the whole world economy and advocates a 'new international economic order'. Nor are prospects really increasing. The tripartite pact between Yugoslavia, India and Egypt initiated in 1966, when those two countries took one-third of Yugoslav exports to the Third World, came to an end. Oil relations with Libya did not flourish, while Yugoslavia ended up subsidizing Iraqi oil supplies instead of vice versa.

As well, Yugoslavia's foreign policy stance has greatly affected the structure of production in the economy. Attempts to be as self-sufficient as possible in defence has led to purchase of arms from a variety of sources, and to building up import-replacement heavy industries to supply defence needs. The structure of exports and imports has changed to meet such things as Stalin's attempt to destroy their economy in 1948–52 and the more recent need to draw closer to the Western European economic boom.

Table 9.1 shows that today Yugoslav exports are mainly manufactured goods (72 per cent), the rest are ores and 'simply processed goods'. One-third of exports is made up of electrical goods, machinery and transport equipment, a very high proportion for a country at the lower end of the European per capita income scale. Many consumer durables (radios, television sets, washing machines) produced with German partners are exported. One-third of exports, mostly composed of consumer goods, goes to the Soviet Union. It is a very big change from both pre-war Yugoslav patterns of trade and even those of the 1957–61 economic plan which laid the foundations of the industrial economy when timber and bauxite still dominated exports.

On the imports side Yugoslavia imports a huge volume of raw materials (notably coal) and intermediate goods; clearly domestic producers cannot meet local industrial demand. Oil is a major item, and inescapable, but machinery and transport equipment, exported in great value by Yugoslavia, is also a large item on the nation's import bill.

Table 9.1 Structure of exports from Yugoslavia (percentages)

	By end use	
	1984	1985
Intermediate goods	51.2	49.7
Investment goods	17.7	19.2
Consumer goods	31.1	31.1
Total	100.0	100.0
	By degree of manufacture	
Crude articles	6.0	5.3
'Simply transformed' articles	23.0	22.3
'Highly transformed' articles	71.0	72.4
Total	100.0	100.0
	By commodity groups	
Food	8.4	7.9
Beverages and tobacco	1.4	1.1
Raw materials (excl. food)	4.6	4.1
Mineral fuels & lubricant	3.5	3.1
Animal & veg. oils and fats	0.1	0.1
Machinery & transport equipment	31.3	32.7
Miscellaneous manufactured goods	17.9	17.5
Chemicals	9.8	11.2
Commodities	22.7	22.1
Other	0.3	0.2
Total	100.0	100.0

Source: *Statistical Pocketbook of Yugoslavia*, 1986, p. 104.

Industry

Industry employed (out of a total active work-force of 6.4 million persons) more than 2.52 million workers (36 per cent of whom were women) in 1985

compared to 800,000 in 1955 (*Statistical Pocketbook of Yugoslavia*, 1986, p. 41).
It meets a considerable part of the domestic requirement for consumer goods
and, as just noted, provides an increasing share of exports.

An accelerated development of industry began with the first Five Year
Plan in 1947 and effort was concentrated in developing power-supply
resources, production in ferrous and non-ferrous metallurgy and machine-
building capacity. After 20 years, production per capita in electric energy had
increased from 80 to 1,000 kwh; crude steel from 17 to 96 kg; cement from
60 to 190 kg; cotton from 1.3 to 5 kg; all energy from 180 to 1,030 kg per
head; fertilizer from 3 to 96 (SG, 1969; Table 10.1 in Chapter 10).

By the 1980s total production in all these industrial products had
increased substantially (see Table 9.2). At first equipment was imported and
obtained as war reparations, but domestic factories now account for a high
percentage of generators, turbines, textile machinery and shipbuilding.
Geographically, industry was mainly concentrated in the northern part of
Yugoslavia where manufacturing had taken place before the War. Since the
1957–61 plan, there has been a rapid development of new industry in
Montenegro and Macedonia, where industrial raw materials are concentrated. Organizationally there has been a strong trend towards gradual
specialization of plants, and since the 1960s, mergers into bigger units in
order to get economies of scale, a process known in Yugoslavia as *intergracija*
(Mrksa, 1963; Jakić, 1965a; McFarlane, 1966, pp. 124–5). As well, German
partners have invested in Yugoslav joint-ventures, especially in the production of consumer durables. Availability of radio sets rose to 66.4 per cent of
households in 1968 and 69.5 per cent in 1978 (*Statistical Pocketbook of
Yugoslavia, 1986*, p. 57); of television sets from 21.8 per cent of households in
1968 to 71.2 per cent in 1978 while automobiles rose from 7.9 per cent of
households (1968) to 29.2 per cent in 1978 (*Statistical Pocketbook of Yugoslavia,
1986*, p. 58).

Table 9.2 Industrial production of selected goods 1965–85

	1965	1975	1985
Electricity (m.kwh)	5,523	40,040	74,740
Pig iron ('000 tons)	1,115	2,000	3,119
Cement ('000 tons)	3,102	7,066	9,219
Cotton yarn ('000 tons)	86	107	132
Fertilizer ('000 tons)	185	2,196	2,410

Source: *Statistical Pocketbook of Yugoslavia, 1986*, pp. 80–3.

What is the importance of industry to the shape of the Yugoslav economy? Industry facilitates its own growth by the method used in Marxist planning of trying to keep a balance between growth of industrial and agricultural sectors. Early development was difficult as industry had to be financed by heavy taxation of peasants and burdens on sectors like forestry, handicraft and industrial raw materials. It was not really until 1961 that ploughed-back profit from within industry itself was becoming the source of its own investment, allowing recompense to be paid to agriculture in the form of higher rural prices (McFarlane, 1966, p. 121).

The Yugoslavs, of course, did not always have the correct balance between industry and agriculture, between the capital goods sector and the consumer goods sector.[13] Other Communist countries fared little better in the 1960s and 1970s.[14] Today statistics indicate that the State budgets of the federation and republics pay more attention to agriculture and the consumer sector than in the pre-1961 period.[15] While in the first Five Year Plan there was disinvestment in agriculture (Čobelić, 1959, ch. 2; Bićanić, 1973, pp. 120-1) in order to finance the accelerated heavy industry drive, by 1956 at the time of preparation for the new Five Year Plan of 1957-61 gross investment per employed person in agriculture was also very low at 1,671 thousand dinars compared to 17,899 thousand in electric power; 15,581 thousand in shipyards; 8,360 thousand in iron metallurgy; 2,929 thousand in metal manufactures (Federal Planning Commission, 1957).

Another problem, not corrected until the 1960s, was that there were inadequate returns for agricultural exports. Industrial prices in Yugoslavia were 81 per cent above average world prices and agricultural prices 20 per cent lower than world prices in 1952 (Bićanić, 1973, pp. 146-7). The terms of trade were working seriously against agriculture and such low prices drove down incentives for peasants, the value of their farms, and the possibility of peasant household accumulation—the major source for new (minor) investments. In 1961 and 1963 action was taken to raise agricultural prices differentially after admissions by Yugoslav leaders (Kardelj, 1960) that the private sector was suffering low productivity. In the 1980s this process was repeated (*SG*, 1986, p. 89).

Agriculture

Another way of looking at the change in the assigned role of agriculture is to note that in 1952 agriculture accounted for 25 per cent of net national product rising to 30 per cent in 1955 (Institut Za Ekonomiku Investicije, 1965, 47-8; Vasić, 1963) by which time 'market forces' were also influencing the rural sector (e.g., growth of precontracting between cooperatives and trading enterprises for 12 per cent of crop area in 1954, loans to farmers for buying means of production). Beginning in 1957,[16] and especially after the 1960s, agriculture received more funds (inadequate as it turned out). As a result of the new economic plan for 1961-6 extra allocations (Federal Planning Commission, 1960a, 1960b) and price rises awarded to agriculture in 1962-4 (McFarlane, 1966), a further boost was given in a revised development strategy for 1964-70 (Federal Planning Commission, 1964). Since then, despite disappointing results in some years (weather still causes fluctuations), improvement in cereal, vegetables and industrial crops (tobacco, cotton, sugar beet) has been considerable.[17]

The problem of agriculture is at once a problem of productivity and of social tensions in the village. Yugoslav leaders have recognized this from the time that collectivization was made voluntary in 1950, and especially in the 1960s when improved results in agriculture were vital to sustain the accelerated industrialization and general economic growth anticipated in the 1961-6 economic plan (Bakarić, 1960; Kardelj, 1960). Although Communist leaders were outspoken on the problem, they did not go as far as the critics (Citrić, 1971) on causes of strains in the 'social relations of production' emergent in agriculture. What were these?

From the outset the problems were (a) relative overpopulation in the agrarian sector; (b) incentives; (c) level and structure of investment. A limit of ten hectares on any individual's ownership of land, and taxation on cadastral yield of the land, remained basic aspects of government interference since collectivization was, in effect, abandoned. The aim was to prevent a large *kulak* class from arising in the countryside and to give some land to each family in the large rural population to avoid agricultural unemployment. Gradually, both the implementation of the ceiling and other imposts and laws affecting ownership and hiring of labour have been either not enforced or have been relaxed. By the 1960s social relations had also been transformed. There was a growth of *kulak* farmers on the one hand and agri-business corporations on the other, eclipsing the small peasant. In 1969 some 278,000 people owned 3.5 million hectares out of 10 million in total while at the bottom 1.027 million people owned only 0.9 million hectares (Citrić, 1971). However, the private sector dropped from 64.3 per cent of agriculture production value in 1961 to 52.4 per cent in 1969 (Citrić, 1971). The reason was the growth of agri-businesses such as PKB (a Belgrade based firm involved in milk, vegetable and fruit processing) as major economic agents in the agrarian economy. These new organizations were allowed to raise prices much faster than individual peasants. On a measure with the year 1955 as index of 100, the individual sector raised its prices from 113 in 1961 to 135 in 1969 whereas the 'social sector' (mainly agri-business and state farms) raised their prices from an index of 252 to 545 over the same period.

Those peasants who were not 'go ahead' *kulaks* found themselves subcontracting to agri-businesses and falling under their control. The consequent loss of incentives was shown in the steady decline in private agricultural output from an index of 119 to 98 (1961-9) with 1955 taken as the base year. Pig output fell from 1.7 million in 1965 to 0.9 million in 1968 and 1969; cattle from 335,000 in 1966 and 316,000 in 1969. By 1984 there were increases of a moderate size in output of these products: beef output rose from 393,000 tons in 1974 to 350,000 in 1984 and pork from 393,000 to 569,000 tons (*Statistical Pocketbook of Yugoslavia, 1986*, p. 73). A good deal of this increase was on non-private farms.

Hence, rural society has been polarized into successful trading and production companies contracting with *kulaks* on the one hand, and a large struggling sector of small peasants on small plots of land on the other. In 1987 discussions were under way to amend the Constitution to encourage successful farmers further.

The correction in proportions between investment allocated to industry (and its share in the structure of production) on the one hand, and agriculture on the other, have been significant in stabilizing the economy but perhaps have not gone as far as some economists would like. This question of the balance between industry and agriculture remains a source of concern at the heart of Yugoslav economic policy. It took sixteen years for economic authorities in FPRJ to realize that the *order* of development was not a clear-cut issue, that a dogmatic answer had been given to the question: should industry be developed first and then its funds be extended to agriculture or should investment be given first to food and raw materials as a base for subsequent advancement in other fields? By the 1970s the idea that both policies—or rather a mix of them—was needed had gathered force but was not universally accepted until the economic problems of the 1980s concentrated attention on the issue.

It was a complex of social and cultural factors, such as the 1971 Croatian and Slovenian revolts against 'unitarianism', which were at fault. Only a few economists (Horvart, 1964; Samardžija, 1968) saw that there was a purely economic issue as well—too high a *rate* of investment had been carried out in the economy and had destabilized it, and this investment contained an inappropriate structure. This is examined in the next section of this chapter.

Investments

Apart from the industry/agriculture balance, a key 'proportion' in a socialist economy is that between the capital goods sector (called by Marx 'Department I') and the consumer-goods sector (Marx's 'Department II'). This is because (Sirotković, 1966; Jakić, 1965a) the crucial allocation of new investments each year between the two departments greatly affects the *rate* and *structure* of future economic growth. Too big an allocation to Department I can destroy incentives by creating shortages in the availability of consumer goods to the new and existing work-forces, with consequent falls in productivity (Stojanovic, R., 1970; Čobelić & Stojanović, R. 1966; McFarlane, 1984a).

It took a decade after 1950 for Yugoslavian economists fully to absorb this lesson, and further, to realize that a cycle of investment was operating in Yugoslavia. Of what did the investment cycle consist and what was the cycle's overall impact on policy towards investment planning? In general, the economists involved in this research saw the cycles as *fluctuations in the rate of growth* (Horvart, 1971a); a number of interesting features were unearthed: the rate of investment had risen very sharply to four times the pre-war level to set the cycle moving in its first phase; other phases followed (in which a four-year movement up and down was characteristic) until the 1970s.

As shown in the next chapter there was a very high rate of growth of investment in the first Five Year Plan, leading to serious imbalances in the economy when 40 per cent of investment financed equipment and buildings in heavy industry. It was not till the 1960s that a combination of planners (Sirotković, 1961; FZZPP, 1964; Pertot, 1966; Horvart, 1962) economists (Vasić, 1963) and some officials (Jakić, 1965a) insisted on a more institutionalized method of rectifying structural proportions in the 'real accumulation fund' (total investment fund) of the economy. At this later time, too, some attention was given to the issue of the *effectiveness* with which new investments were being used (Institut Za Ekonomiku Investicija, 1963). After this the idea of 'heavy industry at all costs' lost any ideological hegemony it had enjoyed (Medenica, 1968).

The serious problem of an investment cycle was gradually perceived by academic economists as a significant feature of the Yugoslav 'market-socialist' system (Čobelić and Stojanović, 1966; Bajt, 1971; Horvart, 1971b). This cycle of economic growth is now seen as something that can also emerge in all planned economies (McFarlane, 1984b) but at this time concentration was on finding Yugoslavia's particular mechanisms.

A. Bajt (Bajt, 1971) argued that consumer demand rather than investment was the autonomous movement that put a floor on the cycle and helped produce movement at the lower turning points. Then it was noticed by the researchers of the cycle referred to above that *inventories accumulated in downswings and decumulated in upswings* —very different behaviour from that in other socio-economic systems:[18] the 'acceleration' principle was not operative;[19] prices varied inversely with the cycle; changes in import and export 'elasticities' (of supply and demand) produced the cycles' upper turning points, but this whole process also ends in an explosion of the balance of payments deficit.

What was not, perhaps, admitted was that the *use of market mechanisms*, the high level of management uncertainty, and the fact that the economy-wide rate of growth and not just development in a particular sector exerted a volatile influence, all pointed to problems at the very heart or *modus operandi* of the system: In a market socialist economy:

the only way of precluding a large measure of chronic unemployment may be to maintain the total rate of investment at a given arbitrary level, which might be quite different from that level which would be dictated by other considerations. Moreover, it is not difficult to show that, unless some stabilizing mechanism is introduced, in addition to or as a substitute for the pricing mechanism, a socialist economy may inherit the instability of capitalism in an even more pronounced form . . . As soon as it is realised that the demand for capital is a function, interalia, of the *current rate of investment* and that this demand will vary directly and not inversely, with the rate of investment, *ceteris paribus*, the existence of a powerful destabilizing influence inherent in the relationship becomes apparent.[20]

Overview

The review above of prices, trade, banking and investment patterns has outlined various *allocation mechanisms* of the SFRJ. However, in this chapter I have suggested that apart from the allocation mechanisms one needs to look at institutions. Any society decides the rate and structure of investment via the particular institutions it designs to meet its own needs (Spulber, 1961, pp. xi-xii, 102). In Yugoslavia, decentralization in both the banking and investment fields has increased the role for allocative mechanisms influenced by trends in supply and demand. The institutional framework, however, is that of 'labour economics'—workers' control, the role of unions in a socialist economy, the attitude of unions to workers' control. The enterprises tend to maximize net income per worker; inflation and fluctuations in investment result from the fact that 'in a market socialist economy there is almost invariably an excess of ex ante investment over ex ante saving, owing to the special psychology of entrepreneurs, even though in Yugoslavia savers are not the same people as investors and a market link subsists between them' (Wiles, 1961, p. 92).

Some of these issues are pursued in more detail in Chapter 13, but first, the next group of chapters outline the changes over time in Yugoslavia's economic fortunes and the economic policies pursued in the period after the establishment of the Marxist regime by the SKJ and SFRJ.

10   The Yugoslav Economy, 1947–1961

The record of economic performance under review in this chapter is divided into a number of periods: reconstruction (1945–7), which consisted largely of repairing the transport network and clearing the rubble from bombed cities; then a first Five Year Plan, which was suspended after four years due to the blockade imposed by the East European countries and the Soviet Union; the relatively successful results for the period 1952–60; and finally, a plan that launched accelerated economic development under more normal conditions, a program of economic development which ran from 1957 to 1961.

The First Five Year Plan, 1947–51

The tasks to be tackled by the new Marxist regime in 1946 were daunting indeed. War had killed up to 10 per cent of the population and all but completely destroyed railway rolling stock and most factories. As well, illiterates constituted close to 40 per cent of the adult population and these people were largely amongst the agricultural population (77 per cent of the total). This was the 'human raw material' which would have to be tapped for rapid development. The pre-war economy had been largely pre-industrial, sustained by export of foodstuffs and raw materials, especially minerals. It was decided to change this, but a new Soviet-style industrialization, seen as the answer to development problems and as a model by the Yugoslav Communist movement still basically loyal to Moscow, had to start virtually from scratch. Table 10.1 tells the story of the low level of 1939 and the recovery by 1968.

A start was made by reconstruction gangs rebuilding broken capital stock. Next, nationalization of most private productive capital was undertaken—in industry, mining, transport and banking in 1946 and in retail trade and catering in 1948 (Bićanić, 1973, ch. 2). The detailed bureaucracy and statistical service necessary for a highly centralized planning system was set up in 1947. By 1949, 13,000 groups of commodities were being planned from the SZZPP, the Belgrade-based Federal Planning Commission. The State Budget controlled an incredible two-thirds of the national income in 1948–9 (Kidrič, 1950, p. 453). Bićanić and others wrote that the annual economic

Table 10.1 Trends in per capita output, 1939–68

	Before the War		1968 Yugoslavia
	Yugoslavia	Western Europe*	
Production per capita			
Electric energy, KWH	80	500–1,300	1,000
Crude steel, kg	17	150–300	96
Cement, kg	60	100–190	190
Cotton yarn, kg	1.3	5–11	5
Energy, kg	180	2,100–4,300	1,030
Fertilizers, kg	3	20–65	96
Sugar, kg	5	24–47	25
Stocks per 1,000 of population			
Radio sets	9	110–200	160
Automobiles	1	17–50	20

*France, Germany, Sweden, United Kingdom.
Sources: *SG*, 1969; *UN Statistical Yearbook*, 1956.

plan weighed 3,300 lb, although no one seems to know what its specific gravity amounted to in detail.

It was under these conditions that the abortive first Five Year Plan was launched in 1947. It gave overwhelming emphasis to capital formation in basic industries (power, processing of raw materials, metals) as Tables 10.2 and 10.3 illustrate by showing the dramatic rise in their share of fixed capital. Investment in the Five Year Plan launched in 1947 had been targeted to increase to a level of 3.5 times that of 1939 and as a *rate* of total national

Table 10.2 Index of fixed capital and employment in basic industry, 1938–56 (1938 = 100)

	1938	1953	1956
Production in industry & mining	100	183	266
No. employed in industry & mining	100	202	275
Value of fixed capital investment in industry and mining	100	248	342

Source: SZZPP, *Materiali Za Perspektivna Plan 1957–61*, Belgrade, 1957.

Table 10.3 Share of 'basic industry' branches in value of fixed
capital of the economy, 1938–56

	1938	1953	1956
A. *Basic industry*:	54.5	69.5	74.9
Energy	27.6	29.7	29.3
Metals	11.1	14.7	15.7
Processing of raw materials	3.4	13.3	17.9
Other basic industry	12.4	11.8	12.0
B. *Other industrial branches*	45.5	30.5	25.1
Total	100.0	100.0	100.0

Source: SZZPP, *Materiali Za Perspektivna Plan 1957–1961*, Belgrade, 1957.

investment it reached 27.3 per cent in 1951, having hit 28 per cent for 1948–50. Eminent economists in Eastern Europe later explained the enormous strains of such high accumulation rate (Kalecki, 1965; O. Šik, 1967) but at this time Yugoslav planners did not have a hard and fast idea of an optimum rate of investment (Stojanović, R. 1970, pp. 111–33; Horvart, 1964, pp. 165–20). They often seemed to assume an unlimited demand existed for capital and that personal consumption was a sort of passive residual, which could be reduced 'flexibly'. All problems of bottlenecks seemed solveable by new investment allocations.

As a result of these attitudes, 40 per cent of the national investment fund went to the *fixed capital* (equipment, machinery, plant, buildings) of heavy industry during 1947–52. Over the same period collective consumption (schools and hospitals) got 20 per cent. For 1947 to 1956 some 58 per cent of investment (net of collective consumption) went into heavy industry (*Yugoslav Survey*, 1957; SZZPP, 1960).

As an inevitable outcome, by 1954 the 'leading link' priorities of the regime such as power (31 per cent), iron and steel, machine-building and shipyards (51 per cent) ate up the allocation from the total investment fund earmarked for industrial investment. Left in the wake of this 'super industrialization' were, in the first place, the consumer-durables section of the consumer goods sector as a whole (only 18 per cent of industrial investment) and such sectors as agriculture, transport and trade (see Table 10.4)

What was the impact on improvement possibilities in the area of the standard of living in this early period of the regime? Table 10.5 shows that

Table 10.4 Percentage share of sectors in gross fixed investments, 1954 and 1957

	1954	1957
A. *'Economic' Investments*	78	74
Industry and mining	51	33
Agriculture	5	11
Forestry	1	2
Construction	2	3
Transport	14	19
Trade	4	5
Craft	1	1
B. *'Social' Investments*	22	26
Housing and communal	14	17
Cultural and social services	5	4
Administration	3	5
Total	100	100

Sources: As Table 10.3; Yugoslav Investment Bank (1958).

Table 10.5 Index of individual personal consumption per head, 1952–7 (1952 = 100)

1952	100.0
1953	101.2
1954	106.4
1955	114.2
1956	121.1
1952–6	106.9
1957	119.7

Source: As Table 10.3.

after the blockade and excessive consumption sacrifice (to release funds for investment) up to 1953, there was a jump in personal consumption per head. To go further into the share of the working class in the economic growth of 1947–61 we now have to take account of the improving rights after 1952 of workers' councils to determine income distribution problems.

Innovations of the 1950s: New Mechanisms for Distribution of Net Income of Firms

It was in the 1950s that a dramatic but perennial issue of Yugoslav political economy arose in quite an acute form. This was how the net income (profit after taxes and minimum wages had been paid) should be allocated between higher wages, workers' welfare, depreciation funds of the enterprise and 'ploughing back the profits' in expanding the equipment of the firm. In the West this problem would come under the rubric of managerial prerogatives and industrial relations. In a 'worker-managed' firm the situation was to be more complex. A considerable part of Chapter 13 is devoted to explaining why this is so; here we will mention the impact in the 1950s of these new ideas on Yugoslav planning as seen by participants (Sirotković, 1961, 1966; B. Jelić, 1961; Horvart, 1964; Uvalić, 1962; Kardelj, 1961b).

Under the Law on Contributions from the Income of Economic Organizations (1950 and as amended) and the Law on Contributions from the Personal Income of Workers two aspects of 'industrial relations' stood out. First, there was the right of workers and their delegates to *full information* on assets, production and investment plans, pay scale, health and safety issues. Second, there was the *right to manage* of workers' councils elected from workers' assemblies. Sometimes these two aspects were compatible, sometimes not; both functions were obviously threatened if superior organs imposed a level of taxation that made the 'net income' of enterprises so small as to cramp the planning of assets and the administration of things at factory level.

The law of 1950 *began* the process of implementing the goal of self-management but the actual experience of the operation of workers' councils allowed new insights and forced new regulations throughout the 1950s.

In the 1950–6 Yugoslav system (and in the Soviet system) the way that net profits of an enterprise were distributed was strictly controlled by law: so much had to go into extra wages, so much to an amortization pool, so much in social investment (grants to local communes to build workers' flats, etc.). The abandonment of this system in favour of complete independence in the distribution of net income or 'profit' in Yugoslavia suggested that a conflict can emerge between the self-interest of members of the factory, and the interests of the community. For example, wages might be increased, and, in the face of short-run inelasticity in the supply of consumer goods, might inflate the price level or at least cause harmful differential price increases, which, through the price mechanism, might distort the allocation of resources. Or again, freedom of firms to make minor investments might strain the supply of savings and the supply of capital goods. All this raised the problem of the development of means of hedging-in the operation of spontaneous factors, and also forced innovations to be made in the taxation system. That is, instead of interfering with 'net profits', the authorities were told to operate on those 'payments to society' (taxes, rents, interest) which were obligatory on firms and whose size, when subtracted from income, determined the level of profit. As later experience showed, planners also went too far in this direction, forcing a major reform in 1965.

In Yugoslavia itself, opposition to the new scheme came from the Trade Union Organization. For the 'price' of the extra freedom in distribution of assets was the imposition across the economic sectors of a more uniform rate of 'payments to society'. This, in practice, weakened the marginal, less efficient, firms which had been kept alive by discriminatory tax charges in their favour in the previous system. Some sackings from these enterprises seemed inevitable—a source of much trade union worry—but in practice fall-out was limited by the exercise of political pressure to protect such enterprises from bankruptcy and closure. Rather, there was a sustained attempt in the 1960s to 'integrate' such firms with others as a result of some new schemes that advocated the breaking down (in Yugoslavia) of industries into autonomous units, which, however, proved too small to reap the benefit of modern technology and management. This meant that specialization and coordination of plants was lacking and the economists' 'external economies of scale' were not achieved. These 'economies', it will be recalled, had been claimed as the main advantage of Soviet-style central production planning in which detailed output programmes for each enterprise were dove-tailed by plans drawn up in a central planning commission.

There is little doubt that in the period 1950–9 this was a valid criticism of the efficiency of the Yugoslav system. Together with worker disincentive flowing from dissatisfaction with low wages, this explained why it was that labour intensity and *gross* output had been increasing, yet productivity per head had risen very slowly (Horvart, 1964; Sirotković, 1966). At the same time it was stressed that a hyper-centralized planning system, with different industries separated from each other by virtue of control by different ministries, can also neglect the possibilities of plant coordination and external economies of scale. Again, a half-way house between centralist coordination and autonomy of industrial firms seemed called for, and Yugoslav experiments in this regard at first seemed encouraging. The functions of these 'combinations' were to write yearly plans for the particular branch of industry, to assemble and distribute financial resources of firms in consultation with the banking system, to give advice on price policy and wages policy, and to exchange information *between* firms in the industry. In the new framework each firm's directors had to sit on a 'college of instructors' and techno-economic councils composed of experts. All these methods seemed to be aiming to combine the virtues of Soviet central control and Yugoslav-style 'autonomy' for enterprises, seen as a half-way house between plan and market, and the Yugoslav economists decided to attempt to improve the 'chambers of commerce' to have them work on similar lines. A conference on productivity held in March 1959 recommended increased standardization of production, the setting up of 'associations of factories' and their cooperation in the manufacturing process of their industry.[1]

The workers councils, at this stage were 'managing state property on behalf of society'. That is, state ownership prevailed over the means of production in most areas of social life (although housing and building sites were not nationalized until 1959). The ground for this form of public ownership had been laid by the nationalization of banks in 1946 (Vučković, M. 1956) and by the 1948 Acts covering industries, transport retail and catering (Bićanić, 1973, p. 26).

However, as Chapter 13 indicates, this situation was ambiguous. When does total 'self-management' of an enterprise become *de facto* enterprise ownership rather than state ownership? A new concept of social property began to be discussed in the 1950s, with the idea evolving of the various taxes and 'contributions' to communes and government at higher levels being regarded as a kind of rent for the use of state property. Certainly they performed this function in practice until codification of new concepts of social property in the 1960s (Djordević, 1966).

The Economic Performance of the 'New System', 1952-6

The extra data that follows (Tables 10.7 to 10.12) show how the economy grew[2] and how the structure of production and investment changed. First, however, it is necessary to start with an image of the short-term disruption caused to Yugoslav trade (and through that to the entire economy) as a result of the Soviet East European 'blockade' which followed Tito's expulsion from 'the camp' in 1948. The figures below are self-explanatory; the only melancholy interest is in noting the differential rate of response of each 'socialist' trading partner.

Table 10.6 The Soviet camp's blockade of Yugoslavia's foreign trade, 1949

Trading partner	Yugoslavia's imports by country of origin (m. tons)					Yugoslavia's exports by country of destination (m. tons)				
	1945	1946	1947	1948	Blockade 1949	1945	1946	1947	1948	Blockade 1949
Albania	4,686	—	2,322	—	nil	3,751	20	40	6	nil
Bulgaria	914	9,193	17,914	12,747	12,528	914	9,193	17,914	12,747	865
Hungary	85	16,380	590,843	976,685	190,263	85	16,380	590,843	976,005	190,463
GDR	—	113	4,776	22,689	1,460	—	113	4,776	22,089	1,460
Poland	366	2,040	53,916	183,150	26,083	306	2,040	53,916	183,150	26,303
Romania	75	921	19,585	5,011	32	75	921	19,585	15,011	32
Soviet Union	28,985	211,800	200,797	262,321	104,208	28,945	211,800	200,797	223,210	104,208
Czechoslovakia	7,192	67,594	181,346	366,781	76,733	7,192	67,594	181,346	366,781	76,372

Source: SZZS, *Statistička Spoljne Trgovine FR Jugoslavije* (Yugoslav Foreign Trade Statistics), Belgrade, 1953.

The National Income

(a) Between 1952 and 1956 the national income rose by 8.5 per cent per annum (if we include the period of blockade, the rate of increase for 1947–56 was 4.5 per cent per annum); (b) this rate of increase compared with 7.9 per cent in Austria (1948–54), 10 per cent per annum in West Germany (1949–55), 6.8 per cent Italy (1949–55).[3]

Value of Production of the Main Branches of the Economy

It is usual in planned economies to break the total figure for national income down into source according to seven key sectors. Table 10.7 shows the story from 1947 to 1956. The longer-term influence of the Cominform blockade on Yugoslavia (1949–53) is clearly shown in all fields. Only in industry, where great sacrifices were made, was production expanded. In agriculture, fluctuations in value of production were mainly a result of climatic influences, which (because of inadequate investment in agriculture in this period) had a disproportionately large influence on the harvest in Yugoslavia, and 1957 produced a record harvest due to favourable weather conditions. The reduction in the contribution from forestry was part of an overall plan to slow up the exploitation of timber resources. The economic performance 1952–6 does not show a remarkably successful increase in production in some branches but the industrial base of the economy, necessary to launch future growth was, on the whole, achieved by 1956. The structure of the total production of the economy by sector over 1952–6 was as follows: industry 42.1 per cent of the total; agriculture 29.1 per cent; forestry 2.8 per cent; construction 6.5 per cent; transport 5.8 per cent; trade and commerce 8.6 per cent; handicrafts 5.2 per cent (SZZPP, 1957).

Earlier we noted the small allocation of gross investment to agriculture of 1952 being doubled but still far too small in relation to industry. Clearly an adjustment of 'proportions' in the economy was becoming necessary by 1957. However, the planners ignored this. The decision of the Five Year Plan of 1957–61 was to upgrade trade and commerce to 9.4 per cent of total production by 1961 and to upgrade transport to 6.5 per cent by 1961, but agriculture's *proportion* was cut back to 23.2 per cent for 1961 from 29.1 per cent over 1952–6 (SZZPP, 1957).

A number of other sectors were not only starved for a share in the overall investment fund but also experienced raw materials' shortages which held up

Table 10.7 Indices of the value of production by sector, 1947–56 (1947 = 100)

Year	Industry	Agriculture	Forestry	Construction	Transport	Trade	Craft
1947	100.0	100.0	100.0	100.0	100.0	100.0	100.0
1948	124.0	116.3	133.7	98.3	146.7	118.1	102.5
1949	138.0	119.3	162.2	107.5	171.5	121.9	110.4
1950	142.2	87.0	132.7	105.6	189.7	114.8	127.8
1951	137.2	128.2	114.3	88.9	181.9	105.0	136.7
1952	135.5	84.6	110.4	84.8	120.0	112.8	149.2
1953	151.3	121.6	88.1	98.5	148.2	140.2	152.3
1954	169.0	107.3	86.6	100.6	166.6	178.4	169.5
1955	191.0	122.4	86.8	88.9	203.7	190.3	174.7
1956	206.6	105.9	98.4	70.4	224.9	194.0	193.7

Source: SZZPP, Draft Plan for the FPRJ for 1957–61, Belgrade, 1957.

their expansion. Those results which were (in the main) satisfactory were at the level of the regimes' two goals of expanding the annual rate of growth of total product and expanding employment. We saw in Table 10.7 the growth of output. Also important was the growth of employment (Table 10.2). In the period 1952 to 1957 the average index of employment in industry rose from 70 to 107 (with the year 1956 − 100) and for the economy as a whole by 39 per cent (ILO, 1962, p. 16). However, wages of workers, except for skilled workers, were stagnant during the plan (Horvart, 1964, p. 125).

Critics have pointed to serious structural weaknesses during this first plan, such as neglect of investment in agriculture and consumer goods, while leading Yugoslav experts like Bićanić commented on the relatively slow growth of the economy in the first Five Year Plan followed by better results in 1952–60. However, inevitable gestation lags in finishing projects should be kept in mind in looking at the times in which a jump was recorded in total output. Table 10.8 can be misleading as to the best performed period if one forgets about the gestation lags before key projects come 'on stream'. Many construction works were started in the late 1940s and did not come into production until later, thereby boosting rather artificially the output figure shown in Table 10.8 for 1952–60 output growth rates.

Table 10.8 Growth of the Yugoslav economy, 1946–68 (rates of growth, per cent per annum)

	Central planning 1946–52	Decentralization 1952–60	Self-government 1960–8
Gross National Product	2.3*	9.8	6.8‡
Industrial output	12.9	13.4	7.9
Agricultural output	−3.1*	8.9	2.1
Export of commodities	−3.1†	11.7	7.0
Import of commodities	3.6†	9.7	7.0
Employment§	8.3*	6.9	2.4

* 1947–52.
† 1948–52.
‡ 1960–7.
§ Persons employed outside private agriculture.
Sources: SG, various years.

Incentives became a brake on economic growth as the period 1952–60 drew to an end. Among key problems here was that wage relativities were being squeezed in this period (Table 10.9), while managers faced bewildering changes in the way enterprise taxes were being levied. Lack of incentive and 'too many' small firms combined to produce low productivity in the 1950s. Nevertheless, the rhythm of production by 1960 had stabilized labour productivity, while the economic proportions in the economy, as well as export performance, had greatly improved. This was largely because strenuous efforts were made to improve the structure of investments, to encourage efficiency by lowering the rates of some enterprise taxes and by introducing better rural incentives.

Table 10.9 Index of wage rates, 1938–57

	1938	1951	1957
Wages of unskilled workers	100	100	100
Average wages of *all* workers	100	100	100
Wages of skilled workers	330	133	149
Salaries of government employees	166	103	135

Source: *Information Bulletin about Yugoslavia*, no. 18, 1954 (quoted Horvart, 1964, p. 125).

The Five Year Plan, 1957–61

The new self-management rules for distributing enterprise income and the gradual tapering off of the impact of the Cominform blockade encouraged planners in 1956 to make a new start and to promote a new economic plan. It proved to be one of the most successful episodes in the post-War economic history of Yugoslavia, primarily because inflation was very moderate and agricultural results improved.

The 1957–61 Five Year Plan set targets for value of gross output of the sectors in the 1957–61 plan as shown in Table 10.10. If we look at these as rates of increase, Table 10.11 shows high results were expected. This series of planned output increases was to be brought about by changing the distribution of investment funds as compared to the 1952–6 period (for which earlier period see Table 10.4). The new *structure of investment* for 1957–61 was to be as shown in Table 10.12.

Table 10.10 Output targets of the 1957–61
Five Year Plan (billion dinars)

	1956	1961
Economy as a whole	3,338	5,260
Industry	1,778	2,986
Agriculture	686	979
Forestry	69	71
Building	214	358
Transport	218	336
Trade	197	278
Crafts	176	252

Source: SZZPP, *Draft Plan for the FPRJ for 1957–1961*,
Belgrade, 1957.

Table 10.11 Planned rates of increase of output,
1957–61

	(1956 − 100)	Index of average yearly increase, 1957–61
Total economy	157.6	109.5
Industry	168.0	111.0
Agriculture	142.7	107.4
Forestry	102.9	100.6
Building	167.3	110.9
Transport	154.3	109.1
Trade	141.1	107.1
Craft	143.2	107.4

Source: SZZPP, *Draft Plan for the FPRJ for 1957–1961*, Belgrade,
1957.

Table 10.12 Target investment in fixed capital: economic branches, 1956–61

	1956 (b. dinars)	1961 (b. dinars)	1961 index (1956 = 100)	Yearly av. amount (b. dinars)	Percentage in each economic branch, 1957–61
Industry & mining	167.4	187.4	111.9	174.8	44.0
Agriculture	30.5	90.0	295.6	68.6	17.3
Forestry	8.7	7.1	81.6	7.3	1.8
Construction	8.1	15.5	191.4	13.7	3.4
Transport	72.4	110.9	153.2	95.2	23.9
Commerce	18.3	31.3	171.0	26.6	6.7
Craft	3.5	5.2	148.6	4.3	1.1
Water power	3.5	8.0	228.6	7.0	1.8
Total	312.4	455.4	145.8	397.5	100.0

Source: SZZPP, Draft Plan for the FPRJ for 1957–1861, Belgrade, 1957.

The Share of Consumption

In the period 1952–6 the level of consumption increased by an average of 6 per cent per annum. During the same period the increase of national income was 8.4 per cent. However, the figure of 6 per cent per annum for consumption was itself made up of an average of 4.6 per cent increase per annum in *personal* consumption, and a 17.6 per cent increase per annum in 'social standard' (public health, social services, etc.). The Five Year Plan 1957–61 provided for an increase in *individual* consumption of 7 per cent each year—the 'consumption fund' was to increase by 350 milliard dinars (40 per cent) over the whole period. 'Social standard' was to increase by 90 milliard dinars or 70 per cent over the planning period, which gave an average increase of 11.5 per cent each year. Thus resources aimed to raise the standard of living were to increase on average by 8 per cent per annum or 45 per cent over the period to 1961.

The Balance of International Payments Problem

This was the weak link: Yugoslavia had to rely heavily on imports of machinery for industrialization. At the same time, with unpredictable harvests, the country had difficulty in finding enough marketable surplus agricultural production to export in exchange for these capital imports. The deficit in the balance of payments (1952–6) was as shown in Table 10.13. Therefore, the 1957–61 Five Year Plan tried to close this gap by exporting more and more manufactured and semi-manufactured goods and by altering the types of imports (less food to be imported and more consumer goods and raw materials were to be produced domestically).

Table 10.13 Balance of trade, 1953–6 (in milliard dinars)

	Internal prices			World prices		
	Imports	Exports	Difference	Imports	Exports	Difference
1953	207.2	130.0	−77.2	86.1	48.6	−37.5
1954	200.2	155.2	−45.0	83.3	53.1	−30.5
1955	234.8	171.0	−63.8	95.8	54.8	−41.0
1956	261.6	221.8	−39.8	97.5	64.8	−32.7

Despite the problem here the new plan and the earlier results of 1952–6 seemed to hold promise for the 1960s—the promise of faster growth[4] *with* more consumption rather than *at the expense* of more consumption.[5]

Overview

From the early 1950s up to 1956 agricultural production had developed relatively slowly, its 1956 level exceeding pre-War by only 3.2 per cent (Yugoslav Bank for Foreign Trade, 1960, p. 11) although its share in net national product had risen to 30 per cent from 25 per cent in 1952. After the new Five Year Plan was put into effect for 1957–61, agriculture jumped to 6 per cent above the pre-War level, with much of the improvement taking place in 1959. Industrial results also were satisfactory after 1955, rising from an index of 52 (with 1959 = 100) in 1955 to 82 in 1957 and more than 113 in 1960. Exports followed this trend: using the same index (1959 = 100) they rose from 61 in 1955 to 119 in 1960 (Yugoslav Bank for Foreign Trade, 1960, pp. 6–7). From 1956 to 1960 alone there was a big jump in production of between 17 and 26 per cent in metal manufacturing, crude petroleum production, electrical manufacturing, chemicals and food processing (Yugoslav Bank for Foreign Trade, 1960, p. 8).

However, the period of the later 1950s was not problem-free. Although improvement in economic use of raw materials and electric power, improved management and economies of scale from amalgamation and concentration of enterprises boosted labour productivity in the period, inflation at a worrying rate appeared as an unwelcome curtain on the 1950s. A big increase in investment outlays destabilized the capital goods market, and exacted a scarcity of building materials while a number of sectors were working at full capacity; as well, bank credit was expanded rather too generously. As a result, prices rose 7 per cent overall in 1960 after a period of price stability in 1956–9. Agricultural prices within the overall movement of the price level rose 10 per cent and industrial services by 9 per cent. Action taken in the early 1960s by the Investment Bank and the National Bank to restrain inflation were hampered by bad weather in 1962 and by a catastrophic earthquake in Skopje, the reconstruction of which required the diversion of the best equipment and labour from other sectors.

Yet even by the mid-1950s the long-term inflationary trend that was to pulverize the Yugoslav economy after 1965 was evident in the *structure* of the accumulation (investment) trends. In 1955, the consumption fund at 1,187 milliard dinars (in current prices) was simply too small when compared to

2,079.5 milliard dinars in the capital goods industry,[6] given that a great mass of peasants were being given new jobs in expanding industries and required more and more wage-goods, while those peasants who remained had insufficient access to consumer goods even where they had made money by raising their productivity. The inevitable imbalance in supply and demand for consumption goods alone put pressure on the price level, forced accelerated imports and with this set in motion the possibility of the development of that other 'twin' of Yugoslavia's economic woes—a balance of payment deficit.

11 The Yugoslav Economy: Experiments of the 1960s

Crisis Tendencies

The outstanding feature of the 1960s was that the sound foundation to faster economic growth given by the 1957–61 Five Year Plan did not result in sure building on that foundation. Instead a series of economic and political experiments dominated the decade, which ended with a balance of payments crisis, problems in the area of income distribution and a looming dissatisfaction in Croatia and Slovenia concerning their economic role in the federation.

Since the decade saw a new Constitution introduced in 1961 and a major economic reform tried out from 1963, we may regard 1961 as a convenient cut-off point from which to analyse the *second phase* of development while regarding the period 1947–61 as the first phase. This may also be a justified bit of periodization because a new planning methodology was applied from 1961[1] and a new system of allocating investments was set up (Yugoslovenska Investiciona Banka, 1963, pp. 25–6), a system later justified by leading figures of the regime (Tito, 1971, p. 185); as well, a new foreign-exchange and customs tariff system was introduced (Yugoslav Bank for Foreign Trade, 1960, p. 26–7; Domandžić, 1966, pp. 345–8).

Action taken here as well in the money and banking area[2] indicated that a number of the more serious economic issues were already being tackled in 1961. First, there was the problem that the dinar was overvalued and the exchange rate regime confusing, so that it was decided to reduce tariff protection and liberalize imports in the hope of encouraging more competition in the economy (Domandžić, 1966). Multiple exchange rates were abandoned and sectoral coefficients of foreign exchange earnings also abandoned. In their place was a single exchange rate, no protection for agriculture and timber but a customs tariff giving 10 to 40 per cent protection for consumer goods and 17 to 60 per cent for industrial goods. National Bank foreign exchange allocations and import quotas determined the flow of imports (Yugoslav Bank for Foreign Trade, 1960, p. 26).

The result was that imports accelerated, exports were retarded and the ensuing balance of trade deficit soon threatened the foreign exchange reserves secured from foreign loans in 1960-1. Another 'reform' was therefore attempted in 1965, a drastic one aligning many domestic prices with international ones. Nominal tariffs were cut from an average of 23.3 per cent to 10.5 per cent and an IMF loan was secured as a result. The whole idea was to integrate the Yugoslav economy with the world market and begin steps to full convertibility of the dinar. This had to be abandoned, when, after initial success with increased exports, a balance of payments crisis set in (see Figure 11.1) which required the return of import restrictions and some 'help' to exporting firms.[3]

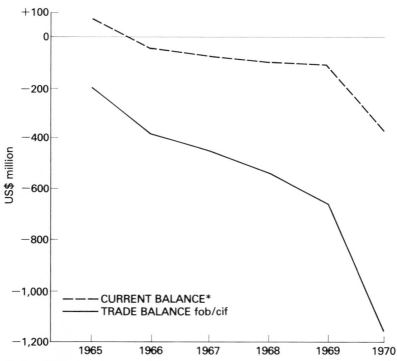

Figure 11.1 Yugoslavia's balance of payments, 1965–70

Source: *The Economist*, 21–7 August 1971.

* Visible trade, plus invisible earnings from tourism, shipping and hard-currency remittances from Yugoslavian workers in the West

Inflationary upsurge in 1961 alarmed the government. By the end of the decade this problem had not been solved. In fact, as Figure 11.2 shows, the inflationary price movement, especially in services, which took off in 1960

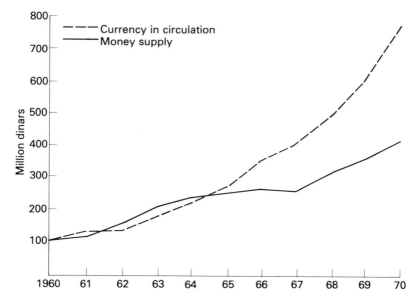

Figure 11.2 Money supply and currency in circulation, 1961–70
Source: National Bank of the Federal People's Republic of Yugoslavia, *Annual Report*, 1970.

accelerated markedly 1967–70—the cost of living index rising from 100 in 1966 to 111.3 in 1970, with agriculture and food prices forcing up the figures. Some economists blamed wages rising above the productivity trend during the decade but Figure 11.2 shows a further important variable was at work: a surge in currency supply.

While burgeoning household demand and consumer credit largely accounted for the trend in Figure 11.2 (National Bank of Yugoslavia, 1970, p. 31), lack of control over the monetary policy allowed this to happen and only in the last years of the 1960s was a serious effort made to keep money supply increases below a target of 12 per cent per annum (National Bank of Yugoslavia, 1970, p. 27).

The cycle of economic reforms by decentralization using market forces leading to balance of payments deficits and inflation had begun by 1965. The gloomy observation of this same cycle repeating itself in the 1970s and especially in 1984–6 can be made. For that reason some effort will be spent in finding causes at work in this and later chapters (12–13).

It is best to begin with the main thrust of the whole economic experimentation process of the 1960s—decentralization of decisions about investment

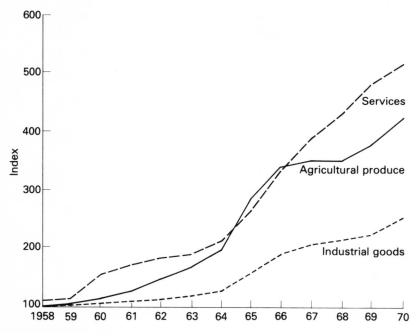

Figure 11.3 Retail prices, 1958–70   Index 1956 = 100
Source: National Bank of the Federal People's Republic of Yugoslavia, *Annual Report*, 1970.

Table 11.1 Indices of price movements, 1967–70*

	1967	1968	1969	1970
Industrial products				
Retail prices	104.1	106.2	108.2	110.5
Producers prices	101.0	101.0	104.0	111.7
Agricultural products				
Retail prices	105.0	102.9	107.0	115.6
Producers prices	91.3	102.0	117.6	115.0
Services	111.0	114.3	109.7	107.3
General index of retail prices	105.1	105.1	108.2	110.4
Cost of living	106.2	106.1	110.3	111.3

* Data for each December in relation to December of the preceding year.

to enterprise level and then further decentralization *within* firms to smaller 'economic units' (parts of the plant having power of income formation for workers under their ambit). Later we will refer to the problem of the pattern of investments in the economy, as it has long been this author's view[4] that economic reforms (important as they are) probably contribute even less to an improvement in the pace and basic stability of growth than a carefully determined, appropriate structure of investments.

Experiments with Income Distribution: the Economic Unit

Reference has already been made in Chapter 5 to the New Constitution and the debates around it. Another key issue was the 1961 decision to give workers' councils a much freer hand in distributing net income (i.e., profits of the firm after deduction of all costs and government charges). The result was a rise of industrial wages of 30 per cent by the end of 1961 and the National Assembly was forced to pass a Resolution ('Recommendation on the distribution of the net income in workers' collectives') calling on workers to rid themselves of the 'psychology of the salariat'. As well, there was a new decision at the beginning of 1961 about new rights for *economic units* within enterprises, which were described as 'the process of creating new social relations in production organization' (Confederation of Yugoslav Trade Unions, 1964, p. 29). One result of these new initiatives, was that a series of questions linking income distribution issues to problems of rate of investments and outputs in individual sectors and the economy as a whole had to be solved.

Economic units, which became the new focus of attention in 1961–5, are one example of an ill thought-out institutional change. The claim made for these bodies having increased rights was[5] that they represented a new stage in the perfecting of self-management socialism, in that workers' councils would now be able themselves to adjust (without outside tutelage) expenditure of enterprise profits on both 'fixed capital funds' and 'circulating capital funds' (including the wage bill). One economist has also remarked (Horvart, 1971a, p. 113) that the reform was necessary to restore wage differentials that had become too narrow after 1961, having widened until then (Wachtel, 1973, ch. 6). It was also a way of overcoming the resentment of workers' councils against the progressive taxation system of the 1950s. After a brief experiment with a flat rate tax on enterprise income replacing progressive tax schedules, even this flat rate tax was abolished in 1965, to mitigate discontent within workers' councils.

This meant that by 1965 the self-managers—workers' councils and the smaller 'units' within the plant—now had *total independence* in setting wage rates within their ambit *and* in distributing the net income of the enterprise. This soon was dramatically translated into changes in the share of gross wages in total value added which rose while the share of 'rentals' (Yugoslav polite word for profits, interest, capital taxes, net profit) fell from 54 per cent in 1961 to 45 per cent in 1966 and 1967 (Horvart, 1971a, p. 116). Some, though not all, economists traced wage-inflation to this aspect of the economic reforms. But perhaps the problems associated with 'sub-optimizing' within the same enterprise, requiring some *parts* of the plant to *lose* money, as against the needs and powers of the smaller economic units, led to the eventual abandonment of these smaller loci of decision-making by the end of the decade. A perusal of documents of the government[6] and the unions[7] shows that the ramifications of sub-optimization were not comprehended or taken into account. The one-sided preoccupation of this crucial part of the economic reform package was, to use the words of the Yugoslav Trade Unions (Confederation of Yugoslav Trade Unions, 1964, p. 16), 'how to ensure that in the distribution between an economic organization and the community the money left to the enterprise is proportional to its produc-tivity and profitable operation.' In other words, in exchange for *freedom* to set wages, the economic units and the enterprise council would use a productivity-geared wage policy. This, however, was too dependent for success on the 'subjective factor'. That is, while theoretically, a wage policy (income-distribution policy) under the control of worker collectives that was strictly geared to productivity would have suited the regime by stabilizing inflationary trends in the economic sectors, the reality was almost certain to be otherwise: that wages higher than indicated by productivity would be voted by such collectives.

Investment Problems of the 1960s

There was a moderate rise in overall investment 1959–63 (Table 11.2), but the *pattern* of investments[8] in the 1960s played an equally important role, with wage policy, in influencing the growth rate and structure of the economy. The structure of investment was, for example, unbalanced in 1960–5 on some criteria (McFarlane, 1966, p. 119; Vasić, 1963) but because of a 60:40 ratio of central:decentralized control, growth of annual gross investment in the economy was relatively stable.

Table 11.2 Gross investments, 1959–63 (milliard dinars, at
constant 1962 prices)

1959	1.019
1960	1.207
1961	1.338
1962	1.432
1963	1.564

Source: Institut Za Ekonomiku Investicija, *Investicije 1947–1963*, 1965,
Belgrade, p. 11.

After the Economic Reform of 1963–5 settled down, things changed.
Republics and enterprises used their new-found freedom to rapidly construct
new investment projects rather than modernizing and/or improving the
effectiveness of existing ones. Some of this was due to the rapid expansion of
households' demand for housing and consumer durables (National Bank of
Yugoslavia, 1970, p. 23, 35) and was of the form of 'induced investment', but
new construction also contributed to the investment boom 1964–8, a boom
largely financed from foreign exchange credits which rose from −47 million
dinars in 1963 to 6.3 million dinars in 1968 (National Bank of Yugoslavia,
1970, p. 39). By 1968 more controls on bank financing by investment credits
had to be imposed and slowed down fixed investment growth from a 22 per
cent rise in 1968 to 8 per cent in 1969 (National Bank of Yugoslavia, 1970,
p. 4).

The necessary slowdown in investment was achieved in 1969 but
something disturbing also happened when fixed investment fell sharply,
while producers' prices rose (Figure 11.4), indicating that the sort of
'stagflation' which later became well-known in the West had made its
appearance: monopolized firms reacted to a fall in demand by raising prices
(notably for cement and various machinery plants) in order to maintain profit
margins.

Social and Political Problems in the Economic Reform

As the economic reform was widely applied to all units, enterprises and
government departments (not yet called 'associated labour' in the 1960s),
social tensions intensified. As debate focused on the changes made in the

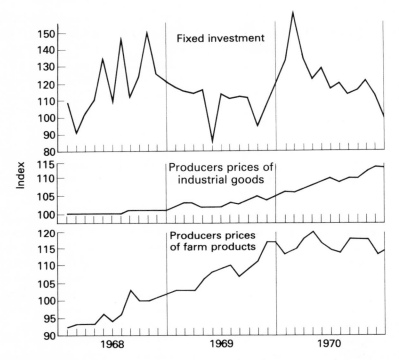

Figure 11.4 Movement of fixed investment and producers' price indices, 1968–70
Source: National Bank of the Federal People's Republic of Yugoslavia, *Annual Report*, 1970, p. 4. Index: data for December in relation to December of the previous year.

locus of economic decision-taking, social and political unrest, accentuated by inflation increased. For example, a basic issue of social policy arose. If the economic base of society was to be governed by the laws of the market, did this mean that analogous criteria of 'effectiveness', 'productivity', 'rate of return on state funds' should also apply in welfare, health and education? After all, on Marxist principles it would seem impossible to isolate a 'superstructure' containing these elements of daily life from the powerful forces unleashed by a commodity-based economic system operating through market forces.

So it proved. Education, health, the arts and welfare were affected as some zealous cadres tried to put everything in these spheres on a productivity basis, with consequent political uproar and distress for 'consumers' of collective goods.

In health, for example, tensions began to develop by the end of the decade. A much-discussed case was that of the town of Kovačica in the Banat. The local council abandoned the polyclinic causing a political furore.⁹ Those medical staff dismissed under rationalization procedures protested that self-management ought to mean *agreement* between self-managing units and government departments; hence subsidies and permission to operate could not be dictated by a government apparatus. The courts were resorted to as the dispute spread, but the underlying problem was the reform itself. As one commentator put it:¹⁰

From the outset of the Economic Reform, hospitals and clinics were required to pay careful attention to their own funds, and were to some extent exposed to market pressures . . . the objective was that various institutions of the health service should be more responsible in the way they handled their resources.

The critics were vocal in pointing out that hospitals were not factories, could not choose their business partners or clientele or formulate accurate prices. The uproar showed that it was no easy task to adapt a social service like this to a mainly 'economic' framework. Health costs were difficult to define and 'cutting costs' could be detrimental to patients; the price of skilled services might not cover costs but could hardly be raised sharply without disenfranchising patients' access.

Health was probably the most seriously affected as a by-product of the new line. In the late months of 1969, patients were already being asked to buy and bring their own gauze, bandages, pyjamas and dressing gowns to hospital. The whole atmosphere of free health and hospitalization familiar to Western countries like Britain and Australia (though not in the United States) was beginning to disappear. With resources to health and hospitals squeezed through decisions of Assemblies' budgets, and allocation of resources *within* the health sector geared to 'productivity' rather than to 'need', a serious contradiction was emerging between traditional socialist goals and the new attitudes in economic units and government departments flowing from the economic experiments. The *Praxis* group in particular began underlining the political embarrassments of the regime arising from this basic contradiction in welfare policy and education.¹¹

Even the arts was not spared cuts—unusual in Communist regimes with their record of lavish subsidies to opera, ballet and art. The Zagreb Comedy Theatre were 'obliged to stop work' and Drama Theatre companies threatened strikes as a result of months of cuts'.¹² Among causes of unrest was a new relative pay structure, redesigned to meet 'profitability' criteria, and the choice of plays according to potential revenues. Self-management, which in principle, was supposed also to function in cultural organizations, had to be modified when it was found that stage-hands and manual workers, following the SKJ's line, cut wages of actors and dancers since they had 'the numbers' on the workers' council. The artists in these cases cited 'were not satisfied with their reimbursements or general artistic policy'.[13] A number of regional and village drama troupes were disbanded as subsidies dried up under new policies of 'profitability' in the arts.

The critical response of Western commentators, especially supporters of the welfare state, artists and others in the cultural field was felt in Yugoslavia. In an interview with the German Social Democrats, Kardelj conceded that the more serious social differentials became in a country like Yugoslavia, the more necessary was an adequate awareness of the process of evolution of socialist society as a whole.[14] No solutions were proffered by the Yugoslav leader except ideological understanding: 'to think in the name of the whole movement—as Marx called on the early communist movement to do—is indeed difficult for persons who are themselves involved in these disputes'.

Overview: Some Economic Results of the 1960s

From 1960 to 1964 there was a moderate investment rate, a rapid rise in personal incomes, followed by a consumer-durable boom. Poor harvests in 1960–2 accentuated inflation and caused a move to raise agricultural prices. Despite the inflation and balance of payments problems discussed earlier, some solid results were achieved over the 1960s in industrial growth and in some social indicators, though bottlenecks remained in coal, power and transport. Instability in investments had become serious by the mid-1960s and capital need was increasingly being financed externally; but by the end of the decade this source was being modified and bank investment credits controlled. Yet the international trade balance of the late 1960s contained the seeds of trouble, while political experimentation concerning the new outspokenness of the republics and problems with self-management in the sphere of income distribution and wage policy continued, under the surface, to create uncertainties. In the 1970s, these more fundamental pressures came to the boil.

12 The Yugoslav Economy: the 1970s and 1980s

As the 1970s opened, two serious shadows hung over the economy. The first was the political confusion in the northern republics which was quietened by the Constitutional amendments of 1974 giving legal strength to regional economic power; the second was a sharp deterioration in the international balance of payments, necessitating a credit squeeze, which created a liquidity crises for a number of enterprises.

Regional Interests and Yugoslav Development

A new mid-term economic plan for Yugoslavia was launched in October 1971 and was to run till November 1975.[1] It was to include a less restrictive foreign trade regime; simplification of the exchange rate system; and devaluation of the dinar on foreign exchanges. A new feature was the official establishment of a 'fund for development' to assist the south: Kosovo, Macedonia and Montenegro. Immediately Croatia complained that its compulsory contribution, a levy of 1.9 per cent of its gross product in the socialist sectors, was too high at 6 billion dinars for the plan, and 0.9 billion dinars for 1971 alone (*Borba*, 26 October 1971, p. 6). The President of the Assembly of Croatia stated that the Republic would have to renegotiate the size of the levy or abandon many of its own public works programmes.

To meet this challenge, Croatia's leading politician and economist, a man at the centre of national life, Dr Vladimir Bakarić, negotiated with the republics' leaders. In a major report (*Borba*, 2 November 1971, p. 5), he outlined the economic problems facing Yugoslavia in the 1970s and the responsibilities that Croatia would have to shoulder as a result. The main issues to be solved were a more effective utilization of resources, reform of the banking system, linking wage rises to productivity increases and overhauling the system by which firms distributed income. The prescience of the Bakarić report can be seen in the fact that failure to clear up these issues led, in large part, to the serious economic crisis of the 1980s. Within Croatia itself, however, the trade unions were asking for a program of subsidies to cover losses of 130 milliard dinars incurred by local factories—precisely the kind of thing Bakarić was trying to avoid.

The need to organize the regional dimension of developmental planning, to take into account the special needs of underdeveloped areas, had already posed dilemmas in the 1960s (McFarlane, 1971). The main ones related to geo-economic disjuncture: the coast, central-eastern and south-east regions contained minerals and other industrial resources, yet the people lived there in primitive agricultural conditions, and, at the same time, in northern zones land was plentiful and over-population rare while manufacturing was developing despite local scarcities of natural resources. Some ironing-out of the huge disparities in the standard of living were being seen as vital in the context of a socialist system of society. What was lacking was the political will at the centre to set about achieving a more balanced regional pattern of industrialization and urbanization. Certainly the post-Tito leadership failed to do what was necessary. Instead it encouraged a break-up of the Yugoslav national market as a political compromise. It took the easy way out and allowed the strengthening of regional étatism. The deep, useful process of widening the extent of the market to promote the social division of labour was seen as less attractive than keeping the regional party machines happy. The present social crisis in Yugoslavia is very much a product of this political cowardice and the mistaken 'compromise path' that was taken from 1974 on and especially after 1980.

As part of the process set off by the 1974 Constitutional amendments a new institutional framework emerged in which economic agents (and indeed the national economy itself) were forced to operate. The banking system was 'politicized' by regional mafias; the national market weakened with much less trade between the republics.

At first the idea of competing regional economic interests did not worry the Titoists. They thought that ethnic rivalries *as such* were becoming less important, that access to resources was part of a political bargaining process and no longer merely a matter of sub-cultural identity. What they did not expect was that they were only at the beginning of a transition process and they underestimated the amount of pain that there was going to be in the process of putting 'regionalism' on a sound enough footing to make it compatible with socialist goals. Certainly they did not foresee that local political mafias linked to huge enterprise conglomerates would become as laws unto themselves.[2]

The 1970s: Balance of Payments Problems and Inflation

The second problem facing the economy in the 1970s was centred on the international trading and payments account. On the side of agricultural output and its potential for export there were already problems in the 1960s. Yugoslavia had ceased to be a net exporter of agricultural goods, a fact of some embarrassment to planners and government officials. Nor could industrial exports be expanded quickly to take up the slack. The 1965 Reform had not raised labour productivity as much as had been hoped. The success on Western markets of such exporting firms as Gorenje (Slovenia) and Koničar (Zagreb) was not matched in the area of ships, railway wagons, bauxite and copper. What was available in these categories went largely to the Soviet Union in exchange for oil, natural gas and steel.

Moreover, in Yugoslavia consumers and industries alike had become highly dependent on imports. Hundreds of thousands of workers returning from assignments in West Germany and Sweden brought with their bankbooks a high marginal propensity to import which they imparted to their families. On the breakfast table, Kellogg's cornflakes replaced eggs cooked in *kajmak*.[3]

As the 1970s unfolded, the balance of payments was increasingly threatened by the underlying structural weaknesses in commodity trade. Even in 1970 the balance of trade deficit of US$1.2 billion had to be offset by tourism (US$0.35 billion) and borrowings plus remittances from the labour power that had worked abroad (US$0.4 billion). By 1975 the overall balance of payments deficit was still US$1.03 billion and in 1979 it rose to US$3.6 billion (6 per cent of GDP) leading directly to the economic troubles of the 1980s (see Table 12.1).

Inflation accompanied the deterioration in Yugoslavia's external economic relations in the 1970s. By 1977 the inflation rate was 24 per cent and accelerating as shown in Table 12.2.

Trouble had begun, as already noted in Chapter 11, when the economic reform of 1965 failed to establish firm market discipline or usher in an era of economic stabilization.[4] In the mid-1970s (especially in 1976-8) there was a 33 per cent rise in the total investment rate of the economy.[5] This put a big strain on resource supplies, on the balance of payments of the republics and the federation. Then, money supply injections into the economy, higher than in other countries, were a feature of the 1964–74 period, so an inflationary surge was always on the cards for after 1974 (see Table 12.3).

As Yugoslavia coped with the new system brought on by the Constitutional amendments of 1974, the 'time-bomb' of very rapid increases in money supply was already present and stirring up inflationary tendencies.[6]

The rise of the inflation rate in the 1970s caused Yugoslav economists to look more closely at the deeper causes of inflation and to take more seriously the notion of inflation as a monetary phenomenon. In 1974 the Society of

Table 12.1 Balance of payments, 1965–80

Year	Amount US$ million*	As % of nominal GDP
1955	+23	0.4
1965	−39	0.5
1967	−75	0.9
1968	−95	1.1
1969	−63	0.6
1970	−348	2.8
1971	−357	2.6
1972	+419	2.9
1973	+488	2.7
1974	−1,003	4.2
1975	−1,032	3.5
1976	+165	0.5
1977	−1,582	3.7
1978	−1,256	2.5
1979	−3,661	6.0
1980	−2,291	4.0

* Different exchange rates have been applied in this table as they changed substantially over the period.
Source: Various *Biltens* of the National Bank of the Federal People's Republic of Yugoslavia.

Economists in Yugoslavia held a special session on the issue and published a summary of its conclusions.[7] An interesting debate followed and in a special issue of *Ekonomski Pregled*, organ of the Society of Economists of Croatia, three schools of thought emerged. The first, associated with members of the Ljubljana Law Faculty, argued that inflation was caused by rapid increases in personal income and consumption flowing from a slow-down in the rate of investment and they opposed monetary restrictions as inhibiting investment and worsening the problem. A second group headed by Perešin countered with the argument that it was rather a *too-rapid* rate of investment which unsettled the economy and fuelled the money supply, leading to inflation.[8] A third school, headed by Vojinić and Korošić, one that was to become much more influential in the 1980s, held that inflation had to be linked to mistakes in development policy and to errors of fiscal and monetary policies of governments.[9] Even at this relatively early stage of an unfolding economic

Table 12.2 Inflation, 1975–85: price index (1975 = 100)

Price movements for:	1976	1977	1978	1979	1980	1981	1982	1983	1984	1985
Industrial goods (producer prices)	106	116	126	143	182	263	328	433	679	1,232
Agricultural goods (producer prices)	114	128	143	179	243	372	501	730	1,654	1,623
Cost of living index	112	128	147	177	230	324	426	601	921	1,597

Source: SG, 1986, pp. 93 and 210.

Table 12.3 Comparative trends in money supply: Yugoslavia and other countries, 1964–74

Country	Increase in money stock ΔM	Increase in national income ΔY	Ratio ΔM:ΔY
United States	5.7	3.5	1.5:1
Sweden	7.5	3.1	2.2:1
Yugoslavia	17.0	6.0	3.0:1

Sources: SG, 1975; *UN Monthly Bulletin of Statistics*, December 1975.

crisis they worried that liberalism in the economy, without respecting the discipline of market forces, simply would not work.

With uncontrolled social investment and outrageous increases in the stock of money the link between 'freeing up the economy' and price discipline was broken. After 1974 these trends intensified (as shown in later sections of this chapter), and it may fairly be said that this school of economists has been retrospectively proved correct in its diagnosis.

Had the external account been more favourable, the inflationary impact for 1975–80 might have been less. However, as shown in Table 12.4, there was no improvement in Yugoslavia's terms of trade.

With the efforts to expand exports not paying off, with money supply stocks rising (total credits to the population rose from 50.8 milliard dinars to 219.1 milliards 1976–81), the underlying health of the economy was undermined. The conditions for rescuing the patient were not there either. I believe that these conditions related partly to the lack of stability in the political system. The economic system required respite from the vacillation and opportunistic pragmatism so evident in the political regime. As well, no self-management system could put down healthy roots while self-managers voted themselves wage rises that were totally out of step with the actual trend in real product per man-hour. Suggestions by sympathetic economists along these lines (Samardžija, 1968) were available. Regime leaders, however, did not take them up in a consistent way, and political uncertainties were actually increased as the need to consider a post-Tito scenario were increasingly imposed by the advancing age of the president.

Table 12.4 Terms of international trade, 1975–85

Year	Price indices		Terms of trade
	Exports	Imports	
1975	100	100	100
1976	104	103	101
1977	117	117	100
1978	128	122	105
1979	147	146	101
1980	175	175	100
1981	196	193	98
1982	203	197	103
1983	179	197	101
1984	189	203	93
1985	186	207	90

Sources: SZZS, *Biltens*, No. 3, 1985, No. 1, 1986; *SG*, 1986.

Economic Drift in the Early 1980s

Tito's death in May 1980 coincided with rising prices for oil imports and the beginning of a deterioration in the terms of trade that was to persist in 1985 despite a very brief interruption in 1982 (see Table 12.4). The lack of a successful export strategy led to unemployment and inflation because it was neither offset by a rational investment plan to stimulate growth and restrain non-productive expenditure, nor by a banking system quick to enforce rational economic criteria in its credit emissions.

A rise in unemployment from 600,000 in 1982 to some 912,000 in 1983 (*SG*, 1984) was a sign of deep trouble especially with another 700,000 working abroad. When this combined with rising prices, stagnating industrial output and ballooning national debt, the SKJ and the government were forced into action. They decided to reduce real wages and to mobilize people around an austerity package. In 1983 they mobilized SKJ members and other loyalists in a campaign to bring down inflation and to curb the freer spending republics. Some results were achieved in the short run. The inflation rate in 1984 dropped to 15 per cent and in 1985 to 10 per cent.

And then price controls were lifted, and with it the lid on inflation. In the mid-1980s, then, Yugoslavia was again adrift in a sea of economic turbulence. The superhuman effort to get a grip on the economy in 1983-5 failed. The beginnings of net repayment of external debt, the moderation of inflation, and the improved balance of payments were all for nothing.

The 'halting of the slide' in 1984 proved to be a false dawn, since inflation became much worse in 1986 and 1987 (with annual rises of 115 per cent and 130 per cent respectively). Two reasons for this stand out: policy errors and lack of monetary rectitude.

The post-Tito collective leadership had missed an excellent opportunity, in the two years after Tito's death, to get a firm grip on the economy and to insert some 'grit' into economic regulation of practices harmful to the system: councils awarding themselves wage-rises above productivity trends; subsidies to bankrupt enterprises; and unpaid debts to banks, suppliers and creditors in many enterprises. The sense of drift communicated itself to the republics and provinces which stressed strongly for their own interests, sometimes to the detriment of the Yugoslav economy as a whole.

A long-term stabilization programme had been drawn up and agreed to by the National Assembly at the end of 1983. This was not adhered to by republics, communes and enterprises. The government itself also made a series of premature relaxations to the austerity measures. First, important restrictions were slackened; second, quite a few measures imposing price restraint were withdrawn; and third, an attempt was made to accelerate the growth of GDP for 1985-7 in the hope that it would generate the resources to allow living standards per worker to catch up.

These 'relaxations' raise the question of whether economic agents and the government apparatus in Yugoslavia are not working on too short a time horizon. Clearly, if there is a general atmosphere of 'let's have jam today rather than put aside for tomorrow', underlying structural weaknesses in the economy will not be tackled consistently as a precondition for the success of medium-term stabilization programmes.

Also not tackled was the basic monetary anarchy of the financial system, which is quite graphically illustrated by Tables 12.5 and 12.6, where the acceleration in credits and money supply after 1983 is portrayed. According to my calculations, the average rate of increase of money stock was 142.7 per cent per year for 1976-85 and of internal loans, 126.8 per cent per year (see Table 12.6).

In the absence of a wage freeze or improving external results (better exports, terms of trade), the movements shown in Tables 12.5 and 12.6 are conducive not only to inflation but to hyperinflation and Table 12.2 showed

Table 12.5 Credit supplies to population, 1976–85 (milliard dinars)

	1976	1981	1982	1983	1984	1985
Total credits	50.8	219.1	276.1	310.1	417.5	590
Short-term credits	4.0	12.6	11.6	12.3	15.7	26
Long-term credits	46.8	199.3	264.5	297.8	401.8	565

Source: *SG*, 1986, p. 212.

Table 12.6 Money supply trends, 1976–85: money stock and total internal loans (assessment values)

	A Total money stock at end of year in *milliard* dinars	B Total internal loans at end of year in *million* dinars
1976	180.6	42,114
1980	584.6	130,655
1981	726.5	192,965
1982	1,019.6	265,037
1983	1,579.8	284,664
1984	2,385.4	329,152
1985	4,425.9	355,806
Average annual growth rate (%) 1976–85	142.7	126.8
Index of growth (1976 = 100) 1985	2,450	845

Source: *SG*: 1986, pp. 212–13, and author's calculations.

levels of price movements that *are* consistent with an underlying situation of Weimar-republic style hyperinflation.

There was no such relief on the external account forthcoming; as Table 12.7 shows, the improvement in export values was checked by rises in the import bill, while export values had to recover from a slump which 1982 and 1983 had imposed on the economy. The invisible or 'non-commodity' items

Table 12.7 Movement of exports and imports in the 1980s

	Export value US$ billion	Exports volume 1980 = 100	Exports unit value in US$	Imports volume 1980 = 100	Imports value US$ billion
1980	224.3	100	100	100	314.0
1981	387.9	108	108	87	502.1
1982	525.8	96	116	66	624.0
1983	943.3	97	114	72	1,062.5
1984	1,603.0	—	—	—	1,714.4
1985	2,934.8	—	—	—	3,049.6
1986	5,486.1	—	—	—	4,112.0

Source: International Monetary Fund, *International Financial Statistics*, vol. 40, June 1987; M. Cirović, *Nova i Stabilizacija*, 1982 p. 87.

Table 12.8 Balance of trade and payments on current account, 1980–5

	1980	1981	1982	1983	1984	1985
Commodity trade	151.3	123.4	144.0	99.0	159.9	136.3
Non-commodity trade	−90.9	−102.9	−124.2	−116.6	−222.8	−291.0
Crude balance on current account	60.4	20.5	19.8	−17.6	−62.9	−154.7

Source: *SG*, 1986, p. 156.

after the brief recovery of 1982 also refused to improve, leading to a rising deficit in the overall current account (see Table 12.8).

This left only foreign borrowing on the capital account to balance the deficit on current account. But loans are difficult to obtain when the external value of a currency is dropping as shown in Table 12.9.

The Rush to Crisis, 1985–8

The period after Tito's death, short as it had been, revealed the weaknesses of a system where a number of very large enterprises acted as if they were above the law and could avoid any guidelines for austerity drawn up by economists

Table 12.9 External value of the dinar, 1980–7

	Dinar per SDR of IMF	Dinar per US$
1980	37.30	29.36
1981	48.60	41.82
1982	69.93	62.49
1983	131.57	156.67
1984	207.56	211.75
1985	343.59	312.87
1986	559.22	475.18
1987		
January	571.89	—
February	643.30	—
March	652.17	—
October	na	850

Sources: International Monetary Fund, *International Financial Statistics*, vol. 40, June 1987; *Biltens*, Narodne Banke, 1987.

and government officials. Yet this was nothing to the anarchical system of regional interests, 'pull' from local party machines and irresponsible compact-making between enterprises and banks which broke out between 1983 and 1988.[10]

At the heart of the matter was party indecision, indeed helplessness, in the face of the economic tornado and the strength of regional étatism. Some politicians even denied there was a crisis at all, claiming that the 'system' was sound and only bad behaviour by individuals was preventing Yugoslavia from achieving stability and growth.[11] Eventually, however, some sanity was restored, if temporarily, by the 13th Congress of the SKJ in June 1986, which upheld the long-term stabilization theme. As well, this Congress made a number of important findings impinging on political economy for the 1980s: that changes were necessary in the practical operation of self-management to prevent outbursts of small-group interest and heavy-handed treatment of local communities by state organs; that a one-sided preoccupation with manufacturing over many years had unbalanced the economy; that investment rates had been too high given the stock of material resources; and that a stream of heavy foreign debts had been unwisely allowed to build up (Trifunović, 1987, pp. 26–31).

In the meantime, the academic community had been galvanized into action. Already they had been prominent in the work of the commission set up under S. Krajger to produce the 'Long-Run Program of Stabilization' which went to the Federal Assembly at the end of 1984.[12] The section headed 'Conclusions' in the original document makes interesting reading as it spells out the theoretical framework and ideological theses that had informed the overall recommendations.[13] Here no defence of the existing 'system' of political economy was countenanced and the influence of Professor Pjanić was clear from the bold use of the rarely-used phrase 'economic crisis' and by various references to the lack of objective criteria in banking policy. Lack of action around the 'Long-Term Program', however, alienated the intelligentsia, especially in Serbia, where the Academy of Sciences criticized the inactivity of the politicians in keeping the urgent recommendations of the Program from the public.[14]

While the centenary of the Serbian Academy had to be cancelled after a series of attacks on it by politicians resenting any 'loyal opposition' role being attempted by academics, the real world was teaching the SKJ a lesson. Real per capita GNP fell from US$3,100 in 1984 to US$2,120 in 1986. The political regime had had some three years to develop the 'long-term stabilization programme' and in December 1986, many members of the federal *Skupština* admitted that it had *not* been fully or consistently applied.

As 1987 opened the public were informed as to what would be required to get the economy on its feet again.[15] The 'Resolution on the Country's Socio-Economic Development in 1987', adopted in the closing days of December 1986, announced that the main targets set were:

(a) the total product of the economy to rise 3 per cent at least in real terms—of this 2 per cent to come from more employment in production and 1.1 per cent from higher productivity;

(b) a 1.2 per cent rise in living standards;

(c) a 4 per cent rise in gross investment;

(d) a 3.5 per cent increase in industrial production;

(e) a 4.5 per cent rise in the goods and services section of exports;

(f) contraction of growth of collectivist consumption (schools, hospitals, art and culture), which was to be pared back to a figure of '10 per cent less than the growth of income generated in the socialist sector of the economy'.

These goals were thought of as feasible, given the constraint of a simultaneous target of bringing the balance of payments on current account into surplus and repayment of some of the country's external debt. In order to ensure plan 'follow-through' and to put 'teeth' into the Resolution, a number of separate legislative acts were passed during the Assembly's December 1986 sitting. The first group dealt with the accounting and taxation treatment of depreciation funds (funds for financing replacement of plant and equipment). The law on depreciation introduced the compulsory use of real rates of 'writing down' the value estimate of the capital stock being used by firms and other economic units. It was expected that this would, by incorporating inflation, make a more realistic tax base for government charges, thereby 'protecting socially-owned property', presumably from the ravages of worker-management boards seeking to minimize tax liability. It also made it more difficult for enterprises to use depreciation funds for unauthorized purposes: paying higher wages, increased flat-building for members of the plant, and so on. An accompanying Law on the Total Revenues and Incomes also demands more periodic evaluations of the value of fixed assets and stocks of investing capital (raw materials, semi-finished goods, etc.).

A second group of bills further imposed controls on enterprise spending. The Law on Financial Re-Organization of Enterprises introduced penalties and withdrawal of subsidies and credits to 'unsuccessful collectives'. The Law on the Social Accounting Service required enterprises to repay debts and bills owing to creditors *before* taking any decisions on the distribution of net income, especially payments to the wages fund of the firm.

The idea of tough implementation 'follow-up', while not new in Yugoslav economic experience, seemed for a time to have more purpose. The dire economic straits of the nation presumably spurred the politicians to 'bite the bullet' in adopting policies of allowing bankruptcies to happen, of a severe credit squeeze and severe financial rectitude in fiscal policy. They were suitably cautious about the prospects of a fast turnaround in economic fortunes and, as well, were appealing to all economic agents to change their expectations and attitudes to economic life in the 1980s, above all to work for greater labour productivity while sticking closely to 'responsibility, more economizing, and stricter discipline'.[16] It was realized in ruling circles, during December 1986 and January 1987, that such a programme was not only needed for the successful recovery of the economy *as they saw it*, but to coax an increasingly reluctant IMF and creditors' group to lend more to the country.[17]

The workers' response was quite otherwise. Strikes broke out in February and March and by mid-March 1987 had assumed the character of a *general strike*. This was because the government had panicked, and ordered a wage 'claw back' in early March when production figures came out to show industrial production in January 1987 was 2 per cent lower than in the same month of January 1986, while the mid-February dollar value of exports was 22 per cent less than in the corresponding period of the previous year. Money wages were soaring, the rises bearing no relation to 'agreed criteria or real product per man-hour increases'. Inflation increased in January by 6.6 per cent in one month, and the freeze on 'non-productive investments' had failed to materialize.

A shocked government said it would allow acceleration of liquidations of loss-making companies, which meant more unemployment, and immediately cut wages. Its strategy was to make the crisis of the economy a crisis for the working class, in order to attract foreign credits and thereby to prop up the faltering political regime.

Wages were frozen by decree to the average level of the last three months of 1986 and pegged strictly to productivity movements. The price of bread rose by 25 per cent. The strike wave that followed involved tens of thousands of workers—the biggest uprising of the 1980s. Police were called out in Zagreb during the middle of March as thirty-five companies in the city were strike-bound while there was a workers' march on town halls (that is, in Celje) as loss-making factories closed their doors.[18]

By March 1987 the Prime Minister was threatening to put the army into factories and transport networks to break the strikes. But he also agreed to lift the wage-freeze in successful firms, tourism and seasonal industries after angry debates in the Federal Assembly. In November, however, wage controls and cuts were reintroduced and miners joined thousands of others on strike throughout Yugoslavia, demanding a 100 per cent wage rise to offset the falling purchasing power of the dinar. At least twenty strikes and many street processions were in progress during the month.[19]

How Did It All Happen?

First, let us take the views of rival expositors in Yugoslavia itself. In one view, that of the *dohodaše* group, corporatism could work in Yugoslavia but is frustrated by too much political interference or too liberal a stance towards the price mechanism. In the views of Korać in Belgrade and Sirotković in Zagreb, groups of associated workers have every right to enter into social compacts that are mutually beneficial. An incomes policy, which is a social contract across the board, should have been negotiated but was in fact imposed.

A second opinion is that the market forces and self-management have not been free enough. A number of economists (largely in Croatia and Slovenia) feel that the logic of the market has been stifled by regional and central interference of the political realm with the economic sphere. A growing sentiment, possibly strongest in Serbia (Pjanić, 1986) but including Korošić (Croatia) as well as A. Fabinc and A. Bajt in Slovenia, want to criticize the *dohodaše* concept of social compacts and blame these arrangements for Yugoslavia's mid-1980s impasse. They believe the hyperinflation was largely of monetary origin[20] (in the sense that corporation losses have been covered by a budget deficit blow-out and by printing money). They also blame the break-up of the national market after 1975, the weakening of the market forces and lack of a perspective plan for the 'drift to crisis'.

Comment on the Crisis

There are those who like to see a proliferation of regional interests and a sort of pluralistic 'self-management', but often they are people who think they can retain power within the anarchy that is produced in the body-politic.

Others fear commodity-money relations as incompatible with socialism. This trend was often associated with Soviet Communism, Stalin, Mao and Pol Pot in the past. In Yugoslavia they are only a small group and their explanations of the 1980s events are too abstract to be really helpful.

If the present author could venture an opinion of his own, there is another serious problem at the heart of Yugoslavia's faltering 'progress' beyond the obviously disastrous results of the break-up of the national market, which now cannot play its 'Adam Smith' role of deepening the division of labour while at the same time unifying disparate economic communities and economic agents. I refer to the lack of a planning mechanism that could identify new investment requirements and possibilities. The very idea of a controlled *industrial strategy* is disputed by regional leaders of party and government. Yet a combination of indicative planning and renewal of a unified national market does seem to hold out the best hope, in Yugoslav conditions (Pjanić, 1986, pp. 25–75), for a recovery in the medium to long term. Certainly this combination would be needed as a lever to bring about structural change.

It also seems that the situation in the 1980s had reached a point where it approximated the 'oligopolistic indeterminacy' that Kalecki thought could overtake a market-socialist economy wherever a group of powerful firms set their own sellers' prices. What happens is this: where firms operate on a cost-plus mark-up, there is inbuilt cost-push inflation once prices of raw materials and labour escalate (under conditions of constant returns to scale). The constellation of forces can, however, produce a fireball. The cost-push type of inflation lasts only till inflation reaches a 25 per cent annual rate, or thereabouts (as in mid-1970s Yugoslavia), after which the situation changes. As Kalecki argued this threshold sees a breakdown of ordinary checks and balances, confusion in monetary and fiscal policies pursued by the authorities, and the collapse of those institutional arrangements making for rectitude in new issues of currency and credit.[21] The result will be that the previous funds of inflationary pressures get absorbed into the upward draught of prices fanned by escalation of the money supply.

This surely comes close to a description of the unfolding economic instability in Yugoslavia in the 1980s. When one adds the 'anarchy of regional étatist tendencies' (so clearly shown up in the Agro-Commerc affair of 1987)[22] and the break-up of that national market (Pjanić, 1986, chs 3–4), a picture emerges that closely resembles Kalecki's worst-case scenario for economic systems of the market-socialist type.

Future Prospects of the Yugoslav Economy

Yugoslavia faces three critical problems as it enters the 1990s. It has a serious structural problem at the base of the economy with inadequate infrastructure in the form of power, water and transport availability. It has entered the early stages of hyperinflation at levels reminiscent of Argentina and Brazil, if not the Weimar republic (as yet). It suffers technological lag *vis-à-vis* European countries, to say nothing of the level of technique commanded by modern multinational corporations such as Phillips, IBM and National.

Two recent texts by Yugoslav authors have tried to come to grips with these realities. The first (Pjanić, 1986) sets out, from an economist's point of view, the stark alternative: either Yugoslav regimes will allow the market to be unified, to operate properly and the political realm allows the logic of the market to work itself out *or* there will be lurches to crisis, and possible collapse, under the present system of rule by regional étatists and greedy enterprise managers linked to them. Pjanić also stressed the need to raise technological levels by coming to terms with MNCs and tapping in to their technology.

The second book, prepared by a group of writers from the Belgrade Economics Institute in 1986 looks at Yugoslavia's likely situation in the year 2000.[23] The overall tone is lugubrious: if Yugoslavia does not seize the chance to overcome its technological lag in the next twenty years it will quite simply vegetate. In that case, the very basis of the system—self-management—will come under fire. To prevent this, short-term productivity must rise, and the effectiveness of resource-use improve, so the authors recommend a quicker integration into Europe and the world economy. The report was backed by 'qualitative indicators of development' being presented, showing a discreditable performance since 1975 including decelerating economic growth, structural imbalances in the economy, technological lag and ecological neglect.

To overcome the past record displayed in the report, the authors consider that a 'growth scenario' would be required in which the GDP would grow by 3.7 per cent per annum up to the year 2000, while employment would grow at 1.4 per cent per annum, annual investment at 4 per cent per annum and exports at 3.2 per cent per annum.

The report is saying what has already been put in this chapter. Without a major change in societal attitudes, restoration of social plans, consciousness of the need to think about 'jam tomorrow', rather than always 'jam today', such a growth scenario will be very difficult to achieve. In that case the failures of the economy will certainly be putting big question marks over the processes set in train by the 1974 Constitutional amendments and over the self-management system as it operates today.

A system in which productive property is managed by non-state bodies, collectives or 'groups of associated labour' (to use the Yugoslav term) up to the point of *de facto* ownership of such property also has laws of motion of its own. This will be brought out by looking at the legal and economic basis of the operation of Yugoslav enterprises. This chapter then moves on to consider some case studies of some of these firms and various theories that have been put forward to explain the role of the firm under market-socialism.

The Legal Status of Yugoslav Firms

Legally each enterprise 'exhibits a principal economic activity' which is registered by a court at the time it is constituted formally and then various by-laws are passed by the Assemblies governing the operation of this 'principal activity'. In the paper work of planning agencies and banks the firm is put under a classification for product-group, industrial branch and economic sector. Enterprises may, by giving notice, move into new or 'adjacent' fields of production and are assisted in doing this economically by the practice of keeping internal depreciation funds and ploughed-back profits for financing investment expansion.

Another legal aspect is that the enterprises have the character of legal persons with concomitant responsibilities (to pay taxes, control pollution, etc.) and obligations. They cannot be liquidated by the arbitrary decision of any state organ. Only a series of court procedures can lead to liquidation and the workers' collective cannot itself make such a decision—it can only take part in discussion before an economic court with the founders of the enterprise also entitled to take part.

If an economic court does rule that an enterprise is insolvent and should not continue, the *fixed* capital, land and amortization funds are handed over to local governments (communes) and only the working capital (plus *other* internal funds) are used for debt repayment and liquidation. There is an order laid down for the payment of creditors starting with claims of the social insurance institutes and banks and ending with claims of the workers themselves for back-pay, severance pay, etc. The Yugoslav approach here is that property-rights of collectives over capital are to be severely restricted. Cooperative members can *use* the capital stock as they wish but cannot sell it. Nor do they have good prospects, legally, in recovering from their firm, should it be illiquid or bankrupt, any investments they may have made in labour time or in purchase of debentures during their association with the enterprise.

Firms usually join 'associations' (similar to trusts) covering the technical dimension of their productive activity. These 'associations' do report in general terms to state organs, and at times, have had some powers (e.g., to ensure credit and investment policies have been followed). On the whole, however, the wider use of 'market laws' has meant that working collectives or 'units of associated labour' in production spheres are independent managers of the funds and technical means of production entrusted to them by the 'social community'. Fixed capital assets, for example, are formed as (a) initial founding grants from communes; (b) investment credits from banks; (c) capital formation within the firm itself by means of 'ploughed-back' profits. Although conversion of fixed into working capital (and vice versa) has been prohibited in various laws and regulations, this has tended to be ignored since 1968, with many firms paying wages and bank interest from fixed funds or using working capital to buy machinery and plant. A new law passed in 1986 aims to stamp out this practice.

As noted in Chapters 9–10, a great deal of the energy of collectives is devoted to the distribution of the income earned by the firm according to laws and regulations laid down. With each major 'economic reform' attempted by the regime, these regulations have had to be adjusted— sometimes in a rather bewildering fashion. The overall trend, however, has been towards more freedom of the enterprise to allocate revenues itself and for the total investment process ('capital formation') to take place as the sum of what economic units decide about investment plans rather than as the result of decisions by state organs.

In Yugoslav ideology and legal practices, income accruing to firms is seen as being influenced not only by the intensity of work and the productivity of labour but by external influences. Some of these would be market-windfalls, the historical pattern of relative prices and the availability of foreign exchange and imported 'inputs'. For that reason, taxation of the firm has tended to incorporate levies or special rents to eliminate these external influences as far as practicable. 'Evening out' earning differentials of this sort has proved impossible in practice, so that one consequence of market socialism is that two workers of equal skill might earn a widely-divergent wage according to which enterprise they belong to.

Economies of Scale, 'Integration' and the Degree of Monopoly

Much of the theory of market-socialism (e.g. Kidrič, 1950) envisaged an economy in which small and medium-scale firms in relatively large numbers competed with each other to form 'market prices' based on 'the laws of supply and demand'. In reality the Yugoslav economic structure soon developed into one in which managers (whether at meetings of 'associations' and 'economic chambers' or clandestinely) acted in collusion over prices. Moreover, the technological imperatives soon reduced the number of firms participating in each industry because the larger-scale production runs needed to reap economies of scale and higher necessary investment reduced ease of entry. This was already a well-known trend in the West[1] but apparently the Yugoslav theoreticians had overlooked the theory of 'monopoly capital', assuming that a totally new system would obey new economic 'laws of motion'. In fact the very same processes emerged, requiring new analysis[2] but also practical studies of reality to guide decisions about whether to oppose or support vertical and horizontal integration within industry on efficiency grounds.

By 1960, the federal statistical office, banks and the SZZPP were taking an interest in two aspects of the degree of monopoly: concentration and 'integration'. It was reported, for example, that from 1955 to the end of 1959 there had been a sharp increase in size of firms and concentration ratios (Yugoslav Bank for Foreign Trade, 1960, p. 718). See Table 13.1, which shows that the problem of oligopoly—a smaller number of larger firms in each industry—had already become obvious within a decade of the regime establishing itself and within a few years of the newer market socialist system.

In the 1960s, *integracija* received official support. Books and manuals came out of new institutes of research concerned with it, explaining to managers and workers' collectives what was permissible by way of merger and integration (Mrska, 1963; Institut Za Ekonomiku Investicija, 1963). Ship-building, electric power, metals and food-processing were encouraged to integrate vertically. By the 1970s a 'Commission for Integration Trends and Self-Organization of the Economy' was operating and reporting to the federal economic chamber of the national parliament. With the decision to allow joint ventures with foreign investors (e.g. German capital with Yugoslav firms and workers producing radios and washing machines), the

Table 13.1 Concentration in Yugoslav
industry, 1955–9

No. of employees	No. of enterprises at end of	
	1955	1959
Up to 30	469	264
From 31–125	897	739
From 126–500	799	909
Over 500	365	527
Total	2,530	2,439

reality of integration and monopolistic industrial structures became even more widely accepted.

Inevitably integration, larger-scale and industrial concentration became a feature of economic life. A more recent study for the period 1966–72 (Estrin, 1983, pp. 87–105) concluded that whereas in 1966 the smallest 20 per cent of firms produced 1 per cent of output and the larger 5 per cent of firms produced 41.2 per cent of output, by 1972 the smallest 30 per cent of firms produced only 2 per cent of output and the top 1.7 per cent of firms produced 41.2 per cent. In terms of use of capital assets, there was a similar trend to concentration: 'the top 15 firms in 1966 used 12.4 per cent of industrial capital assets, and the top 124 firms controlled 38 per cent of capital. The top 15 also used 9.9 per cent of workers. By 1972, the largest 75 firms used 34.3 per cent of all industrial capital and 24.8 per cent of labour'. He noted (Estrin, 1983, p. 103) that some firms have become very large indeed, especially in relation to the domestic economy. Ten industrial firms are responsible for 18.4 per cent of Yugoslav sales while a further five trading firms are responsible for another 11.2 per cent: compared to the United Kingdom and the United States, Yugoslavia had already reached a very high level of concentration by 1965.

It was, of course, always intended to 'counter' the rising degree of monopoly by some fiscal and social policies. Before 1955 taxes on the earning power of enterprises had been levied according to the size of the wage bill. With growing evidence of monopoly this was changed to a profits tax levied on the ratio of actual profits earned to the wage bill (Niketić & Pejović, 1958).

Actual profits were defined as income minus tax minus the cost of legal minimum wages. If this category reached 25-40 per cent of the total wage bill, a tax of from zero to 9.4 per cent was payable. A ratio of 60 per cent attracted a profit tax of 37.3 per cent.

Yet anti-monopoly measures remained *ad hoc*. Sometimes an excess profits tax was introduced; sometimes price control over goods in short supply. This approach often merely increased the atmosphere of uncertainty in which industrial managers had to operate, disrupting investment plans and other measures already taken in order to raise productivity. The more basic issue of how to make compatible a rising degree of monopoly, 'market forces', equity and self-management remained unsolved.

Yugoslav Enterprises: Case Studies

A number of firms that the author of this book studied on field work trips will now be referred to as background for finding out more about the implications of their behaviour for the economy as a whole and for policy (e.g. enterprise taxation, anti-monopoly legislation, etc.).

The sugar refinery, Dimitrije Tucovic, near Belgrade was established in 1962 with an enterprise legal structure of some 257 articles and clauses protecting its rights and 850 workers. By 1964 some sixteen smaller 'economic units' of decision-making within the firm had been reduced in number to eight units. This was done to make both planning and policy over distribution of income of the firm more manageable. The firm attempted to do without bank credits except for foreign exchange, and to expand by means of self-financing. Within four years it had decided to plough-back *half* of all net income after tax, and to devote the rest to workers' amenities, bonus wages, etc. This was quite a high ratio at the time, as many local factories were ploughing back 30 per cent and distributing 30 per cent. Later the Yugoslav authorities were to *require* successful firms to achieve these higher ratios thereby ensuring that the gap in productivity and earning rates between them and the less successful regularly widened. This practice meant that much of what Western economists' *theories* of Yugoslav firm behaviour implied was undercut, as the 'higher accumulation' rule contradicted the fear that self-management would most likely result in richer firms producing a result whereby workers voted themselves a higher and higher share of wages. Government action here did *aim* to even up distribution of income, e.g. by improving the Kosovo workers' relative position compared to Slovenia's by restricting 'consumption-payouts' to workers in the northern firms. In this it did not really succeed (Berković, 1969; Bajt, 1986).

Another firm with lessons implying that many theoreticians should remain cautious was the Bor Copper Works (Jakić, 1965b). For many years copper refiners and manufacturers using copper experienced shortages in supply. In Banja Luka a major electro-mechanics and electronic-parts factory consuming large quantities of copper complained that in the period before the 1965 reform copper was cheap but scarce and irregular in supply. After the economic reform Bor was put on a new basis—no more subsidies. It was allowed to raise its prices, a move previously frowned on because copper ores, like cement and coal, were regarded as special kinds of capital goods—as intermediate goods, which entered into the production processes of many sectors, whose prices should be kept low and stable—as in Eastern European countries. However, a workers' collective at Bor negotiated with regional electric authorities the right to determine prices on the same business criteria as other firms. The result was that the new profitability ensured higher productivity and modernization of the works, and promoted both the willingness and ability to supply customers at the new, higher prices. More copper at higher prices came in regularly and buyers found this situation to be cheaper, for *them*, than the copper at lower prices in irregular supply (Jakić, 1965b, p. 145).

The significance of this Bor case-study is that pricing a raw material too low makes it impossible for the workers' council to cover rentals for hired capital, taxes on capital assets *and* give bonuses. This indicates there is some level of mark-up that allows the 'surplus' of such enterprises to cover costs and encourages diligence in meeting the demand. Should the manufacturers who buy the copper have objected (in fact they did not), it would have been better to subsidize *their* taxes/wage bills than to continue a *general* policy of keeping copper prices down.

Another firm of some interest is Iskra[3] the largest enterprise in Slovenia; in the early 1960s the workers' collectives there decided to produce electrical goods (radios, washing-machines, etc.). They decided to avoid Yugoslavia's shortages of materials, erratic economic policies and unpredictable price movements by entering into production and marketing agreements with foreign corporations: with Italian firms for 'auto-electrical' goods, with American enterprises for small h.p. motors; with a number of West German companies. The problem that this created was that being inextricably bound this way and with a rising proportion of Iskra's output going for export (and hence out of the power of the workers' council on the issue of price formation) was weakening of 'self-management' in relation to the business affairs of the firm. If much of these affairs were governed by pooling agreements and prices depended on oversea events, what power did the elected workers' council have? And, in particular, what choices remained for new entrants into the cooperative? Clearly a firm like this was not, in its main dynamic, being driven by self-management, by deliberations of workers, by ideology. It was being driven by purely commercial objectives.

An important Belgrade enterprise, PKB, is a growing agri-business venture with investments in tourist hotels and debentures in a range of Yugoslav firms. Starting as a milk supplier to Belgrade's urban population, PKB has moved into all sorts of food processing and sub-contracts to Vojvodinian and Serbian peasants for fruits, vegetables and dairy products. From its phenomenal success it has expanded, first into adjacent lines of production and then to activities far from its original intention. PKB is something of a show-case for oversea visitors and researchers. Questions about the decision-making processes behind these major turns in policy have been in the main met by the reply: 'our investment, technical and financial experts put these proposals before our workers and they always agreed'. This seems to confirm an impression, earlier suggested by Ward, that sometimes an invisible power network of technocrats operates behind the scenes and takes such a share of actual decision-making that blue-collar workers are rather swept aside (Ward, 1957).

A final case to be considered here is the Kluz clothing enterprise. When created in 1952 in Belgrade it employed about 200 workers. By 1984 it had ten factories under its wing, employing 7,000 workers. Some 80 per cent of output is exported and 20 per cent is put on the domestic market through 130 chainstores. In 1980 the relative proportions in sale direction was 70:30.

As a result of its successes, *earnings per worker* were rising at 12 per cent in the 1980s, a rare occurrence in Yugoslav factories. As well some 2.5 million dinars annually have been allocated from enterprise funds to free canteen meals, medical attention and other workers' amenities, including a rest home. The enterprise believes its success has been due to its rising export receipts, its productivity-geared wage policy and to a consistent policy of self-financing of its asset expansion rather than the sort of reliance on bank credits that has been the cause of the bookkeeping bankruptcy of many Yugoslav firms. Each of the enterprises discussed in this section has had experiences that throw light on the *modus operandi* of Yugoslav firms. They also serve as a reference point to theories of the 'Illyrian' firm to which I now turn.

Theories of the Behaviour of Worker-Managed Firms

The intellectual roots of self-managed socialism have been referred to earlier in this book. Certainly 'participatory socialism' has appeared in the early Utopian socialists (Fourier, Proudhon), anarchist theory, and the guild socialism of G. D. H. Cole. However, as Wachtel pointed out (Wachtel, 1973, p. 9), participatory socialism is not only reactive. Its study must be approached by way of a realization that it has a theory, a set of principles of its own: a theory of social property (Djordjević, 1966). Its main lack is a notion of how to reconcile what particular workers' groups want and what society needs.

After Yugoslav experiments with widening the scope of workers' control in factories had been operating about eight years, the neo-classical school of economists, mostly Americans began to publish highly theoretical works trying to explain the economic principles behind worker-managed enterprise (Ward, 1958). Later contributions claiming to be based even more firmly on a study of Yugoslavia were made by such economists as Horvart (1964, 1969); Vanek (1970, 1973); Ward (1967b); J. E. Meade (1972, 1974) and Estrin (1983).

In the remainder of this chapter two things will be attempted (a) a *critical* review of the neo-classical (orthodox) economists who have turned their attention to the Yugoslav self-managed economy as a special case where workers hire capital for rental instead of capitalists hiring workers for wage-labour; (b) an outline of an alternative approach to the Yugoslav firm, which avoids the methodology of neo-classical economics and takes into account the sociological aspects of corporate behaviour occasioning perverse results such as dismissing workers from the collective as profits rise or gaining when output is reduced.

In the model of B. M. Ward, an 'Illyrian' firm is portrayed acting in ways analogous to those in a Yugoslav 'market-socialist' situation. Crucial to the theory outlined, however, is that eight very abstract and restrictive assumptions are made at the beginning and these must constantly be referred to before any sensible (or even any concrete) policy implication can be drawn out.

The assumptions of the Ward–Vanek–Meade (WVM) approach are: (i) decisions in the plant or factory are made by elected workers' councils, who are free to set prices and outputs in terms of their own material interests; (ii) free markets operate to allocate all resources; (iii) technical means of production belong to 'society' on whose behalf the state charges a rental (or capital tax) on enterprise assets being used in production; (iv) the capacity of plant and equipment is fixed in the short run (only current prices and output are relevant in the model); (v) net revenue of the firm (i.e., after taxes and costs have been paid) are fully distributed to the workers—*there is no self-financing*, no regular process of reinvestment out of profits; firms have to go to the capital market for funds; (vi) the 'contractual wage' is fixed by the state. The workers' take-home pay then consists of the contractual wage and any bonuses to personal incomes eventually paid out of profits; (vii) workers are 'free' to change jobs but hiring and firing is the province of workers' councils; (viii) machines, raw materials and stocks of semi-processed goods bought by firms, as well as the sale of the firm's own product, are done at market prices. While Ward later relaxes a few of these assumptions, these eight assumptions are the key to implications drawn from the use of his models.

Even at this stage, however, it is clear that the assumptions of free competition are going to clash with the fact of a very high concentration ratio in Yugoslav industry and the heavy influence of law and politics in promoting self-financing in firms and encouraging it to remain at high levels.[4]

When put to work, the Ward–Vanek–Meade (WVM) model purports to demonstrate a 'startling' phenomenon: a perverse short-run supply curve of output appears for the worker-managed firm, according to which the quantity of output X declines as market price increases (Ward, 1958, pp. 574–5, 579). This is because the *maximand* (what is being maximized in the firm) is average *net income* per worker *if* the worker in practice acts as the model assumes—solely from material self-interest. Instability in market behaviour develops as with the negatively-sloped supply curve for output, especially in the case of one factor of production and even more in the case of more than one factor of production. Only when profits are zero in an Illyrian firm and in a market capitalist firm will the choice of combination of inputs or factor utilization be the same. When profits are positive the model yields the result that Yugoslav firms have a bias towards capital-intensive technology, but with negative profits more labour-intensive techniques are chosen.

In the long run, the WVM model allows the orthodox economists to relax a little, at first sight, because in the long run (where economic agents are assumed willing to establish new cooperative enterprises and are able to dissolve existing ones) things look more 'normal'. Consumer sovereignty produces a demand for commodity X, new firms enter, as under competitive capitalism, and the 'perversity' disappears; the 'Illyrian' firm (WVM model firm) is shown to be as efficient as the capitalist one. Enter Estrin and Benner (1986). Empirical study of Israeli worker-managed (unions in control) firms indicate such firms perform better than capitalist enterprises in terms of labour productivity, capital productivity, and ability to pay higher wages. The main source of this superiority is the *relatively* cooperative nature of worker-run firms and the reduced conflict in industrial relations. Some improvements in performance comes through indirect effects of these factors, operating through mediating variables such as lower labour turnover which facilitates accumulation of a specific form of *human* capital that suits the union-run firm.

While differences exist between union-run firms in Israel and workers' councils exercising control in Yugoslav firms, these findings raise issues not clearly considered in the WVM approach.

There are some minor variations in the WVM models on the issue of who can make the key decisions on hiring. In one version (Vanek, 1970, 1973) existing members may decide about the admission of new members to the enterprise, whereas in Meade's model (Meade, 1972, 1974) *potential* members also participate in this decision. As the membership grows the potential for conflict between members and between personal desires and collective mass psychological traits also increases.

Meade (1972) also allows for the possibility of an inegalitarian cooperative in which members can hold varying shares, and people have to purchase their release from the cooperative. This also means that a series of results of perversity can arise *within the neo-classical paradigm about 'Illyrian' firms* used by Meade (Meade, 1974). First, if new members of the workers' collective are coopted, the *net income per worker* of all may fall, producing a permanent bias against expanding employment; second, if prices of final output rise *and*, at the same time, the *value of marginal product* rises by less than the average earnings per worker (in value) then a gain accrues to the whole sector (and per member) if someone is expelled. This, Meade and Ward indicate, will happen even if *output* also falls. This means that despite any socialist ideology coming to the work-force out of socio-political bodies, the workers' collective tends to have a vested interest in 'natural wastage' as their colleagues leave. It follows that social and economic policies would need to be designed to counter any such perverse effects.[5]

This leads also to the question of the degree of monopoly, also discussed in the next section. If Meade is right, in any context *outside* of his neo-classical construct, as well as within its restrictive corset of abstract assumptions, a monopolistic cooperative will often act in ways to restrict output and employment which would be even more severe than in the case of the capitalist monopolies of Western countries.

Three criticisms of the basic methodological framework set up by Ward, Meade and Horvart may now be offered; the weak psychological postulates of what motivates members of collectives; the excess level of abstraction in the assumptions used and the circularity of the concept 'value of capital' fundamental to their neo-classical paradigm.

Motivation and Psychology

Economic agents, here the workers' collectives, are supposed to maximize marginal utilities (satisfaction) as individuals and the firm's profits as a collective. Workers are assumed to be looking after their narrower interests on the one hand and to be pursuing a different 'collective' interest on the other. The two are made consistent only by the 'lynchpin' argument that 'all will gain' if maximum profits and personal incomes per worker are aimed for, and other possible psychological feed-backs between the two sets of 'psychological' inputs remain unexplored.

In fact, the psychological link between individual behaviour and mass behaviour is nowhere spelt out. Yet this is an important issue, long familiar to psychologists[6] and only detailed understanding of it will help explain things about Yugoslavia: for example the collapse of worker morale within enterprises in the 1980s.

When many factory workers have recently been rural dwellers, they have some memory of collective decision-making. Second generation urban dwellers might not. There may be a struggle between the phenomenon of recollectivization of the psychology of the individual in the mass situation[7] and that individual consciousness and spirit which is familiar in the work of Freud and Jung and a bowdlerized version of which is used by neo-classical theorists of the 'worker-managed firms'. To submerge oneself into a collective group decision is only possible given an extreme process of cleavage between ego consciousness and unconsciousness attitudes and the consequent loss of 'centroversion'.[8]

This is not the place to pursue these psychological issues but enough has been said to indicate two possibilities exist in filling out the 'psychological assumptions' that would need to be set out for behaviour of the Yugoslav-type firm. The first is *despair*, as the need for group solidarity collides with the individual conscious and unconscious instead of the basic mechanism of compensation by the unconscious being allowed to do its work. The second is the possibility of anarchism and lack of regulation leading to a centreless agglomeration of individual egotisms. This might explain, for example, the rising incidence of strikes and *violence* in strikes that have accompanied both the post-Tito political paralysis and the severe economic decline of the Yugoslav economy and personal incomes throughout the 1980s.

Whatever the subtleties of these considerations for the understanding of views about the bodies of 'associated labour' in action, the Yugoslav situation still throws up the continuing problem of the 'informal' control of the enterprise by technicians and managers. Many surveys have shown this (Ward, 1957) and it is encapsulated in the comment of one worker on self-management: 'That's only on paper. When the managers choose their people, workers have to obey. That's how it is here' (quoted in Perlman, 1973, p. 18).

Excessive Abstraction of the Neo-Classical Model

A glance at Ward's eight assumptions suggests immediately the difficulty such a model must have in setting itself up as a reference point for Yugoslav microeconomic business and group behaviour. This needs to be taken together with the general criticisms that have been made in the area of neo-classical theory of the firm in this regard.[9] However, the problem with Ward, Meade and Horvart's approach goes further. Behind it is the dubious proposition that in a socialist society and even in a future communist society, commodity production and markets would remain the central 'social relations'.[10] This conclusion, as well as those specifically drawn from the WVM models, depends too much on abstract theory and not enough on Yugoslav concrete practice. The peculiar behaviour patterns that have been detected in Yugoslav firms can probably better be explained as the result of cultural and political traditions and confused psychological reactions, or as stemming from regional party politics. A further point to remember here has been pointed out by Hutchison, a conservative economist alive to what fences neo-classical economics must mend if it is to be taken seriously.[11] This is that the postulate of *correct expectations* has too much logical weight to bear in equilibrium economics and its model-building. For Frank Knight, G. Shackle and others have exposed the lack of utility in any assumption of certainty for the theory of the (innovating) firm and with it a serious limitation of 'equilibrium economics'. Hutchison comments that Cliffe Leslie in 1879 had already made this point in 'his remarkable essay' yet the maximization-under-certainty postulate 'has proved, as a piece of simplificatory scaffolding, very difficult, or virtually impossible to remove'.[12]

Taken in conjunction with the reality of mark-up pricing methods typical of Yugoslav firms operating a degree of monopoly, the limitations of the Illyrian model are manifest.

The Theory of Capital in Self-Managed Firms

The assumptions set out by Meade (1972) will serve here to illustrate the third severe drawback for any serious use of the 'equilibrium' models of the Yugoslav firm. According to Meade, to study the worker-managed firm we *start* with a firm in an industry 'in which there are only two inputs—a homogeneous worker L, who works a given number of hours at a given intensity, and a fixed capital good K, these two factors producing an output X with a production function $X = X(L, K)$'. He goes on to assume P_x the price of a unit of X; W the market wage rate of labour and the price of a machine (a unit of K) is P_k. Then come two important points; the rental paid for the hire of a machine is iP_k if 'i' is the market rate of interest. A cooperative of workers may be postulated as also hiring machines and using them up to the point where the value of marginal product of the machine equals the rental. What is wrong with this? Simply put, it is that you cannot treat rentals earned by existing bits of equipment as prices paid for their hire and use. Nor can the size of the rental depend on the *amount* of equipment nor even on its technical capacity to produce saleable products. Especially, it cannot depend on the price for which the firm's final output is sold. All of this chain of argument has been blown to smithereens by Sraffa.[13] As shown by the Cambridge critique there is no unambiguous measure of 'bits of plant and equipment'; and it is *not* true that additions to capital will always tend to be associated with a lower rate of interest because of an improvement in the relative scarcity of capital. As one Cambridge critic of this sort of theory has aptly put it; even moving to a 'financial' rather than a *physical* concept of capital cannot solve these problems because,

if capital is regarded as paper titles to ownership of assets, it cannot be independently valued except in terms of its yield, capitalised at some assumed rate of interest. In other words, it is not something that can be measured in units of itself, and any measure of it in money inevitably involves circularity so far as an explanation of the return or yield on capital is concerned.[14]

Unfortunately, therefore, we have to say there is *no theory* of the self-managing 'Illyrian' firm that stands up.[15] In order to develop one for the future the following minimal steps should be taken: first, the degree of monopoly and its effect on pricing and income distribution needs to be incorporated. Second, there must be a look at corporate strategies—at the sociology of bureaucracy—in the Yugoslav context. But first we will look at some new attempts to improve theory of the 1980s.

The 1980s Theories of Worker-Managed Firms

Two further lines of development of a formal Western theory of Yugoslav firms based on a study of Yugoslav data may be noted.

(a) a new approach to worker-managed firms by Derek Jones, Jan Svejnar, Espinoso, Estrin and Levin which has a flavour more empirical and sociological than neo-classical theory with a new emphasis on dynamics, growth and property-claims of members of collectives (Jones & Svejnar, eds, 1985).

(b) a further development of Ward–Domar by learning from empirics and altering the theory to fit new facts at the hands of Ireland & Law (1982).

The first trend in re-appraising the theory of Yugoslav firms is related to the question of how economic agents behave in the face of different choices for a set of 'self-managers' concerning whom they should admit to their circle, concerning their relationship to capital markets (albeit of the constrained Yugoslav kind). Also taken up are those implications one must trace out to promote understanding of the differences in *incentives* and *organizational structures* that exist between traditional firms and self-managing ones of the Yugoslav type. The exercises collected by Jones and Svejnar were an important project in clearing the ground and finding out what were the *specific* laws of motion affecting Yugoslav firms as compared to (say) cooperatives in Chile and other Latin American countries and especially as compared to worker-managed and participatory firms operating under *capitalist* economic environments.

An aspect of the contributors grouped around the Jones–Svejnar approach is their attack on the 'Texas' School of Furubotn (1974 and 1976) and remarks on Aoki (1980). Thus McCain shows (McCain, 1982) that Aoki uses bargaining theory to eliminate the case of zero profits in long-run equilibrium. Aoki assumes that in a self-managed firm there is enterprise-specific human capital embodied in the skills of long-time workers. There are also positive economic rents accruing to the firm, even in long-run equilibrium, these being relative to the alternative costs of the inputs used, not necessarily the prices paid for them: for example, the entire economic profit might be paid to the worker (in the form of wages) so that accounting profit would be zero even though economic profit (rent) is positive. Aoki's model is useful for thinking about *Yugoslav* firms (though he does not do this himself), because it does *not* use a neo-classical production function (a fatally-flawed aspect of orthodox theories of the firm). Output is in fixed proportion to the labour input but a capital input is not mentioned (except for informal discussion of human-capital specific to the firm), so many of the earthquakes opened up by the 'Cambridge Critique' are avoided. Interestingly, too, Aoki posits a given relationship between the firm's chosen growth rate and the *growth expenditure* incurred (especially advertising, fixed investment, personnel retraining). He shows that a change in the 'environment' can strengthen the workers' bargaining power: if prices are unconstrained this will encourage the planned rate of growth and the firm is under pressure not to lay anyone off as incomes rise.

The 'Texans' are a different kettle of fish. Their leader, Furubotn (1974) sketched a model of codetermination in which workers costlessly move from firm to firm if they are dissatisfied with wages. This also puts a constraint on a labour-managed firm and it may have to put a restriction on the number hired (as in the 'Illyrian' conclusion). Hence profits are lower under codetermination and lower profits will lead to reduced investment. Hence codetermination is likely to be a sub-optimal game. McCain argues that there are many ideological fudges in the Texan approach (McCain, 1982, p. 26) and more generally that it is necessary to make a clear distinction between individual bargaining, collective bargaining and codetermination. Once this is done, 'the whole set of Illyrian-theory predictions about the impact of co-determination must be reconsidered', while Furubotn's model is held to be too rigid in not seeing that constraints on the maximization of income program of a firm are relaxed in the nature of 'opportunist' collective bargaining by workers. McCain also denies that any real operational meaning can be given to the 'Furubotn effect' in Yugoslav conditions—i.e. to the idea of the shortening of the time horizon of firm intertemporal planning in the case of worker-ownership where the individual worker cannot appropriate the product of an investment after leaving the firm. Here the complication is in the possibility that workers will ignore the productivity of the capital good in the earlier period of its life and will vote for a less than efficient programme of investment out of retained earnings of the enterprise.

Ireland and Law's Approach

Once again assuming the 'competition' of the textbooks this approach considers the importance of long-run entry of competitive firms on the process of equalization of incomes and value marginal products; it raises the strong possibility that absence of new entry will create income differentials between enterprises. In this case, 'homogenous workers' with similar skills will not get the same wage. With some enterprises 'rich' relative to the others, members of enterprises with above-average assets enjoy above-average incomes per man hour.

The theorists therefore suggest (Ireland & Law, 1982, p. 154) that great caution is needed before belief in a positive correlation between relative incomes and assets of technological knowledge leads to 'evidence' being accepted on the existence of the 'Illyrian' model firm. They also raise doubt as to whether one can clearly distinguish in practice, and in dynamic conditions, a Yugoslav firm that is profit-maximizing and one which is maximizing income per worker.

As well as earnings differentials appearing between Yugoslav firms there is the question of arrangements to meet changing tax requirements in Yugoslav conditions. Ireland and Law draw attention to the impact of low real interest (due to enterprise control over bank lending policy) as an incentive to economize on the use of labour; similarly with reduction in capital tax which has followed a number of 'economic reforms' put through in Yugoslavia. Such a shake-out of labour seems at odds with regime policies and points to the need to readjust real interest rates upwards, a view shared by many Yugoslav economists in the wake of the 1986–7 inflationary spiral. An important contribution here is that Ireland and Law call for a *new* analysis quite separate from the older Ward–Domar model because with the 1974 Constitution the whole integument within which Yugoslav firms had to work also changed (Ireland & Law, 1982, p. 171). With the evolution of the decentralized system featuring polycentric foci of power (described in the last chapter) there are fewer 'pure economic' signals and criteria. The political realm has influenced the prospects of economic units much more directly. Social compacts, social ('self-manager') agreements are drawn up by autonomous divisions within enterprises known as 'Basic Organs of Associated Labour', which can veto managerial decisions and which can separate their own enterprises and join another. This development further undermines models making 'Illyrian' firms behave like those in a capitalist market environment (admittedly with distortions) and points to the need for re-examining the goals or objectives of labour-managed enterprises, including Yugoslav ones. Behavioural interpretations and attention to the *de facto* power of managers, to sales maximization and to growth maximizations become more important.

It is about time textbooks caught up with the economic analysis of self-managed firms and with Yugoslav experience; and it is about time that names like Obradović, Estrin, Ireland, Law and Levin took their place alongside Vanek, Meade and Ward in the index of such texts. However, the

'faith economics' of the neo-classical school dies hard; dynamics and growth
have to struggle to get on economics syllabi side by side with static
equilibrium; and it seems that Yugoslavian puncturing of the stereotypes
used to 'explain' socialist economies in the hands of the textbook men has not
yet penetrated their consciousness to the point where they can cope with the
interesting problems the Yugoslav case throws up.

The Theory of Monopolistic Firms under 'Market Socialism'

Unlike the assumption made in the WVM model, Yugoslav reality has
encouraged monopolistic competition and oligopoly: first, the official policy
encourages 'integration' as an alternative to *state*-based coordination in
industrial planning; second, managements collude on prices to be charged as
they do in the textbooks about 'imperfect' competition in the West.[16]
Business associations provide the integument in which this can happen, and
only occasionally do officials frown on this (or on attempts to form larger
business units) as contrary to genuine self-management.

The reality has been that only between 1952 and 1957 was there anything
approaching the situation of small or medium-scale businesses competing in
isolation from each other on a free market. Multi-plant firms and integration
upwards into conglomeration has been the order of the day, as shown in an
earlier section of this chapter. As well, the tendency for high rates of
ploughing-back of profits to be required of richer firms entrenches the
ideology of oligopoly rather than competition. As a result, a different theory
of this situation is required to that of the WVM-style models we have
considered.

The 'degree of monopoly' may be seen as the determinant of the extent to
which firms offset rising labour and raw materials expenses by increasing
their prices in the same proportion as the cost increase. In the less competitive
industries a given profit margin will be targeted and maintained by this
method. Unlike their capitalist counterparts, Yugoslav firms do not as a
policy carry much excess capacity due to shortage of capital and its expense in
a system based partly on taxation of equipment hired by collectives. Hence
the response to an increase in demand will not be to increase output to absorb
sudden demand increases; rather there will be a temptation to raise prices
even more.

In this way inflation *via the method of price formation* is allowed free rein,
even when the underlying causes of that inflation are rising unit labour costs

(fanned by some greedy workers' councils) or careless monetary policy. For example, in 1965 and 1966 when the Economic Reform reduced subsidies and taxes on enterprises and allowed relative prices to freely adjust, agricultural prices rose by 43 per cent and then 16 per cent (in the agri-business areas) and by 15 per cent and then 11 per cent in manufacturing (Horvart, 1971a, p. 12).

The strong implication is that Yugoslav firms behave in ways that get the worst aspects of monopoly capitalism (mark-ups to maintain profit margins and no output expansion to meet sudden demand rises): another case of market-socialism embracing the worst of both worlds. The only means for the state/society to combat this institutionally built-in method of inflation-ary adjustment have been (a) to introduce arbitrary excess profits taxes (as in 1955–60), with unsettling effects on entrepreneurial behaviour or (b) to introduce price control, which it has done from time to time (e.g., more than 50 per cent of prices were controlled in the 1960s Horvart, 1971a, p. 111), but each time in contradiction to both the *official* ideology favouring 'the market' and a genuine desire that the state should vacate decision-making in the microeconomic field.

Once *inter-sectoral* relations are affected also by monopolistic price practices, problems arise which do begin to produce excess capacity, as with the theory[17] and practice of Western monopoly capitalism. Why is this so?[18] Where *all* profits are ploughed back, there is not, in a neo-classical model of the 'Illyrian' firm any 'exploitation' in the technical sense of the term.[19] Yet the reality is that the mark-up profits and 'full cost pricing' of firms do determine the share of wages in enterprise output and ultimately the share of wages in national income. Hence the firm's policies in pricing must affect sectoral relationships and income distribution.[20] We now compare the 'capitalist' and 'market-socialist' cases to illustrate this mechanism.

Assume no international trade, and that prices are based on cost mark-up rather than demand. The relationship of prices to costs will then be determined, in both the 'capitalism' and 'market-socialism' models, largely by monopolistic and semi-monopolistic factors.

The national income depends purely on movement in investment (I) and in consumption (C). We can, following Marx, divide the economy into two 'departments'. The first (Department I) includes investment goods, the second (Department II) includes final consumer goods.

For the 'capitalism' model, we will assume also that workers do not save and that the consumption of capitalists is stable. For simplification we can also assume that wage rates are stable or else move in the same proportion as prices.

Change in 'Department I' will represent a change in the value of investment-goods, while the movement of Department II signifies a change in the value of consumption-goods.

Writing ΔC — changes in consumption, ΔI — changes in investment, m — share of profit; $(1 - m)$ — share of wages (these depending on the degree of monopoly), we have the following picture as investment grows:

(a) In Department I, ΔI consists of changes in wages and profits, given by $(m_1) \cdot \Delta I$ (i.e. changes in profits) and $(1 - m_1) \cdot \Delta I$ (i.e. changes in wage rates).

(b) In Department II, ΔC changes according to movement in $m_2 \cdot \Delta C$ and in $(1 - m_2) \cdot \Delta C$. How then are I and C related, and what will happen when the rate of investment increases?

When the output of the capital goods sector is increased, wages will go up by $(1 - m_1) \cdot \Delta I$; consumer goods are produced to meet the demand for wage-goods and workers are added to employment levels in Department II. Such workers consume part of new output in Department II as well.

The unconsumed part of additional consumer goods output corresponds to profit, i.e. the surplus of Department II is $m_2 \cdot \Delta C$.

Equilibrium is reached when this surplus is adequate to meet the demand from additional wages and salaries caused by the expansion of investment (the increased employment in Department I), i.e. when

$$m_2 \Delta C - (1 - m_1) \cdot \Delta I.$$

This means that whenever the rate of investment is changed, there will be a resultant change in consumption, the rapidity of which depends on m_1 and m_2. Thus if investment is reduced there will be a consequential change in consumption.[21]

Now assume that there is a given productive capacity in Department II. If Department I expands, consumption will gradually increase according to the formula and installed capacity there will increase to meet extra consumption demand. But it immediately follows that if investment is reduced, the capitalist system is doomed to under-utilization of capacity in Department II through the 'multiplier' effects of the equation. If the rate of investment is less than required to ensure full utilization of capacity in Department II, then excess capacity in Department II will persist unless either (a) prices of consumer goods are reduced or (b) government intervention reduces the degree of monopoly. However, even the introduction of these doses of realism into the 'pure' capitalist system suffices to show that this can only be a purely theoretical solution. The government has not the power, and the monopolies are unwilling to order price cuts since their profit margins are inflexible in the face of a fall in demand.

Now 'market-socialism' will also involve monopoly and oligopoly. Directors of socialist firms producing the same good will evolve tacit or hidden price-fixing. Then, if the rate of investment is reduced, there will be the same effects, sketched above for the capitalist model, operating also under market-socialism. What about the mechanisms producing excess capacity? Does it also apply in the Yugoslav-type case? In my view:

(a) Under-utilization of capacity as a result of a reduced rate of investment and the operation of the price mechanism could only be avoided if the socialist firms fixed higher prices but at the same time paid extra wages in advance of profits. This would be possible for the 'market-socialism' model since it is, after all, still a socialist economy. This way is not open to the 'capitalism' model, whilst increases in capitalists' consumption (a possible alternative mechanism) are only possible after a considerable time lag. But if advance payments to workers are *not* paid in the market-socialist model, consumer goods cannot be sold. (In Yugoslavia there have been many periods in which factories could not sell goods due to high prices and there was also inventory accumulation of such goods.)

(b) If the government wishes to reduce investment without reducing consumption and without increasing the level of excess capacity in Department II, it could lower taxes on enterprises. This would give workers more out of residual profits—it would reduce m_1 and m_2 and raise demand (i.e. it works the same way as increased capitalists' consumption in our first model). The difficulties about this scheme are that the very monopolistic or oligopolistic 'socialist' firms which have raised their prices are now enjoying a lesser tax burden and strengthening their position in the economy. Further, profit-sharing by workers in socialist firms is not as easy as it looks. Some firms are in a better position than others. So if profit-sharing[22] is introduced into a decentralized socialist economy, there will have to be central intervention to ensure justice in the matter of the relative distribution of benefits for firms and their workers. Special consideration might have to be given to firms with unique difficulties such as obsolete machinery for a falling market demand. Thus the decentralized system has to be 're-centralized' (as happened in the Yugoslavia of the 1960s).

(c) The government could levy a tax on the value of fixed capital of the firms to encourage full utilization of capacity and enforce price reductions. This has also been done by the Yugoslav government. But it may be doubted whether these taxes really overcame excess capacity. They tended to be regarded simply as a constant or given thing. Moreover, they were claimed to have reduced the incentive to install capital-using techniques, thereby reducing technical progress. A tax on excess capacity itself would be preferable. But this would be hard to calculate and hard to police; the decentralized socialist firms would borrow stocks temporarily from others to give a 'show' of temporary full-capacity working, then return to 'normal' once inspectors had left.

(d) An excess profits tax can be introduced (as periodically in Yugoslavia). Paradoxically, this tends to distort the profit motive! It increases uncertainty on the part of the socialist Director. He will not be sure of his profits and will be unsure of what prices to charge. An atmosphere of 'fear of excess profits tax' is, after all, not conducive to higher productivity. Moreover this action is really a form of *ex post* control—the *de facto* substitute for central price control, but with the disadvantage of extra uncertainty. Central price fixing, on the other hand, *might* make the profit-motive work in an efficient way. With fixed prices, firms must sell more goods to get profit and a firm producing unwanted goods has to change its product-mix, since it is paying interest on stocks and earning no profits.

It might be thought that the theoretical issues above would not be generally relevant because a market-socialist economy like Yugoslavia will rarely reduce investment. But in fact it does so when: (a) there has been above-plan investment in the immediate past that needs to be stopped; and (b) investment decisions are decentralized to firms and local authorities (say to a ratio of 20:80 as in Yugoslavia today). Under such conditions there develops intense pressure for the standard of living to rise in particular regions of the country (the Croat-Slovene unhappiness again), and for investment to be cut back to fulfil this demand. There must, in any case, be *some* shift from investment to consumption at particular times and the problem emerges again. Anyway, there will frequently be a situation where investment expands more slowly than capacity grows, and this opens the way for all of the mechanisms described in the capitalist model to operate also in the market-socialist system.

Sociology of Corporate Bureaucracy

The notion that one adopts of the *essential nature* of the business firm is important. In the United Kingdom, Marris[23] and Adrian Wood[24] have shown that corporate bureaucracies behave in certain ways—including acting as a financial planning unit. In the United States, Galbraith in his *New Industrial State* analysed the impact of the 'technostructure' (economists, lawyers, accountants and project engineers) on the behaviour of the firm. In Yugoslavia, however, it seems that the *sociology of corporate bureaucracy* has been rather a neglected subject—strange, given the whole system of self-management socialism was to be built on new ways of managing economic units. It seems that a naïve Utopianism has prevailed there.

One of the few to be conscious of the issue was a Yugoslav living abroad, Jan Vanek[25] (brother of Jaroslav Vanek, author of *General Theory of Labour-Managed Economies*). In a study of Yugoslav enterprises he noted that the Yugoslav firm is solely responsible for the development of those functions which Galbraith designated as the province of the technostructure[26] in Western firms and those which Adrian Wood has described as promoting the rationale of the firm as a financial unit.[27]

The first of these in particular is crucial because it lies at the heart of the organic growth of a firm and its ability to survive and compete. Technological progress within the firm is not only a problem of decisions about investment patterns or of relationships with financial bodies supplying loanable funds (although these are relevant in important ways) but of a certain will of the collective and its management to 'learn by doing' and to put inventions to full commercial use.

The second aspect, the firm as a financial unit, is also important. If we think of the state as generally setting the growth rate of the economy exogenously to the enterprises' affairs, then, with investment coefficients given, there will tend to be one value of the firm's mark-up which is consistent with the autonomously determinant growth rate, because of the way business is financed. In a capitalist economy the relationships between profitability, new capital issues, debt and the need for financial reserves all come into the behaviour of firms. Given a firm's retention of profits ratio, the supply of finance for any particular rate of expansion is a function of the mark-up of profit in the value of unit output.

For Yugoslav firms, too, the expectations of managers will relate also more to the economy's investment rate than to competition from fellow firms. The demand for finance will depend more, in the Yugoslav case, on the relationship between its pricing policy, its costs (including selling costs) and the amount of investment required per unit of output. And where the capitalist firm faced restraints on the supply of finance it can attain (due to sensitive financial markets), the Yugoslav firm often gets its finance for political reasons.

With its supply and demand for finance determined in this way, and with the firm's mark-up determined by the economy-wide or sectoral investment and output growth rates, the distribution of income mechanisms outlined in the last section come into play and determine the level of sectoral investment and degree of capacity utilization.

The behaviour of the empire-builders *within* the Yugoslav firm, as elsewhere, sets the 'tone' within which collectives, units, and groups of 'associated labour' all conduct their debates. As noted by French scholars, economic analysis of the firm in the modern world can no longer be satisfactorily carried out with the normal paraphernalia of supply and demand, price formation, etc.[28] Rather, the enterprise must be seen quite differently. It must be seen as a group of human beings with multi-dimensional aspects to their multi-faceted behaviour, things about which orthodox theory has little to say. The new relationships between the 'salariat' on the one hand and blue-collar union members on the other are an important aspect of this.[29] Workers recruited purely for 'Taylorist' ends may be disappearing (i.e., those recruited as 'beasts for the machine'). Nowadays communication between workers themselves sets up a new social relations within the labour process. In Yugoslavia, the 'groups of associated labour' have actively been grappling with this problem. They have realized that the ability to understand what is involved in management is crucial and must become a skill required at all levels. The problem has been that the management's own 'invisible' power network has been slow to pick this up or respond to it.

Hence you have the paradox: the workers know that managerial price-fixing is causing nation-wide inflation and that if their wages depend solely on output and productivity of the economic sector in which they work there would be conflict, no common ground among firms in an industry and that 40 per cent of firms might go bankrupt if the 'outside' forces of supply and demand profit were allowed to function. Hence the workers, far from acting like the 'rational economic agents' portrayed in the WVM model, have moved to curb the technostructure's power: (a) to exercise monopolistic collusion: (b) to let 'profitability' destroy carefully built up experiences in producing a more 'all-round' worker, no longer simply tied to the machine; (c) as well, the fact that workers depend on the enterprise for social benefits (housing, sickness benefit), but on 'outside earnings' (including 'moon-lighting') to meet day-to-day living costs makes them less prone to use the strike weapon but more likely to reduce their productivity while at work.[30] The result is checkmate and paralysis within the whole pattern making up ·corporate behaviour (in the sociological sense) of the Yugoslav firm.

Agro-Commerc Affair

In July 1987 a Belgrade journalist overheard some bankers and their political friends in a fashionable cafe discussing the volume of promissory notes issued by Agro-Commerc one of the country's largest enterprises: an agri-business with substantial property and hotel investments employing more than 13,000 people.

On 15 August 1987 the newspaper *Nedeljna Borba* reported that the case of Agro-Commerc had been investigated by the central bank and the financial auditing inspectorate but had been hushed up by the Party machine of Bosnia. It also reported that at least 22,000 million dinars (US$200 million) of dubious cheques and promissory notes was involved.

In late September, a special issue of *Borba* (newspaper of the Socialist Alliance of the Working People, the Popular Front), uttered a most unusual document for a communist country. Its 'Special Edition', entitled 'Affair of Agro-Commerc' exposed over 48 pages the blow-by-blow account of how this enterprise had successfully expanded into adjacent fields of production and exports, how its director, F. Abdić, had built a luxury home on the coast at Rijeka, and how 'protection' had been given by H. Požderac, the Vice-President of Yugoslavia, as well as local Bosnian Party leaders close to Požderac once financial scandal was suspected.

One of the most startling things to come out was that banks had felt intimidated about refusing loans to the Agro-Commerc conglomerate or about declining to cash its promissory notes, despite clear guidelines from the national bank on stricter control over short-term credits that might be diverted to longer-term uses. This new situation created the conditions under which the banking system adjusted to commercial enterprises and not vice versa. This means a 'wild card' factor in the economy as a whole—a pool of liquid funds unrelated to real production. It was feared that perhaps US$900 million (and possibly even US$2 billion) could be involved once the authorities had tracked down other firms which had been doing the same as Agro-Commerc.

The results of these illegal activities were, of course, that Yugoslav workers as a whole were forced to shoulder the burden via the inflationary spiral such 'printing of money' by large enterprises induced.

The significance of the exposure of Bosnian Party protection for the conglomerate was that it brought to the public gaze for the first time the practice of unlimited credit pipelines to favoured enterprises. This had become something endemic in 1980s Yugoslav practice: the issuing of loans, credit and money supply on political criteria without any regard to the rate of return, followed by State Bank branch cover-up, on the political instructions of regional étatists.

Overview

While the development of theories in the West about the 'Illyrian' firm is of some technical interest,[31] their logical structure is not sufficiently strong or persuasive to act as a further stimulant to, a feedback mechanism for, Yugoslav policies in relation to enterprise decision-making. Indeed, successive laws introduced after 1975 and aiming to force wealthier enterprise to plough back more of their profits, percentagewise, than less successful ones, run counter to assumptions, used in the economic theory of worker-managed firms.

Study of enterprise behaviour in practice suggests, instead, that workers' councils have had to struggle to get accepted in *practice* many of the decision-making powers that are assumed in the theory of Western economists concerning 'market-socialism'. Successive struggles for more popular control (1952, 1968, 1971, 1983) have exposed the gap which exists between the official ideology of the Yugoslav Marxist regime and the social relations it claims to describe. Self-management, for many workers' collectives, appeared less as an operational principle of a socialist economy and more as a mask for a commercial-technocratic bureaucracy to maintain its privileges. The very high rates of 'value of surplus product' extracted per worker, noted in the period 1952–61,[32] continued to pose a problem as workers' councils depended on exchanging the wage fund of the firm for labour of workers (to cover their living costs) while the 'surplus' was appropriated by state or commercial bureaucracies and transformed into capital—some to be used to expand enterprise assets, some for the costs of running government and some for 'social' or 'collective' needs (schools, hospitals, etc.). The main psychological burden on workers has been the existence of people whose 'capital' is not based on their own efforts in production but on private labour, services, middlemen activities and speculation. Such people and the 'black' or parallel labour markets are commonplace in Yugoslavia's large cities and pose problems of equity, of how government under self-management can handle such aspects of market socialism without re-introduction of social controls.

While the managerial system used for the Yugoslav economic sectors cannot be directly blamed for many of the price rises and strikes of the 1980s, the lack of planning and the vague links between sectoral plans and enterprise behaviour, both mean the economic strains from excessive credit emissions and adverse export trends created chaos for wage policy.

Part IV
Contemporary Political Issues

14   Foreign Policy

Only two serious attempts have been made, one in the earliest days of the regime, to present a Marxist theory of relations between socialist countries. Such a theory, as it came forward (M. Popović, 1949; Kardelj, 1961c) had to emphasize the economic issues involved. For example, the main problem facing the chief ideologue in the area, Milentije Popović, was that important differences of interest between newly socialist nations would persist and would even reveal themselves in a more open form. Conflict could arise from divergent standards of life as between regions, especially in relation to the movement of capital between them. Another principal difference which arose was on how far richer socialist nations should suffer a form of 'forced saving' to help their poorer socialist neighbours. As a result of pondering these issues Popović was led to examine the phenomenon of Soviet bureaucracy and its behaviour in the sphere of foreign economic relations.

With the use of Soviet–Yugoslav joint-stock companies to develop transport and minerals in Yugoslavia (Djilas, 1962) the Popović theses were overtaken by events and relegated to abstract theorizing and Utopianism. From now on the hard-heads like Kidrič (1950) and S. Vukmanović-Tempo were emphasizing not theoretical desirabilities in international economic relations between socialist countries, but practicalities. Increasingly there was a trend towards an *ad hoc* series of positions and policies in international affairs. For an account of these the observer has to turn to biographies of Tito (Dedijer, 1953; Auty, 1970; Djilas, 1981), to collections of Tito's speeches (Tito, 1956; 1971), to memoirs of Ambassadors (Mićunović, 1980) and to reports tabled by foreign ministers (Koča Popović, 1959).

Yugoslav Foreign Policy in the 1950s

If there was any guiding principle in Yugoslav foreign policy over this period it was probably encompassed in the phrase 'active co-existence', a phrase which became popular in Yugoslav circles after the joint Tito–Nehru Declaration of December 1954, though the idea had existed before that date.

The 1958 Programme of the League of Communists (ch. iii) stated the principle in this way:

Peace in the present conditions primarily means peaceful coexistence between peoples and states with different social systems. This coexistence must not be passive, entrenched in bloc positions; it must be active, it must aim to achieve ever broader cooperation between peoples.

The policy of non-involvement in power blocs followed from the policy of 'active coexistence'; it became a restatement of this policy from another angle. 'The policy of non-alignment adopted and pursued by their respective countries' (said the Tito–Nehru Declaration) 'is not "neutrality" or "neutralism" and therefore passivity, as sometimes alleged, but is an active, positive and constructive policy seeking to lead a collective peace on which alone collective security can really rest'. On the other hand, suggestions that the non-aligned powers almost inevitably themselves tend to constitute a bloc (a 'third force') was strongly rejected by the Yugoslavs as contrary to the spirit of 'active coexistence'.

Support for the United Nations Organization became another facet of this policy of 'active coexistence': 'This Organization, despite its present shortcomings which are the outcome of the influence of existing inter-national contradictions, could become the active factor of a democratic mechanism which would be used not only to suppress war but also to encourage and promote comprehensive cooperation between peoples', while 'the policy of active coexistence should be based on respect for the independence, sovereignty, equality and territorial integrity of other countries, and on non-interference in their affairs' (League of Yugoslav Communists, 1958, ch. iii).

Another general principle of Yugoslav foreign policy, fairly consistently upheld during the 1950s was support for the independence of colonial and semi-colonial peoples. The Resolution of the 7th Congress of the League of Yugoslav Communists (April 1958) supported 'the struggle of the peoples of the colonial and semi-colonial countries, considering that every forcible retention of those peoples in a subjugated position, as well as endangering the independence of other countries, is impermissible and harmful to the interests of peace'. Communists in Yugoslavia believed that some of these peoples might be able to avoid most of the phases of capitalist development and pass over to socialism rather quickly.

While using foreign ministers' speeches is necessary background, a mere summary of official pronouncements about the basis of a country's foreign policy does not always tell us very much about the actual policy of that country. As the Under Secretary for Foreign Affairs Koča Popović himself stated (*Review of International Affairs*, 15 September 1955):

The formulation of the principles of a foreign policy, like all other formulations, can occasionally seem, and often become, mere phraseology deprived of any meaning, like the ritual formulas and symbols of a faith that are constantly repeated but seldom adhered to in actual life. Although it would be wrong to depend solely on such a formulation in appraising the real policy of a country, it would be equally wrong to consider it to be without any value at all.

In considering the 'real policy' of Yugoslavia we must consider not only the principles enunciated but also the world environment in which these principles are to work, and the basic interests and needs of Yugoslavia which lay behind the official adoption of these principles.

Four special features of the world environment in the 1950s which Yugoslav foreign policy had to consider were: the easing of the Cold War after the Geneva Conference of mid-1954; the relative balance in armed might between the two great blocs; the appearance of a large number of newly-independent Afro-Asian nations; and changes in Soviet foreign policy following the death of Stalin.

These might be described as the external realities. The internal realities which Yugoslav statesmen had to remember when formulating their international policy in this period were predominantly economic. Yugoslavia was the largest country in the Balkan peninsula (17,000,000 people, 99,720 sq. miles); a small country on the world scale, her balance of trade continued to be adverse. This made it important to develop international trade links. In addition, there was a growing need for financial assistance from abroad, from the West or the East, or both.

In the years of the 1950s the overpowering factor in Yugoslav policy was the break with the Soviet Union and its protectorates. Yugoslavia attempted the difficult task of maintaining an independent policy between the two great blocs at a time when the Cold War was at its height: 'Yugoslavia will not bow down to the West any more than it bowed down before the Cominform', said Tito in March 1950, but at times Yugoslavia found it hard to maintain this independent course.[1]

One example was the train of events that ensued when economic assistance from the West was obtained. America was engaging in economic warfare against Communist states (Adler-Karlsson, 1968). In June 1949 the United States had, however, eased the ban on the export of various items to Yugoslavia. Between 1950 and 1954 the United States, Britain and France gave Yugoslavia aid amounting to US$428 million. (In the same period droughts forced Yugoslavia to import foodstuffs to the value of US$350 million.) However, after June 1955 only the United States continued to give economic assistance. The United States also gave arms, but when suggestions were made that there should be a system of inspection with US advisors Tito spoke out bluntly (July 1955):

It is their own affair whether they give us more arms or not, but Yugoslavia cannot accept more arms if the conditions are different from those which already exist—if an attempt is made to impose new conditions in conformity with some US law. It is the laws of Yugoslavia, not those of the United States, which hold good in this country.

The outbreak of fighting in Korea in June 1950 put Yugoslavia in a delicate position when the issue was brought up at the United Nations. However, in votes on the UN Security Council Yugoslavia either voted against the West or abstained from voting.

The threat of Yugoslavia's borders led to closer relations with Greece and Turkey. In February 1953 Tito signed a treaty of friendship with both Greece and Turkey, and a year later this was transformed into a military alliance. A local Balkan bloc appeared to be emerging. But Yugoslavia refused to join the North Atlantic Treaty Organization, and her military agreement with Greece and Turkey stipulated that Yugoslavia would not be committed if the other two became involved in war because of NATO.

Better relations with Italy were held up over the Trieste dispute. In October 1953 Britain and the United States proposed to hand over Zone A of the Free Territory of Trieste to Italy, leaving Zone B to Yugoslavia. The scheme was abandoned after opposition from Yugoslavia. However, discussions led to an agreement twelve months later, Italy taking Zone A less two small sections which, with Zone B, were given to Yugoslavia. Italy had always ranked high in trade relations with Yugoslavia, but after the settlement these relations improved further.

The other two changes which the period of strained relations with the Soviet Union produced in the 1950s were closer economic and political contacts with Asian countries and new links between the League of Yugoslav Communists and socialist parties in Europe and Asia. But it was relations with the Soviet Union which really mattered and these were zigzagging over the whole period of Khrushchev's ascendancy in the CPSU (Mićunović, 1980, chs. 13–18).

At the end of 1954 the economic blockade of Yugoslavia by her Communist neighbours came to an end. These states then made compensation agreements with Yugoslavia to recompense for damage arising from the blockade and the breaking of earlier contracts, while a series of new trade agreements were signed. East European criticism of Yugoslav foreign policy abated.[2] In May–June 1955 a Soviet delegation visited Yugoslavia. Khrushchev wished to make the reconciliation an ideological one and a reconciliation between the two Communist Parties, but the Yugoslavs insisted on treating the *rapprochement* as one between states, not parties. It was only when Tito visited Moscow, a year later, that a declaration signed by both the heads of state and the Party leaders was issued (Mićunović, 1980, ch. 20). This declaration stated that the roads and conditions of socialist development are different in different countries and that relations between the League of Yugoslav Communists and the Communist Party of the Soviet Union were to be based on a complete freedom of will and equality.

A by-product of the improvement in relations with the Soviet Union and its Communist allies, and of the easing of the tense world situation after the death of Stalin, was a modification of the Balkan Alliance. Developing differences between Turkey and Greece over the future of Cyprus also weakened this Alliance. A Consultative Assembly made up of parliamentarians from the three countries was established; but the Balkan Alliance became less of a military alliance and more of a cultural *entente*. 'It is thus clear', stated the Yugoslav Secretary for Foreign Affairs in March 1955, 'that in the present conditions the main stress cannot be placed on military measures', and in March 1959 Yugoslavia, in practice if not by official declaration, repudiated the dormant Balkan Pact in favour of bilateral political cooperation with Greece and Turkey.

A very important neighbour turned out to be Hungary. On the whole, relations with Hungary were turbulent. Yugoslavia's reconciliation with Hungary after 1945 made slow progress. The main matter in dispute was that of compensation to Yugoslavia for wartime damage and the blockade of 1948–54. The Yugoslavs were not disappointed to see Rákosi resign in 1955 as Secretary of the Hungarian Communist Party; but they were not very enthusiastic when Gerő became Secretary. When the Hungarian Revolution broke out Tito condemned Gerő for seeking the first Soviet intervention (24 October 1956). 'To call upon the army of another country to teach a lesson to the people of one's own country is a serious mistake' (Tito, 1956). However, Tito regarded the second Soviet intervention of 4 November 1956 (which permitted Kádár to form a new government) as the lesser evil and Yugoslavia accorded recognition to this regime. Yugoslavia was against foreign intervention in principle, (Kardelj's speech of 7 December 1956), but this one might be justified if it permitted the establishment of a government which would change the political situation in Hungary, rally the socialist forces, and accept the workers' councils which the revolution in Budapest factories had thrown up. The kidnapping of former premier Imre Nagy on 21 November, after he had left the asylum of the Yugoslav Embassy, brought violent condemnation from the Yugoslav leaders.

In the same speech (Kardelj, 7 December 1956) in which he urged support for the Kádár government in the hope that this government would link itself with the working class, Kardelj pointed out that neither the Hungarian workers' councils nor the Communist Party nor the Hungarian intelligentsia were consciously socialist, i.e. they were not seeking full power for the workers' councils:

> Since the Hungarian Communists did not make such an approach and are not so approaching the Workers' Councils, but perpetually keep agitating that work should be resumed, without reference to authority, it is they themselves who are increasingly pushing them under the influence of the petty-bourgeois and nationalistic, pseudo-democratic elements and phrases.

Kardelj believed that Soviet intervention in Hungary was influenced not mainly by a concern for socialism, but by the question of the international balance of power. However, he admitted that this aspect of the Hungarian uprising also influenced the Yugoslav government, while the question of the proximity of Soviet troops to the Yugoslav frontier was also a factor. Yugoslav foreign policy here was torn by a conflict between the desires of socialists to see socialism preserved and improved in Hungary; the need of a small state in international affairs to avoid Great Power clashes on its frontiers; and support for the principle of non-intervention in internal matters.[3]

Relations between Yugoslavia and the Soviet Union cooled after the 1956 events in Poland and Hungary (Mićunović, 1980, ch. 13), though there had been many misunderstandings during 1954–6 also. At the end of 1957 Yugoslavia abstained from signing the declaration approved by twelve Communist Parties in Moscow. On the other hand, from December 1957, she ceased to accept US military aid (Mićunović, 1980, pp. 45–50).

During 1958 the renewed campaign of the Soviet Union, China and their closest allies in Eastern Europe against Yugoslav 'revisionism' continued in the political press of Eastern Europe.[4] Trade and economic agreements between the Soviet Union and Yugoslavia, and even between the Soviet Union and Poland, began to work more fitfully and aid was given on a purely hand to mouth basis (Mićunović, 1980, p. 48). Petty irritations arose, as when, in December 1955, Albanians forced a Yugoslav ship escaping from a storm to put to sea again with the cry 'No shelter in Valona harbour for revisionists'.

With the decisive change in outlook emerging at the 7th Congress of the League of Yugoslav Communists (April 1958) many of the other Communist Parties showed their estrangement and hostility by refusing to send delegations. The Congress gave the Yugoslavs a chance to state their theoretical position again and gave *Pravda* and *Jen Min Jih Pao* yet another opportunity to denounce Yugoslav 'revisionism', since the 1958 Programme of the League of Yugoslav Communists gave a large amount of attention to questions of orthodox views on the role of the Party and of the CPSU in particular:

The interest of further socialist development demands free socialist democratic relations between the parties of the socialist countries. In the struggle for the victory of socialism, the working class of one country or another may, for a certain period of time, be the standard-bearer of that struggle, its vanguard, or possess greater material power; but that does not entitle it to a monopoly position in the workers' movement, least of all to monopoly in the sphere of ideology. Past experience has shown, and is making it even clearer to-day, that cooperation in the workers' movement is possible only between equals. [League of Yugoslav Communists, 1958, ch. 1]

The Programme asserted that the Soviet Union had been the only socialist country; protection of the Soviet Union as the main stronghold of international socialism was one of the principled measures of proletarian internationalism, but this time had now passed. Socialism, peace and 'active peaceful coexistence' called for new policies within the socialist bloc generally.

The 1960s

The 1958 Congress changed Yugoslavia's foreign policy stance. The frenetic activity around the codifying of a new Constitution in the early 1960s was paralleled in foreign policy. In September 1960 Tito delivered a major exposition at the United Nations of Yugoslav policy concentrating on colonialism, disarmament and world peace (Tito, 1971, pp. 93–121). A year later a very large conference of non-aligned countries (of which group some twenty-nine attended) was hosted in Belgrade. Tito's address on the occasion expounded the goals of developing, non-aligned nations and their compatibility with Yugoslavia's own views (Tito, 1971, pp. 123–50).

The UN address featured warnings about the end of the Camp David spirit of better relations between the superpowers due to the U2 flight of an American pilot over the Soviet Union. The rift was leading to such dangerous developments as nuclear arming of the Bundeswehr, the Cuban crisis and the increased US support for anti-left forces in Laos. Moreover, colonialism was not dead; it was operating openly in Algeria and the Congo and its heritage had not been liquidated due to the growth of economic neo-colonialism. Speaking to the 1961 Belgrade non-aligned meeting Tito called for more active steps towards disarmament, describing a 'profound crisis in this field' (Tito, 1971, p. 127). He went on to support the revolutionary trend in Angola, anti-apartheid sentiment in South Africa and to condemn 'outside interference' in Laos.

If Tito's speeches were *ad hoc* in character, Kardelj undertook a systematic ideological defence of Yugoslav foreign policy (Kardelj, 1961c). The context was one of violent assaults on Yugoslavia's foreign policy stances by the Communist Party of China during 1958–60. Kardelj's reply to the Chinese was that so-called 'revisionism' can actually mean a development of the theories of Marx and Lenin to take account of the realities involved in the unfolding of the developments of both the capitalist and socialist worlds, and changes in the nature of relations between them. To ignore these was 'dogmatism'.

Kardelj argued that Yugoslavia was not wedded to 'neutralism'; it did, however, believe in peaceful coexistence of regimes with different ownership and social patterns (Kardelj, 1961c, pp. 16–20). The Chinese, he showed, were trying to impose their own conception of international policy on others. To the charge of 'cowardice' he pointed to the record of the Yugoslav Communist movement in the struggles against the Nazis and in maintaining unity and ideological firmness against Soviet pressure during 1948–55 (Kardelj, 1961c, p. 24). He concluded (Kardelj, 1961c, p. 27) that 'only a policy which combines a clear revolutionary orientation with a realistic analysis of the objective conditions and of all the factors of social development is really revolutionary'.

Relations with China deteriorated further, however, in 1963, when the Chinese published *Is Yugoslavia a Socialist Country?* This was one of the most insulting documents ever uttered in foreign relations between socialist nations. Apart from its attack on a range of Yugoslav policies, reference was made to the high-living style of influential Yugoslavs. The 'anti-revisionist' tirades of the Soviet Communists against Tito's policies were restated with a vengeance by the Chinese.

In 1968, in a speech in Leskovac (Tito, 1971, pp. 153–68), Tito stated Yugoslavia's position on the invasion and occupation of the Czechoslovak Socialist Republic by the Soviet Union and Warsaw Pact nations. In this address the 'Brezhnev doctrine' that the 'socialist commonwealth', headed by the Soviet Union, had the right to intervene on behalf of Communism generally was challenged:

Our positions on the Czechoslovak case have been made clear to the world, and we stand by them forever . . .

The principles of non-interference, independence, integrity and sovereignty must be valid for all countries of the world, whether they be members of a bloc or not.

Yugoslavia's policy provoked a strong attack from Poland, Hungary, the GDR, the Soviet Union and especially from Bulgaria, and some of the older 1948 charges about Yugoslavia and its move towards capitalism were repeated. Self-management was singled out, as well as Yugoslavia's economic reform of 1968, for abuse.

A strong rebuff to the Bulgarians was, however, combined with a policy of not disrupting economic relations with Eastern Europe and there were stepped-up efforts within the non-aligned world to improve Yugoslavia's standing in the face of the East European pressure.

The 1970s

In the 1970s Tito grew more anxious about Soviet intentions towards Yugoslavia under Brezhnev, while his anti-Sovietism led to a break with Cuba and some other radical Third World states in the 'group of 77' at the United Nations. At the conference of these groups, Yugoslavia's policy led to some confusing new proposals,[5] and to criticism of Castro for not being 'even-handed' in attributing blame for world tensions accelerating to a danger point.

Moreover, the shock of the attempt by leading circles in Croatia 1970–1 to discuss Croatia separately joining the United Nations led to re-assessment of foreign policy for the 1970s. As the Croatian explosion of national feeling and antagonism to 'unitarianism' or 'Serbian dominance' reached its height in September–October 1971, any moves by Tito in foreign policy became significant. The major initiative turned out to be spectacularly closer relations with the Soviet Union, with Brezhnev, Secretary of the CPSU visiting Belgrade, 22–25 September. In their joint communiqué, Tito and Brezhnev noted:

The development of all-round Yugoslav–Soviet relations is based on the principles which were expounded in the 1955 Belgrade Declaration and the 1956 Moscow Statement as well as the 1965 Joint Yugoslav–Soviet communiqué.

Co-operation between the SFRJ and the Soviet Union is based on closeness of historical destinies, an identity of the groundwork of the social system, closeness of approach to numerous international problems, devotion to the principles of socialist-internationalism, a common struggle for peace, independence and equal international cooperation, and to the struggle against imperialism. [*Borba*, 26 September 1971]

Before the Brezhnev visit it was reported that Brezhnev had agreed to certain Yugoslav conditions for improved relations. The well-informed journalist Lajos Lederer (London *Observer*, 5 September 1971) listed these as: (a) the Soviet Union to discourage militancy of Yugoslav pro-Cominform exiles in Moscow; (b) the Soviet Union to abandon joint Soviet-Bulgarian military manœuvres in Bulgaria; Brezhnev to modify the doctrine under which the Soviets could interfere in East European affairs in case of emergency; (c) the Soviet Union to deny publicity or support by its agents of any Croat *émigrés* in Western Europe. In return the Soviets got strong Yugoslav support for a European security conference; assistance in neutralizing Chinese pressure on some countries important to Soviet foreign policy (Algeria, Vietnam). The Yugoslav press reported (*Politika*, 13 September 1971) that the Soviets had applauded speeches by Tito at Tjentisk and Koprionik during early September on the theme of 'Unity against Class Enemies and the Dictatorship of the Proletariat'. The desirability of closer relations between Yugoslavia and the Soviet Union was repeated by the Hungarian paper *Nepszabadsag* and the Polish paper *Trybuna Ludu*; (d) the Soviet Union to be more sympathetic to threats to Yugoslavia's borders.[6]

The 1974 stock-taking by Kardelj of the state of Yugoslav foreign policy summed up the flavour of 1970s official attitudes. Kardelj commented that:

The policy of non-alignment has opposed tendencies to divide the world into military and political blocs, but it was not the main, let alone the only substance of non-aligned policy—it was the necessary consequence of that policy, rather than its actual substance. This was [rather] common resistance to the system of economic and political relations among nations that had taken shape in the imperialist era and which was based on colonialism, on semi-colonial forms of dependence, on the scramble for hegemonic power over peoples. [Kardelj, 1974, p. 95]

Socialism and non-alignment were, Kardelj insisted, quite consistent priorities for the Yugoslavs to pursue in foreign policy. By encouraging other non-aligned countries to follow an internal path of socialism, Yugoslavia was objectively weakening the imperialist system, and, by demonstrating a self-management road was viable, it weakened statism, Stalinism and similar structures that had led to an undesirable 'hegemony' in foreign policy (Kardelj, 1974).

Outside Yugoslavia, however, the Western left criticized Tito's foreign policy for finding common ground on international issues with such odious regimes as Abyssinia ruled by a semi-feudal emperor, with the King of Afghanistan and the Shah of Persia. While most of the critics saw Yugoslavian foreign policy as opportunistic, the reasons for Yugoslavia's behaviour between 1954 and 1974 had deeper roots.

First, the Western powers had exerted, via aid and credit, a considerable influence over the economic dimension of Yugoslavia's international relations. This forced Yugoslavia to look for new friends. It also persuaded the leaders that even some pro-US regimes could become friends. Second, its experiences with the growing differentiation of Soviet bureaucracy and policy conflict in the Kremlin led to confusion (Mićunović, 1980, ch. 21). Third, fear of the internal contradictions between Yugoslavia's own republics led to extreme caution in foreign affairs, and a more careful 'balanced' criticism of the East European system for fear of provoking Soviet leaders.

Orientation of Yugoslav Foreign Policy in the 1980s

General

A key element in 1980s foreign policy has been recognition of the inter-dependent character of the economic policies of modern states (Fabinc & Kalogjera, 1987, p. 18). Yugoslavia's relatively open economy has meant that it was going to be inevitably caught up in regional and international restructuring of the world economy. Yugoslav writers on foreign policy like to say that the early participation of Yugoslavia in regional groupings and in the non-aligned movement has put the country in a position where it is quite experienced in such issues of 'integration into the world economy' or in regional cooperation (Fabinc & Kalogjera, 1987, p. 27):

Yugoslavia has been and remains an advocate of various forms of co-ordinating mechanisms within the framework of regional and international organisation, along the general line of its non-alignment, independence and faith in the progress in the world and its aspiration for a lasting solution to . . . problems of development.

Stripped of the 'officialese', what does this mean in practice for contemporary foreign policy?

The post-Tito era, given reasonable performance of the Yugoslav economy, should have seen a more developed Yugoslavia tied more closely to

Europe. While this has happened to some degree it came about perhaps as a result of some disillusionment with the behaviour of the Afro-Asian countries, or at least with the current frameworks of non-alignment. Yugoslavia has been pleased by the development of market socialism within China and with China's more active role in the non-aligned movement, but it has not been happy with the slow progress of UNCTAD and other global gatherings on 'North-South' issues. Little cooperation has been forthcoming from Western industrial nations in solving Third World problems. Yugoslav think-tanks in the area of international relations, as well as Yugoslav diplomats, have expressed the belief that in the 1980s many more new nations are beholden to a superpower and thereby weaken 'non-alignment' as a practical everyday strategy. Politically, the strength of non-alignment has ebbed, and with it a linchpin of Yugoslav foreign policy.

The President of Yugoslavia in 1984, M. Spiljak, tried to come to terms with this in his report to the Federal Assembly on 19 April 1984 (Spiljak, 1984, pp. 12–18). On the positive side, he felt that the fact that Yugoslavia itself was created by a genuine popular revolution gave it a special status with national liberation movements and many members of the Group of 77. This also required Yugoslavia to take responsibility for the continuing vitality of the non-alignment bloc. The ferment and moral questions raised by arming of Third World countries was one great issue on the agenda (Spiljak, 1984, p. 13); another was the need to activate UNO to stand up to the superpowers on the arms race and to break down a growing tendency for powerful UN members to simply resist change; a third was that Yugoslavia was compelled by its own socialist origins to 'give support to those national liberation movements which struggle for the liberation of their peoples' (Spiljak, 1984, p. 16).

On the 'economic relations' elements in foreign policy, the evolution of Yugoslav doctrine in the 1980s has become noticeably disillusioned (Adamović, 1983), about the realities involved in 'a new system of economic relations with foreign countries based on market principles and economic criteria' (Kovač, 1987, p. 77). Yugoslav experts complain that market-oriented foreign economic relations can be realized 'only in a broader and more competitive environment' (Kovač, 1987, p. 77). Common market discrimination against non-members, rigged commodity markets, multi-national manipulation of textiles, alcohol, fruit and other areas—all these portray 'market imperfections' and destroy the foundations of the new system attempted by Yugoslavia symbolized by the abandonment of multiple rates of foreign exchange for a simpler system on 1 January 1986. Moreover, due to economic stabilization measures officially adopted, Yugoslavia itself is forced to take on fewer foreign credits in the new system, and its foreign economic relations after 1986 have been mainly concentrated on repayment of debt, a policy they strongly defend. In future the structure of Yugoslav exports will be changed from the more 'political' dealing with overseas countries to one based on market criteria. This might mean less trade with Eastern Europe and more with Western Europe.

The post-Tito leadership has to juggle two facets of foreign policy: its desire to promote a constructive regionalism, and its desire to switch to market-oriented economic relations with foreign countries. This reflects the leadership's desire to continue in a vanguard role in promoting non-alignment but also the pressure on it to switch to economic criteria in bilateral and trading relations (Kovač, 1987, pp. 78–81).

How much is policy in the 1980s helped by theory, 'think-tanks', analysis? So far, foreign policy has been hampered by lack of analysis of some areas, still taboo due to the Titoist hangovers, although taboos on criticizing foreign policy stances of Yugoslavia have largely been lifted. Only in 1986, however, did a study appear about conflicts among the Group of 77, among the friends of Yugoslavia in the non-aligned states (Tadić, 1986). Similarly there is a relative paucity of published Yugoslav foreign policy texts on such issues as regional imperialism since 1975; the implosion of structurally weak states, the bureaucratic misbehaviour of various UN bodies (UNESCO, UNCTAD, etc.); the presence of serious threats to world peace from countries other than the superpowers, such as Iran, Iraq, Libya and China.[7] None the less, officially the 'non-aligned' approach does remain a major cornerstone of overall policy.

The 'Regional Orientation' in Yugoslav Foreign Policy

While interest in various regions within the non-aligned movement has been a feature of Yugoslav policy since 1961, there has been, since 1980, an intensification of concern with three particular areas: the Mediterranean, the Balkans and the Common Market (EEC) countries.

(a) The Mediterranean   The pressure of US missiles in Sicily is of concern to Yugoslavia. They realize that their airspace would be invaded in the event of an exchange of missiles between the superpowers. So there have been energetic efforts expended by Yugoslav diplomats in support of the concept of the Mediterranean as a 'zone of peace'. The problem has been the differing alignments already entered into by the countries of the region. While some belong to NATO and superpowers control the sea, a desire for independence

and 'consolidation of sovereignty' have led several countries to call for demilitarization, neutralization and the transformation of the Mediterranean Sea into a 'zone of peace and cooperation'. Yugoslavia has been playing a strong role in encouraging this sentiment while being conscious of the desire of the countries involved to guarantee their own security, while it also raised the 'zone of peace' concept at the Seventh Conference of Heads of States, New Delhi, 7–12 March 1983.[8] But to make the Mediterranean a 'zone of peace' is not easy with bristling American missiles stationed in Sicily, and the facts of the Israeli conflict and the Cyprus affair. Yet, with the EEC itself getting involved with the Mediterranean, the danger of Yugoslavia being ignored in favour of Spain, Portugal and Greece was accelerated by way of 'bilateralism as the exclusive form of cooperation between the Mediterranean countries and the EEC'.[9] Hence it is necessary to 'generate stronger feelings of the common purpose in the Mediterranean . . . for Yugoslavia as a European and non-aligned country, this would be of special significance'.[10]

(b) The Balkans   As a response to Stalin's pressures after 1948 and the possibility of a land invasion of Yugoslavia from Romanian and Hungarian territory, joint defence with Greece and Turkey was attained with the signing of the Balkan Pact in 1954. This is now dormant with the threat from the Soviet Union having steadily receded and the tension between Greece and Turkey over Cyprus having increased. Assistance and moral support for Yugoslavia now would be more likely to come from the 'non-aligned' movement.

In the 1980s relations between Yugoslavia and Greece have been warm, and with Turkey correct. Yugoslavia has pressed for Cyprus issues to be solved by active UN policies and intervention, and supports a non-aligned Cyprus.

Perhaps the touchiest Balkan problems for Yugoslavia today are relations with Bulgaria about the past, present and future role of Macedonian people. Dimitrev's domination of Bulgarian affairs in the 1940s and the first ten years of Zhivkov ensured the problem was defused. The 170,000 Macedonians living in Bulgaria were accorded national minority status, to the satisfaction of the millions who live within Yugoslavia and Greece. In the late 1960s this began to change, and gradually the Bulgarian Census ceased to classify Macedonians and Turks, apparently as part of a forced assimilation. Bulgarian historical and cultural works began to mention the current S.R. Macedonia as part of Bulgaria. This pressure eased somewhat after 1984 but it still 'on the backburner' in the event of any general deterioration in relations.

(c) The EEC   The urgent question confronting Yugoslav–EEC relations is barriers to entry of Yugoslav exports. This was less acute in the period 1968 up to 1980 as bilateral deals were possible and a Yugoslav–EEC Cooperative Agreement regulated the commerce. After that, Yugoslavia had problems and lost its automatic preferential treatment. This was a serious blow only partly assuaged by EEC investment in highways and other infrastructure within Yugoslavia that are linked to exports.

Yugoslav foreign policy has also had to come to terms with the revival of the right-wing political parties in Western Europe as electoral forces and with what is described in Yugoslavia as the 'crisis on the West European left'.[11]

Yugoslavia's options, as seen by local experts,[12] are (a) to promote East–West relations through non-aligned and neutral European nations; (b) to switch to more non-governmental contacts with Europe; (c) to break down Yugoslavia's image in West Europe as an alien culture, which 'identifies Yugoslavia's position with the Balkans and Eastern Europe'. This could mean letting Croatia have more contact with Lombardy, and Slovenia with Austria, on the cultural front; (d) gradually to step-up cooperation with EFTA, whose members have an entrée with individual EEC nations; a similar operation might be developed with Greece and Turkey.

Essentially the problem remaining with the EEC is that Yugoslavia's policy had been rather static until the 1980s. Neo-protectionism in the Community has got worse, however, with Spain and Portugal's entry, and Yugoslavia fears it is being left on the sidelines, not only in relation to its wine and machinery exports but in the matter of its urgent need to get access to the all-important technology of the 'post-industrial society'. Two tactics have been sought to overcome this. The first is to get closer to the EEC by first getting closer to EFTA members, European neutrals with strong ties in the economic and technological fields with the EEC. The second is to seek an active role in EUREKA and other multi-nation European consortia.

Holding back a more dynamic policy of integration with the West European economy as a whole is the fact that Yugoslavia itself is not ready to handle the issue of a fully market-based set of external economic relations. Only in 1986 was a single rather than disparate exchange rate system established, while future full convertibility of the dinar into Western currencies still seems decades away.

Yugoslavia and Eastern Europe

Yugoslavia's traumatic relationship with Eastern Europe after 1948 has already been explained and Table 10.6 in Chapter 10 shows how exports and imports were affected in the short run by the blockade on Yugoslavia which was imposed by the Soviet Union and all the other East European countries at the time.

In the 1980s the situation has changed dramatically. There is no great fear of the Soviet Union in the public or in official circles. Relations with Poland, traditionally good, were maintained by official Yugoslav silence over Solidarnost and its suppression. The 1987 reforms in Poland have been welcomed. Relations with Hungary have improved since the 1960s, with support for the Kádár–Gróz wing of the Hungarian leadership. Reciprocal good treatment of the Yugoslav minority in Hungary and of half-a-million Hungarians living in Vojvodina have helped. Romania and Czechoslovakia maintain good relations.

Yugoslavia and other Socialist States

The biggest change in Yugoslavia's foreign relations between 1975 and 1985 was the improved friendship with China, seen as a major enemy during the Cultural Revolution. The process started with Tito's visit to China and improved with official Chinese apologies for their role in 1948. China's 'opening to the world' after 1978 improved things further, as well as the trend to a market-orientated economy. Today the Yugoslavs speak of an identity of views with China on most issues.

One of these is on the Kampuchea situation, with Yugoslav support being given to the 'coalition' against Heng Samrin, the Vietnamese-backed leader governing Cambodia. Yugoslavia supports Prince Sihanouk and says it wants to see an independent country emerge. (Its criticism of Vietnam for sending troops across the border was not one of 'principle' however, since the annexation of Timor by Yugoslavia's ally, Indonesia, was supported.)

Relations with the Indochinese states are described as 'complex'. In fact relations with Vietnam are poor, although both countries maintain embassy staff. Yugoslav Party leaders were not invited to any congress of the Vietnam Workers' Party and this apparently rankled.

Yugoslavia and International Organizations

(a) The United Nations and Yugoslavia

The most interesting aspects of UN work in the 1980s for Yugoslavia were the procedures on Human Rights exposures flowing from the Resolution 1503 of the Economic and Social Council in 1977; the establishment in 1982 of a Convention on the law of the seas; the Middle East Crisis.

Yugoslavia has been positive towards the 1980s developments in the human rights field within the United Nations, considering that the early UN Charter and other covenants 'had been produced in a politically less favourable climate'.[13] With the developing countries, Yugoslavia had put its pressure on UN discussions to get cogent rules, and did not despair of progress—despite criticism of the procedures for double standards and politicization.[14]

A. Vratuša pointed out that a struggle for a new international economic order included a satisfactory law of the sea, ratified by the United Nations.[15] The signing of a convention at Jamaica on 18 December 1982 was a step forward, considering that ten years' work and the participation of 160 states and autonomous territories were involved. The exploitation of the wealth of the sea has been brought under some sort of regulation. The capitalist world had not been able to impose its will. Yugoslavia as a non-aligned maritime state has an interest in ensuring the Convention is put into practice by UN members and the use of the sea regulated as part of the aim of achieving a new international economic order.

However, the United Nations is only one international agenda for Yugoslavia, which is active in such bodies as the UN Economic Commission for Europe (Yugoslav J. Stanovnik was the secretary for this for some years), in UNESCO, etc. It is important, for example, to consider Yugoslavia's dealings with the International Monetary Fund.

(b) Yugoslavia and the IMF

The IMF is, today, a very significant force in world affairs at a time when international monetary disturbances and a growing level of foreign debt is the order of the day. Yugoslavia's large and rising debt has forced it to call on the IMF for many loans. Some Yugoslav leaders feel that the burden of repayment is somewhat unfair to Yugoslavia and have suggested it be renegotiated, although it has been repeatedly stressed that Yugoslavia 'does not want to go to the Club of Paris' and does not seek any moratorium on debt repayments. In the mid-1970s the IMF upset Yugoslavs[16] by hinting that the political system itself was a major cause of economic problems and of inflation; since then they have mostly given 'advice' on purely monetary and fiscal issues and such advice has been mainly accepted.

(c) The Non-Aligned Movement and Yugoslavia

As a founder of the non-aligned Heads of States' Conferences and one of the originators of the charter for a New International Economic Order, Yugoslavia's close ties with the non-aligned movement are clear. It is still a matter of faith that this should be the main vehicle for Yugoslav foreign policy to be conducted and should not be altered in the event of changing relations with the superpowers. Tito's ideas are constantly mentioned and upheld in this area.

However, Yugoslavia has been concerned to prevent the non-aligned movement from moving to the left, believing that this would lead to its disintegration. A nasty moment came in 1977 at the Havana gathering of the non-aligned when Yugoslavia, backed by Indonesia, fought a challenge from Cuba and Vietnam for a more militant stance against US imperialism and a more friendly one to Soviet peace initiatives. This raised the issue of whether some 'nearly-aligned' countries could really play a role in the non-aligned movement as a whole and what effect increasing diversity of membership would have on the movement in the long run. It even posed the question of whether non-alignment would be viable if the world capitalist economy continued to create trade, production and debt problems for Third World countries and hence to polarize views about socialism and communism.

Today there is much more mass media debate about where Yugoslav foreign policy should be going. Such debates were rare while Tito was alive and exercising a strong personal role in this area. There is also much more professional 'input' into decision-making with studies being done by strategic studies centres, and by specialists on economic aspects of international relations for the Presidency and some Parliamentary Commissions. Perhaps for this reason the tone of the research is decidedly *not* 'leftist' as can be seen in the way that moves to the Right in China or to market-based economic mechanisms in socialist countries receive a warm Yugoslav reception.

Post-Tito Foreign Policy

Apart from an intensified 'regional orientation', the 1980s have seen little change in Tito's basic strategy on 'non-alignment', stressing the importance of the Group of 77 in the United Nations and developing much better relations with China.

Feared Soviet pressure on Yugoslavia or even intervention to get a submarine base at Kotor on the Montenegrin coast did not eventuate. Fear of 'Cominformists', pro-Soviet sympathizers within the Yugoslav community, has been endemic among the security forces with 52,000 arrests in 1949 at the height of the Tito–Stalin struggle and, more recently in 1984, the sentencing of thirty-two people in Montenegro for operating a pro-Soviet, clandestine communist group (Amnesty International, 1985, pp. 5–6).

In fact between 1981 and 1986 Yugoslavia received a number of assurances, from Eastern Europe, one of particular importance to the post-Tito leadership (of S. Dolanc, K. Girgorov and others) being that Macedonia was recognized as an integral part of the Yugoslav federation. This followed a serious quarrel between Yugoslavia and Soviet ally, Bulgaria, when Communists there made aggressive statements to the effect that 'there is no Macedonian state'. It seems unlikely that the Gorbachëv era will lead to any Soviet pressures on Yugoslavia of serious consequence. As a result, one can expect foreign policy to continue with the line set at Belgrade airport during Khrushchev's dramatic 'apology' in 1955 (Mićunović, 1980, p. 1): that relations will be 'correct' (if not warm) with Eastern Europe and that bridges will be kept open for Western banks and the World Bank.

Perspective

Whatever the impact of Yugoslavia on Third World affairs and on UN matters (which is considerable), or on Western policy (which is minimal), the major point about Yugoslavia's independent dealings with other nations is the historical impact it has had on Communist states and individual Communists.

Despite denials by Party historians in Eastern Europe, the existence of a different 'socialist road' in Yugoslavia was a factor after 1955 influencing people who want *either* more working-class influence over state economic plans *or* 'economic reforms', as they were called by Hungary in the 1960s, China in the 1970s and the Soviet Union in the 1980s. Yugoslavia did play a big role in helping Kádár come to power and with that the unfolding of a more relaxed atmosphere in Hungary. While Yugoslavia failed to influence either the Czech invasion 'affair' of 1968 or the Solidarity movement in Poland in 1981-2, it has had a general influence over East European reformers, including economists, technocrats and liberal Communists.

At the wider level of the international Communist Parties, the impact of the Tito-Stalin quarrel was important in the long run. The sectarian condemnation of the Yugoslav Party in which most individual Communists indulged was exposed by Khrushchev's 1955 apology. The shock of this, combined with the anti-Stalin Congress of the CPSU in 1956, meant that the whole period of hardening dogmatism of 1948-54 came under scrutiny and many Parties and Communists either left the movement or had to change their methods of operation and thinking in fundamental ways. Yugoslavia may not have cleared the bureaucratic rust that had settled on the various Marxist regimes at that time but it has at least made a fatal dent in the notion of monolithic Communism.

15 Domestic Politics: Current Issues

The 'current issues' dominating Yugoslavia in the 1980s were the ones outlined in Chapter 12—inflation, regionalism, foreign debt. However, there are a number of medium and long-term problems ticking away below the surface which are intertwined with the economic policy issues. These include the rapid change in work-force structure; the status and functioning of major areas of social welfare; problems within the structure of self-management and cyclical movement in investment. These are the issues to be canvassed in this final section.

Work-Force Structure

The *structure* of the work-force had changed strikingly by 1956 with 50 per cent instead of 80 per cent being in agriculture. Since then, as Table 15.1 shows, this has again altered so that only 4.2 million now work in agriculture, many of them older people. In order to offset falls in productivity, the number of tractors supplied has been greatly increased, as indicated in the last column. The squeezing of the peasant and disparity between urban and rural standards of living was a problem between 1946 and 1956, and possibly up to 1963-5 when, under the Reform measures, agricultural prices were raised. For the later (1975-85) period, the figures indicate that prices paid for

Table 15.1 Changes in agriculture, 1956-85

	Index of production (1955 = 100)	Agricultural population ('000)	Cultivated land ('000 hectares)	Tractors (no.)
1956	83	10,316	10,200	14,658
1966	154	9,198	10,200	50,965
1976	189	7,844	9,962	255,851
1979	195	7,844	9,917	415,655
1980	197	4,277	9,938	595,486
1982	214	4,277	9,875	705,847
1985	198	4,277	9,841	881,693

Source: *SG*, 1986, p. 89.

agricultural goods have risen by 1,523 per cent and for industrial goods by 1,132 per cent, suggesting that since 1980 the terms of trade had moved somewhat in favour of agriculture. The 1987 Constitutional amendment suggested to Parliament by the Presidency seems designed to take off all remaining controls on successful farmers in an attempt to raise productivity in agriculture further.

Major Trends in Social Indicators

Health

There has been a great improvement in overall life-expectancy as a result of better provision of health care to rural areas—from 67.7 to 73.2 years for women and from 64 to 67.7 for men. The scandalously high infant mortality rates of the 1950s have been reduced in the last decade to about 9 per thousand.

Social Insurance

The welfare state has been gradually extended since 1951 as shown in Table 15.2 on Social Insurance. The number of old age pensioners has increased from 71,000 to more than ten times that amount, while invalid pensioners have trebled. Clearly these areas are becoming a growing burden on the present generation. Yugoslav social insurance is paid largely out of enterprise and communal funds which are put aside for this purpose out of revenues.

Table 15.2 Social insurance, 1951–85

	No. of insured persons	Type of pension		Inherited pension*
		Old age	Invalid	
1951	1,960,000	71,146	138,965	107,902
1956	2,625,245	121,160	190,665	143,268
1966	4,199,814	356,256	351,998	235,583
1976	5,466,566	507,973	466,819	377,551
1978	5,850,016	546,107	509,413	413,638
1980	6,368,818	609,253	572,754	453,150
1985	7,235,891	766,638	710,238	559,570

* Pension granted to juvenile dependants of workers who die before retirement age.
Source: SG, 1986, p. 98.

The central government looks after war veterans from its tax collections on consumer goods.

It cannot be said that urgent solving of local conditions has invariably been at the forefront of social policy. Kosovo remains a running sore in relation to unemployment; Bosnia neglected women's education for years. Some changes in this direction seem urgent, subject to the constraint on lower-level units in ministries and mass organizations who realize this but are hampered by austerity programmes and financial stringency.

Education

Yugoslav urban dwellers are a literate population. The strong historical influence of France on Serbia and Lombardy on Croatia ensures an interest in literature, philosophy and *pedagogija* which is obvious to any observer who cares to enter Yugoslav bookstores.

As far as school policy is concerned, a successful effort has been mounted to get primary-school level accepted universally. In tertiary education, however, problems remain, for while many have been pressed into education at this level, there has also been a much changed profile. The result by the mid-1980s was the appearance of pockets of high unemployment in specific fields and particular regions. Rapid structural change of the economy is clearly needed and with it retraining of workers and their skills. The Long-Term Stabilization Plan (Parts III and IV) forecast that the economy's need to absorb the technological revolution will intensify while integration of Yugoslavia into the European economy is also likely to be attempted in the 1980s and 1990s. The implications of this would be a complete overhaul of the existing educational attitudes and policies in all areas of the education system. Funds will be required to assist those made redundant to cope with a new life-style.

All the present levels of real expenditure on education, health, social insurance and culture remain threatened by the hyper-inflationary surge of the 1980s. The Long-Term Stabilization Plan in its Part IV mentions this and points out that cuts will have to be severe for the rest of the 1980s if the rate of growth of real GDP were to be *less* than 3 per cent annually, a most likely scenario.

Current Problems from a Longer-term Perspective

Essentially what we consider under this heading is the tendency of Yugoslavia's economic-political system of 'self-managing socialism' to provide surprising, even perverse results in relation to incentives, productivity and income distribution. These tendencies, as they have accumulated, have severely tested the health of the domestic political economy. This point will be further explored in this chapter by looking at the following areas: (a) the problem of the relationship between trade unions and 'self-management' of factories in the context of promoting working-class interests; (b) the relationship between industry planning and financial deregulation as a source of contradictions in domestic economic policy; (c) the tendency of deregulated markets, combined with faults in the operation of the economic units, to produce 'socialist' business cycles; (d) the problem of uneven development of regions.

Trade Unionism versus Self-Management

Perhaps this topic epitomizes a problem that lies in the 'soul' of Yugoslav socialism. If 'associated workers' groups' and their delegates (a) run factories, (b) attend 'assemblies', where extra-factory matters are decided, how can trade unions which *collectively bargain* for working-class interests *as a whole* have any significant input into Yugoslav socialism? Must Yugoslavia, like Eastern Europe generally, 'neuter' the strength of the trade unions, albeit for different reasons?

In the 1970s and 1980s there was a great deal of discussion in Yugoslav Communist circles about the role to be allotted to unions once they had lost their right to influence wage-levels and the right to confront the state over issues they considered to affect the working class as a whole. For, as shown in Chapter 5, successive amendments to the Yugoslav Constitution had devolved such functions on assorted groups of 'associated labour', leaving a role for unions little different from that of advisory bodies or social welfare agencies. Later legislation hardened this tendency (Secretariat of Information of SFRJ Assembly, 1977).

This is an important demotion of unions. Experience in the United Kingdom suggests strongly (Green & Wilson, 1982, 1983) that to avoid Japanese-style business unionism and an 'industrial planning' that has gone too technocratic, trade unions need to directly influence overall industrial planning. Planning left to government bodies or to the market is not a 'planning' that easily accommodates to class interests of workers. It is known, for example, that in Sweden the unions have traded plant-level influence on investment, technological change and safety for the right to centralized wage bargaining with employers and government. The thought has occurred to more than one Yugoslav socialist that they may be getting the worst of both worlds—neither trade-union clout at enterprise level nor any centralized wage bargaining power: the market has more say than the 'working man' (Green & Wilson, 1982, 1983; McFarlane, 1966).

In the 1980s this dilemma has been more sharply apparent than at the time of the Tenth Congress of the League of Communists in 1974 when so many high hopes were held for the new rights of 'associated labour' to influence the distribution of income not only *within* the factory and office but in society *at large*. Go back to the discussion in Chapter 13 about the impact of the 1987 events in throwing into the spotlight the lack of a bridge between what the collectives were doing (voting for wage rises above productivity trends and 'agreed criteria') and the social interest at the time of protecting the working class *as a whole* from the effects of a bumbling government's 'austerity package'. In the 1980s' discussions, the absence of union input was seen as a factor which had (a) allowed the government to pursue overall real wage reductions as a solution to Yugoslavia's economic crisis; and (b) permitted major tax, welfare and investment decisions, nominally decided in 'assemblies' composed of delegates from groups of 'associated labour', to come under the influence of the new technocracy. The result was that the workers went on strike against wage cuts and factory closures showing a serious lack of confidence on their part in workers' councils, trade unions, government policy and the 'self-management' system as a whole.

From this point of view, the 1976 Basic Law on Associated Labour which extended internal enterprise management rights by allowing planning contracts to be signed between groups within the same firm and between a group in one plant and those in another factory with which that plant had relations, left many issues unresolved (Broekmeyer, 1977, pp. 133–40). Such cross-plant dealing atomized the 'groups of associated workers' and the necessary solidarity required to meet any assault on living standards was weakened. In place of collective bargaining over various items in the plan (or affecting the total rate of investment and the total rate of consumption in society) conducted between trade unions and the planners, something highly effective in protecting a class interest (Green & Wilson, 1982), the Yugoslav working class had only a limited protection. This was in the form of what influence their delegates might have in assemblies making recommendations on such matters.[1]

So a fundamental dilemma has not been resolved since the 1976 'Basic Law': how to prevent atomization of the working class at a time when an ascendant technocracy was moving more surely to look after its collective interests. Perfect democracy *inside* a factory cannot by itself ensure 'self-management socialism';[2] there must be a collective voice for workers' *class* interests at those times of economic crisis when government finds it tempting to tackle 'fiscal realities' by attacking living standards.

Industrial Planning and Financial Deregulation

If Yugoslav credit politics were too 'easy' in the 1960s, leading finally to a squeeze and illiquidity for many firms, it was the decision in 1964 to abolish many centralized investment funds—a form of quasi-deregulation of capital markets that lay at the heart of the problem.[3] Later, as already shown in Chapter 6 there was a process of recentralization and more financial control following the Croatian upsurge of 1969–71.

Deregulation of the financial system, however desirable from some other viewpoints (more efficient banking services, diversion of resources to effective investment), has created for contemporary Yugoslav industry planning a series of dilemmas. At a time of rapid technological change and computerization of industry, where involvement of the work-force in structural change is vital, the possibility of orderly change has been undermined by deregulated financial markets. For there must be a mechanism of controls to ensure that finances flow into the development of home manufacturing industry and its absorption of new technology, and away from mere take-overs of existing firms (*integracija*), high yielding investments (Adriatic tourism), or even the export of capital. Nor is Yugoslavia an exception. For years in Sweden firms were required to keep blocked accounts in the banking system which were released to them when changed economic circumstances warranted this (Lindbeck, 1975). In Australia, during the period of the Menzies government (1950–66) and in the United Kingdom under Labour, government 'qualitative credit controls' channelled investment into selected industries and social investment while exchange controls prevented the export of financial resources. Yet in a socialist country like Yugoslavia these controls have been lacking in the difficult circumstances of the 1980s, with pressure on the exchange rate and rising interest rates. Not only has this meant that inflation has been harder to moderate at its source, but industry planning and 'managed structural change' have not received the necessary back-up of financial controls which experience in a series of countries suggests it needs to have. Pressure on the exchange rate from the annual foreign debt of US$20 billion throughout the 1980s could only be relieved in two ways; (a) by making painful structural adjustments such as closing marginal firms, cutting real wages, reducing tariffs; or (b) introducing centralized monetary controls to force liquid funds into new import-substitution industries, a managed exchange rate, and more effective control of banking and the monetary policies of the republics. But, caught in the new *de facto* autonomy of the republics, being unwilling to tackle *all* the structural rigidities (e.g. bankruptcies of marginal firms) but only *some* (real wage cuts), insisting on a deregulated financial mechanism, and lacking any plan for getting import substituting industries moving, the Yugoslav government drifted between its options. Not surprisingly, the 'faceless' post-Tito government leaders have tended to get the worst of both worlds. In 1986–7 they got them with hurricane force.

Socialist 'Growth Cycles' in Yugoslavia

The link between the series of economic reforms and accompanying changes in politics and ideology were discussed in Chapters 5–8 above. One intervening factor here has been the emergence in Yugoslavia of a business or investment cycle (Bajt, 1986 and 1971; Čobelić & Stojanović, 1966) which, superimposed on a cycle of decentralization–recentralization, has led to the ultimate shape of the economic system today. This parallels a similar, but not identical, experience in China and in some East European countries (McFarlane, 1984a).

This mechanism is so important that it deserves special attention. The process of the unfolding of such cycles starts when excessively high national investment is allowed or even encouraged by a Communist government. A large rise in output of capital goods follows. This is the phase of *acceleration* in the socialist investment cycle. However, this very process creates imbalances in relation to raw materials, construction materials and energy as incomplete investment projects accumulate. To cope with the worsening materials supply situation, enterprises build up inventories. This causes a dire shortage of goods. The acceleration of investment also causes balance of payments difficulties as material shortages have to be eased by massive imports, which, in the end, have to be stopped.

Eventually, these economic tendencies restrict further output growth and bring on a severe crisis—economic *and* political. Planners are forced to concede the need to reduce target growth rates in all sectors of the economy and to restrict the runaway expansion of investment. Action now brings on the next phase of the cycle: *economic slowdown*. The slowdown is largely due to the fact that economic units cannot work at capacity as a result of shortages of raw materials; as well, growth slows in this phase because new investment is curbed and effort is directed towards the completion of unfinished projects.

Top priority is now given to mining (to augment raw material supply) and agriculture (to feed more workers). After a lapse of time, the priority completed projects bear fruit and get into production thereby easing the tension stemming from the imbalance between industries. Recovery follows, but after another time lag, planners and enterprises lower their guard against the dangers posed by economic imbalances. They may then ease standards required to get approvals for new projects and we enter the run-up to the acceleration phase; the cycle begins again.

At each phase of the cycle restrictions are 'required' on the consumption and welfare benefits of workers. In the phase requiring new investments, firms are exhorted to plough back profits and the 'self-managers' pressured to delay making increased allocations to wage funds and welfare funds under their control. When the slump is on, the work-force self-managers are asked to cooperate in real wage cuts to expand employment and allow foreign exchange rate adjustment. At each point, the preference of the working class *as a class* about consumption and investment levels are shut out, and in Yugoslavia, the system of technocratic advice to government, combined with participatory planning at the plant level has produced excessive and violently fluctuating investment rates. In fact it now appears that in the case of *market-socialism* there are special factors at work accelerating the ups and downs of the cycle, one being that enterprise expectations now depend not on profits alone but on the movement of total investment in the economy.[4]

Yugoslavia has not succeeded in finding a way out of this cyclical movement with its disruptive effects not only on the economy but on the implementation of economic reform and on political stability (Bajt, 1971 and 1986). The onset of the economic downturn of the 1980s has not only coincided with painful political adjustments for a post-Tito political style and system, but external events such as movements in oil prices and the slump in world trade have acted to greatly attenuate the steepness of the 'economic slowdown' phase of the Yugoslav cycle. At the mid-1980s no recovery phase, let alone an acceleration phase, was in sight.[5]

Regional Economic Conflict

A federation with uneven living standards and differential rates of economic growth is bound to be potentially unstable from the political and social point of view. The legitimacy of regional leaders becomes an issue as they have to be seen to be actively pursuing a 'just share' in the national cake; regional-republican interests are pursued as strongly as federation ones. Many observers feel that the 1980s have seen the Yugoslav national market splintering into eight autarchical regional markets—something like the older economic attitudes of Mercantilism have emerged (Rusinow, 1984).

It has always been difficult to find a methodology that would measure regional inequalities (McFarlane, 1971, p. 83; Fisher, 1968; Gregory, 1973; Ivanović, 1962). Earlier attempts to find such estimates in the 1950s and 1960s generally produced seven major indicators: income per inhabitant, fixed capital per employed worker in the socialized sector, cadastral income yield per person in agriculture, worker and salary earners as a percentage of population, roads longer than 100 km, non-agriculture population as percentage of total population. Relative to population size, Slovenia, Croatia and Serbia always did best on these indicators.

In the 1980s, the following rough indicators are a guide to uneven development. First, growth rate in production of manufacturing and mining since 1955 has been fastest in Montenegro as the index number of 1985 (1955 = 100) is 2,603. The index for Macedonia is 1,981, for Serbia 1,179 and for Kosovo 1,140 (Statistical Pocketbook of Yugoslavia, 1986, p. 78). Since the more developed Slovenia and Croatia had indexes of 778 and 745 this shows the switch of the 'industrialization' program to the less developed republics and provinces over the last thirty years. Power generation per worker in 1983 was also highest at 8.2 kw in Montenegro, with Bosnia 5.9, Kosovo 5.7, leaving Slovenia at 5.2 and Croatia at 4.6. Other indicators are listed in Tables 15.3 and 15.4.

The first of these shows the impact on living standards of inflation has been differential with Slovenia being asked to reduce workers' standards along with Macedonia and Montenegro, but an attempt also to put the poorer provinces in a position of not being differentially worse off.

This has been done by a conscious policy of increasing plant and equipment levels in the underdeveloped areas during the 1950s, 1960s and 1970s and asking Croatia and Slovenia to be 'on hold' (relatively speaking) in the 1980s. This is shown in Table 15.4. They must have found it very difficult to do much about restraint, as the table also indicates that as a result of the relief and economic freedom given under the 1974 Constitution, and before that the 1965 Constitutional change and Reform, Croatia had doubled its investments in its own plant and machinery 1966–80 and Slovenia had tripled its investment.

The question that now arises which links political and economic relations among the republics of Yugoslavia is this: could tension over contrived attempts to correct regional imbalances, differentiate population growth and change relative access to federal resources lead to the disintegration of the

Table 15.3 Index of real disposable income per worker by republic, 1963–85

Year	Total Yugolsavia	Bosnia–Hercegovina	Montenegro	Croatia	Macedonia	Slovenia	Serbia
1963	100	100	100	100	100	100	100
1973	170	168	154	171	156	154	171
1979	204	191	179	199	174	175	211
1980	189	182	173	187	159	160	193
1981	180	175	165	181	149	146	185
1982	172	172	155	175	143	141	181
1983	156	158	122	156	124	128	166
1984	144	145	117	146	114	127	154
1985	150						

Source: SG, 1986, p. 431.

Table 15.4 Gross investment in fixed capital funds of Yugoslav republics, 1956–84 (billion dinars at 1972 prices)

Year	Total Yugoslavia	Bosnia–Hercegovina	Montenegro	Croatia	Macedonia	Slovenia	Serbia
1956	19.7	2.7	0.9	4.7	1.2	2.6	7.4
1966	52.4	7.1	1.1	13.0	4.3	6.4	20.7
1976	99.6	15.2	2.7	22.7	5.6	17.2	35.6
1980	120.7	18.4	4.5	29.3	7.9	16.8	43.6
1981	108.8	16.0	4.5	27.7	6.3	14.6	39.6
1982	102.8	16.4	3.9	25.4	6.0	13.1	37.8
1983	92.9	14.9	2.9	23.5	5.2	11.9	31.2
1984	83.7	12.9	2.9	19.3	4.3	12.2	32.1

Source: SG, 1986, p. 424.

federation? Some Communist leaders do fear this, and Albanian minority citizens who seek Republican status for Kosovo are invariably accused of really wanting to bring about a union of Kosovo with neighbouring (and hostile) Albania (Amnesty International, 1985, pp. 38–40).

However, the new leaders, elected at the first post-Tito Congress of the SKJ in May 1984 and in the State Presidency simultaneously, are as conscious as senior veterans of the Revolution had been in 1971 during the Croatian uproar of the dangers of lack of cohesion and this fear of drift and lack of unity does unite them in a determination to keep together. Yet, perhaps enough *de facto* economic autonomy has been given to the republics (if not to the *provinces* like Kosovo and Vojvodina) to reduce some tensions between republics if not all. In 1986 tensions rose when two of the republics, Macedonia and Montenegro, announced they had no financial resources with which to meet their agreed obligations to make payments into various funds of the federation. The US$1 billion shortfall meant that the bill had to be met by other republics and provinces, causing serious resentment particularly in Vojvodina, the most successful grain-growing area of Yugoslavia.

Centrifugal and pluralist tendencies are undoubtedly strong (Rusinow, 1984) but political and regional leaders are striving for legitimacy and to achieve that by use of the symbols and myths of the Marxist regime: while in the case of a serious threat of disintegration, the SKJ could regain its will to rule.

Up to 1984 Serbian influence had declined somewhat and this fact, together with more 'liberal' leadership in Serbian political circles after Tito, eased the discontent of Slovenia and Croatia. This changed under the impact of hyperinflation and Kosovo tensions, when the northern republics had to watch heavy-handed methods reminiscent of Ranković used in Kosovo. Moreover, it is to be noted that only under pressure from cultural circles in Slovenia and Croatia was the European Cultural Congress of 1980 held in Belgrade, while economists from Ljubljana and Zagreb, rather than Belgrade, have been in the vanguard of attempts to involve Yugoslavia in the European scientific project, EUREKA, in which Hungary is also participating.

Some Croatian and Slovene politicians feel drawn, culturally, to the older configuration of Croatia, Slovenia, Venice, Lombardy, Trieste. Others merely feel that federal politicians are hindering close ties between their republics and such areas. Serbs argue that these ties have already broken up the Yugoslav national economy and fear the political break-up of the federation comes next.

Commodity Society and Alienation

In this book attention has been paid to economic plans and the rhythm of investment and output in particular periods. Also, much has been said about strikes, worker opposition to enterprise bureaucracy and to contradictions in self-management. Such fundamental issues are probably more important in the long run than merely judging the worth of successive Plans or noting how necessary it is to move towards a unified national market. These 'fundamentals' include as well, though, those issues which have been debated in socialist countries ever since the 1920s in the Soviet Union: what is the 'dictatorship of the proletariat' in practice? Has a form of state capitalism developed or is Eastern Europe in a transition stage to something more genuinely socialist? Where does Yugoslavia with its attention to markets and interest in productivity and profits fit into this debate?

A small number of Yugoslavs, mainly sociologists, do worry about man's alienation and his rape of nature in a socialist system based on egoism (I. Bošnjović in Šoškić, 1983, p. 201). Some other Yugoslav Marxists support the idea that market socialism is not merely a method of achieving a transition to communism, but a goal in itself (Horvart, 1964, p. 225). Yet others, like the Praxis group, have concentrated on the by-products of a market system in a context of political monopoly of the SKJ and have seen emerging in Yugoslavia the 'alienation' which concerned Karl Marx: that of the worker from the fruits of his labour. A Party philosopher, Dr Stipe Suvar, in June 1970 agreed with this general line of thought when he said 'most of the social power is wielded, in my opinion, by sections of the political-administrative and technocratic-managerial bureaucracy; even in cases when various competences do not normatively belong to them they dispose with powerful manipulative mechanisms' (Suvar, 1970a). Suvar saw the rise of the technocracy coming out of the fact that self-management had reduced the role of the state and that of the SKJ; that self-management had developed more in 'breadth' than 'depth' and had not taken on many of the powers lost by the older, 'tottering' political bureaucracy. Under these conditions banks and managers formed, via the market system, a new financial oligarchy, restoring a sort of wage-labour relationship and thereby re-establishing the commodity and money-based alienation of the worker from his collective effort. A consumerist and distributionist ethos prevailed over a producers' ethic (Suvar, 1970a).

What Suvar and *Praxis* seem to be telling us is that there can be no easy way of isolating the social superstructure from the effects of commodity-society in the economic base. They suggest that a key contradiction in Yugoslavia exists in the fact that alienation and commodity production cannot be eliminated independently of the other. Therefore, the goal of Marxian socialism (the elimination of commodity production as part of a program for reaching direct association of producers whose output was linked to social need) cannot be established. Perhaps that is why Horvart abandoned the project and made *market-communism* the goal rather than those of Marxian socialism of the old school (Horvart, 1964, pp. 231-4).

The split in Yugoslav Marxism on the problem of reconciling 'market-socialism' with abolishing the 'alienation of commodity society' inevitably was reflected in overseas comment. Khrushchev in 1955 expressed sympathy for Yugoslavia's workers councils but criticized the widespread impact of market mechanisms in influencing the distribution of resources in a socialist system. Many Western economists supported the Yugoslav initiatives (H. D. Dickinson) while others like Joan Robinson and Dobb remained sceptical.[6] At the other end of the spectrum the Stalinist Albanian leader Enver Hoxha perhaps spoke for the Maoist line on Yugoslavia prevailing 1961–71 when he reported (*Politika*, 3 November 1971, p. 4) to the Sixth Congress of his Albanian Workers' Party that:

Yugoslavia has all the characteristics of a bourgeois country and therefore suffered from the same serious and chronic evils typical of capitalism such as deep economic crises, unemployment, competition, anarchism, inflation, bitter socio-political conflicts and national disagreements.

Although some Western political economists wrote in similar vein (Sweezy, 1964) most of the other observers have preferred to treat Yugoslavia's negative features as a 'disease of transition' to socialism.

Overview

Twenty years ago, Yugoslavia seemed to be in the midst of a remarkable revival of socialist thought—even democratic-socialist thought, since it embraced an extension of self-management to many more spheres of social life. Tito's overwhelming presence did not stifle the debate; if anything he was in a 'left' mood.

The attempt by political philosophers and social theorists to push this line of thinking and recommendation for changed policies in the early 1970s was, however, blocked by the fears aroused by Slovenian and Croatian separatism and by the wide-ranging nature of the critique of bureaucracy and technocracy (Pečuljić, 1967; Stojanović, 1967, Suvar, 1970a; Vidaković, 1970). By 1974 Tito's speech as President of the SKJ was that of any orthodox Communist leader (Tito, 1974). In that year, too, there were attempts to beat up a personality cult around him (Štaubringer, 1974).

As leading critics of orthodox Marxism the *Praxis* group had the advantage that they did not internalize problems of Marxist philosophy but, rather, took up concepts one at a time: liberty; property rights under socialism; the nature of modern bureaucracy; community needs. This gave them a longer-term influence than was recognized at the time, for they were saying something relevant (and familiar in the West in the writings of Tom Bottomore): that Marxism must be seen as a method of social investigation not as a comprehensive structure of abstract ideas for which the 'correct' policy can be logically inferred (Bottomore, 1979).

This approach made it easier for the *Praxis* ideas to be unconsciously absorbed into mainstream political thinking in Yugoslavia and helps to explain much of the 'one policy problem-at-a-time' approach of the post-Tito leadership. There was, between 1980 and 1983 something of a liberalist trend in economic and political theory, while in historical studies notions of a non-linear approach (Jakšić, 1985) towards stages of historical development and a tolerant attitude to the controversial 'Asiatic mode of production' concept pre-dated the appearance of these ideas in the Soviet Union under Gorbachëv (Afanasjev, 1987). It was more widely accepted in the 1980s that not all values are ideologically determined by class (Pečuljić, 1967; Suvar, 1970b) or by socio-economic formation (Jakšić, 1985). The nature of Yugoslavia as a federation of different republics had raised the controversial issue (Pečuljić, 1967; Vidaković, 1970) that there was a plurality of working classes, with different regional cultures producing different modes, attitudes and responses. Much of this was being accepted in the 1980s, perhaps the idea of different *occupations* producing these things less so (Djordjević, 1962; Pečuljić, 1967; Berković, 1969).

So it was that the earlier pessimistic view (Djilas, 1972; N. Popović, 1970) that Yugoslav Marxism could not break free of its orthodox Leninist roots became less obviously true of the 1980s scene in Yugoslavia.

The current debates in Western Europe about market-socialism as a new sort of economic system (Nove, 1983; Hodgson, 1984; Socialist Philosophy Group UK, 1986) has benefited greatly from study of Yugoslavia's market-socialist policies, despite the very special socio-historical circumstances in which they have developed in the SFRJ (Milenkovich, 1971). In particular the practical problems of combining collective and state ownership, of regulation of markets to achieve social goals has, on the whole, been of use to international socialists. True, there have been few attempts to relate human needs or the free time of the worker to a system of market-socialism as in the work of the Budapest school (Hegedus, Heller, Markus & Vajda, 1976; Fehrer, Heller & Markus, 1983). Nevertheless, the idea of the limitations of the market economy in this area have occasionally been noted (Djordević, 1962, 1966) while the overall concern that 'associated labour' via delegates to 'social assemblies' can act as a countervailing force to market distortions is now part of the Yugoslav value system. The deficiencies of the practice of doing this in any socialist society (Fehrer & Heller, 1983) and in Yugoslavia in particular has attracted criticism (Hodges, 1981, p. 125; Rusinow, 1984) from those who wonder why no strong consumer or ecological movements have emerged as political pressure groups in Yugoslavia. Perhaps it has to be said that, tragically, fear of cultural pluralism going 'too far', the inheritance of the Slovene-Croatia outbreaks of 1970-1, has set back for some time the eventuality of such cultural pluralism being seen as having a positive value in contemporary Yugoslav domestic policy.

A major claim of Yugoslavia on our interest is the system it pioneered of decentralization and self-management (Adler-Karlsson, 1969, pp. 57-63). The problem of workers' control of nationalized or socialized industry is not a new one—it goes back to the origins of socialism in the nineteenth century—but Yugoslavia has gone furthest in the practical aspects and has valuable contributions to make to the theory of workers' control. Moreover, the notion that self-management is part of a positive move to freedom and not just a passive freedom of rights against the state has taken firm hold in Yugoslav intellectual discussion. However, the negative aspects of the system, as brought out in the 1980s strikes, are also important lessons to be drawn out.

We can conclude that Yugoslavia's socialism is relevant because it offers a special variety of socialism; because it presents new contributions to socialist theory; because it offers in foreign affairs a pathway between subservience to Moscow on the one hand and to Washington on the other; because since 1944 it has been the potential nucleus of a Balkan Federation of Socialist States; because it throws light on the prospects of liberty in a socialist society; and because of its experiments in factory self-government and its assemblies elected from delegations.

It would be just as unwise to overestimate the importance of Yugoslavia as to underestimate it. Nor must we overlook interesting developments of the 1980s in Poland, in the Soviet Union and in China. Already the history of socialism shows that the pattern is going to vary considerably, from country to country, according to the differing social backgrounds and stage of political development of each country (Hodges, 1981; Fehrer & Heller, 1983), according to the size and resources of each region, according to the different conditions under which power is achieved. Undoubtedly there are some disappointing features of socialist development in Yugoslavia. But it is clear that a study of the Yugoslav experiences is of value for comprehending the future of Marxist ideology and Marxist regimes.

Final Comment

In this short book two themes were pursued. First, that the sheer regional diversity of Yugoslavia and the accompanying inevitable conflicts of regional interest caused distortions in economic and political decision-making that a federation and a market economy found difficult to handle. This was the geo-political aspect.

Second, that self-management of economic units by 'groups of associated labour' in practice meant that particular interests were put against wider socialist interests, and the working class as a whole often suffered. This was the class aspect.

An attempt has been made at each important stage of the argument to also indicate the inter-relationship between the two aspects and their impact on the workings and outlook of the Yugoslav Marxist regime. That is why this book has emphasized that the Yugoslav experience in 'building socialism' has been one of holding down strong centrifugal tendencies which threatened to blow up the 'grid' built on four main points, four centres of gravity on which the whole edifice was constructed. These were, as explained throughout,

(a) a belief in rapid industrialization and a policy of transforming the peasantry into a working class;
(b) attempts to cement the unity of the different nationalities making up the nation;
(c) collectivist control over resources;
(d) non-alignment in world politics, active membership of the non-aligned bloc.

Thirty-two years of history have greatly modified these poles of unity.

The attempt to industrialize quickly has created and perpetuated an inflationary economy. Agricultural productivity has not been as high as might have been expected. The peasantry (except in Kosovo) have been transformed, but many of the new urban workers have left the country or are only partly employed in the towns.

Unity of the nation, which had begun to develop, was shattered by the

1970 Croatian revolt and then hijacked by the regime of regional étatism sparked by the 1974 Constitutional change that Tito had hoped would mitigate the dissatisfaction of Croatia and Slovenia.

Collectivization of public assets has been undermined both by self-management (where this led to the pursuit of narrow small-group and personal interests) and by a situation where regional political mafias have dictated to banks and enterprises.

In retrospect, Tito's 'defusing' of the Croatian issue in his 1974 Constitution has become a legacy which has produced the very situation he was trying to avoid: letting each republic keep its own surplus in an effort to stimulate local growth has ended in breaking up market socialism. It has produced decentralized politics without the economic unity that a natural market can produce.

The policy of non-alignment remains, but its practical operation had been thwarted by quarrels within the non-aligned movement and by the new international economic re-alignments which have been to the detriment of Yugoslavia in Europe and to its African and Latin American allies in the Third World.

Notes

Chapter 2

1. Yugoslavia joined the Axis Pact (Germany, Italy, Japan) in March 1941, but immediately a popular movement of protest developed and the government was over-thrown. Germany then attacked (6 April) and the Yugoslav army capitulated after eleven days of resistance. Hitler attacked the Soviet Union on 22 June 1941. The first shot in the Yugoslav partisan insurrection was fired in Serbia on 7 July. In addition to the communist-led partisan movement General Mihailović led the Chetniks, a Serbian royalist organization. In the north Pavelić and the Ustashi maintained a puppet 'Independent State of Croatia' (1941–5), fascist and pro-Italian in orientation. Part of southern Serbia was annexed to Italy's colony of Albania, Macedonia was handed over to Bulgaria, north Serbia was annexed by Hungary, and Slovenia was divided between Italy and Germany. Serbia was under German occupation and Montenegro under Italian.

Chapter 3

1. For an account of this era from the economic point of view see Bićanić, (1973), chs 2–3.
2. The Communist International (Comintern) was dissolved in 1943, when the Soviet Union was following a policy of friendship with her capitalist allies. The Communist Information Bureau (Cominform) was established in September 1947, when the 'cold war' had started. As a recognition of Yugoslavia's importance its headquarters were sited in Belgrade.
3. In 1947 the Soviet Union and the East European Communist states supplied 52 per cent of Yugoslavia's imports and took 49 per cent of her exports.
4. Not all Yugoslav Communists rallied to Tito in 1948: Hebrang led the doubters and severe strains were imposed upon the tolerance of Party leaders (Auty, 1970, pp. 252–6). See Chapter 7 below for more on the split with pro-Cominform Marxists, within the Yugoslav Party.
5. At this time the United States carried on several embargoes on trade and other economic boycotts against all Communist nations. See Gunnar Adler-Karlsson, *Western Economic Warfare, 1946–67*, Uppsala, 1968.
6. The Soviet ideologists could not accept this, and not only Stalin. Seven years later, in March 1958, in his report on 'The Further Development of the Collective Farm System', Khrushchev remarked that 'state property is a higher degree and collective farm property a lower degree of socialization'.

7. For construction and investment cycles in China, see N. Maxwell & B. McFarlane (eds), *China's Changed Road to Development*, Oxford, Pergamon Press, 1984, especially ch. 2 by S. Ishikawa, and ch. 3 by McFarlane.
8. Namely, 1949–55 (the new socialist economic system), 1955–8 the second Five Year Plan); 1958–60 (the new system of worker-influenced income distribution); 1960–5 (new economic system); 1965–70 (decline in economy and balance of payments crisis accompanying economic reform); 1970–4 (constitutional amendments and freer income distribution); 1974–9 (aftermath of oil shock); 1980 to date (sustained economic crisis, falls in real living standards).
9. A major sign was a burgeoning foreign debt which rose from US$6.58 billion in 1975 to US$14.9 billion in 1979 but then shot up to more than US$20 billion in each year after 1980.
10. Real net income per year dropped from 1980 to 1984 and only in 1985 did the index reach the 1980 level; see *Statistical Pocketbook of Yugoslavia, 1986*, p. 451.

Chapter 4

1. Further discussion of the Croatian 'uprising' of 1971 is found in Chapter 8 below.
2. See further discussions on this point in Chapters 5–7.
3. Documents and speeches of the various leaders of Yugoslavia at the Tenth Congress of the League of Communists of Yugoslavia were published in full in English in the Yugoslav journal *Socialist Thought and Practice*, vol. 14, no. 6–7. Among the speakers were Tito, Kardelj, Bakarić, Dolanc, Vlahović and General Ljubičić.
4. See discussion in Chapter 12.
5. See the section 'Agro-Commerc Affair' in Chapter 13.
6. Many individual members of the Academy also want a rebuilding of the whole Yugoslav political system from the bottom up. In mid-1987 twelve Belgrade philosophers published an open letter supporting one of these, M. Zivotić, president of the Serbian Philosophers' society, against constant attack by Party officials.
7. *Verčeni Novosti* (Belgrade), 5 March 1986.
8. *Verčeni Novosti* (Zagreb), 21 September 1987, p. 7.
9. R. Bassett, 'Jokes begin to lose their appeal amid Kosovo crackdown', *The Times*, London, 31 October 1987. This article explains in detail the line-up of the quarrelling factions of the League of Communists in the Republic of Serbia.

Chapter 5

1. However, see the fuller discussion in Chapter 7 under 'The Djilas Assault'.

2. In order to get a fuller picture see Chapter 7 for the discussion about the short-lived theory held in Yugoslavia that the Soviet model amounted to 'state capitalism'.
3. For the ideological debates to which this gave rise see Chapters 5 and 7.
4. In the Soviet Union Leonid Brezhnev in 1977 moved to make President and Party leader the closely linked roles they became, but this was not the case before 1975.
5. In China, Mao, and in Vietnam, Ho Chi Minh fulfilled presidential type roles from the vantage point of Party leader.
6. The proposal was moved by L. Koliševski; see Documents of the 10th Congress in *Socialist Thought and Practice*, vol. 14, 1974, p. 103.
7. Constitution of the Socialist Federal Republic of Yugoslavia, 'Basic Principles', Part X.
8. *Constitution*, 'Basic Principles', Parts I, II, III.

Chapter 6

1. The rapid decentralization of the system was shown in the fact that in 1953 the Federal Government employed 7,200 functionaries, the Republican governments 33,600, and the People's Committees 164,000. That only 3.45 per cent of all functionaries dealing with civilian affairs were employed by the Federal Government is a remarkable fact, as was the very high proportion (more than 80 per cent) who were directly responsible to the popular committees at the local levels (Sweezy, 1958).
2. As the system developed, the input of blue-collar workers dropped, reflecting also the fall in SKJ dependence on partisans of the Second World War struggle and on blue-collar workers for their own membership (Tito, 'Introductory Speech to 9th Congress of SKJ', *Socialist Thought and Practice*, January–March 1969).
3. As Tito later complained, 'the view is sometimes expressed that all attempts to deal with social problems at the federal or republican level means *statism*. We must correct such views. A developed system of self-management also presupposes broader integration at all levels—a reinforcement of the role (although in a different form) of the responsibility of administrative organs—the communal assemblies, the Republican assemblies and the federal assembly.' (J. B. Tito, 'Introductory Speech to 9th Congress of SKJ', *Socialist Thought and Practice*, January–March 1969). Yet within eighteen months Tito had shifted his position and Federal Assembly initiatives were curbed in the new Constitutional amendments.
4. For a similar trend in China in 1958–60 and a discussion of the political as well as economic role of communes there see chapter 'The Communes' in E. L. Wheelwright & Bruce McFarlane, *The Chinese Road to Socialism*, Harmondsworth, Penguin Books, 1971.

5. A list of the respective leaders in both areas is presented as an appendix to this chapter.

Chapter 7

1. It is interesting that by the time Tito addressed the *second* Congress of Workers' Councils in 1969 the number of blue-collar delegates had fallen to a minority.
2. Many of these issues were launched for discussion at an extraordinary session of the Conference of Yugoslav economists in Ochrid, 17–18 October 1970. The topic was, 'The Further Development of the Economic System'. See the report by N. Želić in *Ekonomska Analiza*, vol. 10, 1977, Belgrade.
3. N. Želić, ibid.
4. See, for example, the letter by C. T. Lankowski in *The Economist*, London, 25 September 1971.
5. Ibid.
6. See 'Another Way', Special Supplement of *The Economist*, London, 21-27 August 1971, on Yugoslavia. A detailed account of actions of students, professors, priests, war veterans and the League of Communists of Croatia is given in Chapter 8 on 'Political Dissent in Yugoslavia' of the present book.
7. The article was published in the Soviet journal *Literaturnaya Gazeta*, 1986. It may be noted that the remarks there on secrecy and the bureaucracy as a closed corporation closely parallel discussion by the young Marx in his 1843 study *Critique of Hegel's Philosophy of Right*. See especially those remarks in the translation published in Lloyd D. Easton & Kurt H. Goddart, *Writings of the Young Marx on Philosophy and Society*, New York, Doubleday 1967, pp. 185–6.
8. Radisav Marinković, 'Commodity Production: With Market Forces or Without?', in Serbian League of Communists, *Socijalizam i Ekonomske Zakonitosti* (Socialism and Economic Laws), published by Ekonomska Politika, Belgrade, 1985.
9. Ibid., pp. 124–5.

Chapter 8

1. See the account of the Djilas affair outlined in Chapter 4, 'Splits in the Party'. Interestingly, on his release from jail in 1961 Djilas said, 'some of the government's recent actions are positive. I have hopes'. (*Time*, 27 January 1961). Also in March–April 1987 there were reports of a reconciliation between Djilas and the regime (*The Guardian*, 27 March 1987) at age 75.
2. For a full statement of this case, see T. Hočevar (1968).
3. A key issue of *Praxis* banned was issue no. 3–4, 1971, which had a number of articles very critical of Yugoslav society, including Nebojsa Popov, 'Forms and

Character of Social Tension'; R. Supek, 'Contradictions and Inadequacies in Yugoslavia's Self-Management Socialism'; Milan Kangrga, 'Phenomenology of Ideological Political Growth of the Yugoslav Middle Class'; P. Vranički, 'Socialism and Crisis' and M. Nikolić, 'Class and Nationality in Yugoslavia'.

4. Yugoslav political leaders complained that the image of Yugoslavia as a unified country was damaged; that Yugoslavia's status as a non-aligned country was being questioned abroad. There was also an impression (via the security police) that Soviet overtures were made to Croatian *émigrés*.

5. Hrvatska Matica, through its newspaper *Hrvatski Tjednik*, went beyond pleas for greater official support for Croatian cultural and historical studies. On 5 November 1971, it criticized the term 'Yugoslav People's Army' as used by federal defence and political circles. It also demanded that citizens should serve out their military training in their own republics and that army commands and documents should be in the language of the republic concerned.

6. Ustashi: pro-fascist movement in Croatia during 1940–5, who seized power and enjoyed German patronage under Dr Ante Pavelić.

7. The Petofi Club or circle in Hungary was a group of writers who attracted thousands of people to poetry readings and political discussions during 1956. Dissident Communists also attended including György Lukács and Imre Nagy. (See the account in H. G. Heinrich, *Hungary*, Frances Pinter, London, 1986, p. 33). In China, Mao repeatedly warned against the dangers of such a circle. For China see Wheelwright & McFarlane, *The Chinese Road to Socialism*, 1969, Monthly Review Press, ch. 5.

Chapter 9

1. The question of monopolistic tendencies undermining market competition and free prices is so significant in Yugoslavia that a special section of Chapter 13 has been dedicated to it. In the Soviet Union economic reforms were advocated by Liberman and others. An article by I. Goberman, Chairman of the Chief Administration of Automobile Transport of Moscow City explained that monopolistic competition in transport had to be avoided in Soviet economic experiments (see I. Goberman, 'Trucks on the Way', *Znamija*, January 1966, pp. 162–73). A full review of the issues can be found in two articles by McFarlane & Gordijev (1964, 1965).

2. See T. Pairault's chapter 'An Important Debate' in N. Maxwell & B. McFarlane (eds), *China's Changed Road to Development*, Oxford, Pergamon Press, 1984.

3. Abba P. Lerner, *The Economics of Control*, New York, Macmillan, 1944; J. V. de Graaf, *Theoretical Welfare Economics*, Cambridge, Cambridge University Press, 1987.

4. P. W. S. Andrews, *Manufacturing Business*, London, Macmillan, 1949; R. Hall & C. Hitch, 'Price Theory and Business Behaviour', in T. Wilson & P. W. S.

Andrews (eds), *Oxford Studies in the Price Mechanism*, Oxford, Oxford University Press, 1951.

5. According to one journalist's report the number of strikes from January to August 1984 had been 300, considerably higher than in 1983 (Dessa Trivisan, 'Nation at the end of its tether', *The Times*, London, 20 August 1984, p. 6.) By the end of 1986 there were five times the number of strikes (in twelve months) than during 1980 and a 50 per cent rise in number of strikes.

6. See Marx's 'Critique of Hegel's Philosophy of Law/Right' in Lloyd D. Easton & Kurt H. Goddart, *Writings of the Young Marx*, New York, Doubleday 1967.

7. For more about this factor as an important issue in Yugoslavia's overall development see Chapter 8 about 'the Croatian affair' and remarks in Chapters 12 and 15 on 'regionalism'.

8. For a discussion of causes and diagnoses of inflation in Yugoslavia in the 1960s see Chapter 11 below. The role of the tariff is discussed in Yugoslav Bank for Foreign Trade, 1960, pp. 26–7 and in Domandžić, 1966.

9. *Borba* (13 October 1971, p. 4) reported the 'Commission for Integration Trends and Self-Organization of the Economy' under the Federal Economic Chamber as recommending that new laws must be passed to 'bring about a more coordinated appearance on the world market'.

10. Yugoslavia's foreign investment laws, enacted since 1979, have questioned the size of transfer of profits from joint-venture enterprises, notably those with German partners.

11. A closer look at earlier Yugoslav economic reforms of 1951, 1961 and 1965 reveals that an identical if more restrained policy was adopted.

12. The evolution of this foreign policy position is outlined in detail in Chapter 14.

13. The details are discussed in Chapter 10.

14. In China the proportion between industry and agriculture was out of kilter in the 1960s and up to 1979, when a 'correction' from the top was attempted. See N. Maxwell & B. McFarlane, *China's Changed Road to Development*, Oxford, Pergamon Press, 1984, chs 2 and 3.

15. See Tables 10.4–10.8.

16. The 1957–61 Five Year Plan targeted a 17.3 per cent annual increase in agriculture's fixed investments. While less than industry and mining (44 per cent increase) and transport (23.7 per cent increase) this was much faster than in earlier periods and higher than forestry, trade, craft, hydropower and other sectors. Production for the period was planned to rise 7.4 per cent yearly as a result of higher investment (Federal Planning Commission, 1957).

17. Cereal output and other farm crops have expanded more satisfactorily since the 1960s. Yields for wheat have risen from 1.76 kg per tree in 1964 to 3.61 in 1985; rye from 1.12 to 1.73 kg per tree; maize from 2.86 to 4.12 kg per tree; sugar beet from 32 to 41.6 kg per tree; sunflower from 1.78 to 2.09 kg per tree. Though wheat average harvested dropped from 2.1 m to 1.34 m hectares from 1964 to 1985 total production rose from 3.7 to 4.8 m tons and maize with

also some reduction in acreage from 6.9 m to 8.9 m tons (*Statistical Pocketbook of Yugoslavia, 1986*, p. 71).

18. See, for example, the exposition in R. M. Goodwin, *Essays in Linear Economic Structures*, London, Macmillan, 1983, pp. 144–6.

19. See Goodwin, op. cit., p. 145.

20. M. H. Dobb, 'Economic Calculation in a Socialist Economy' in Dobb, *On Economic Theory and Socialism*, London, Routledge, 1955, p. 43.

Chapter 10

1. *Information Bulletin about Yugoslavia*, no. 31, April 1959.

2. In considering economic growth of the Yugoslav economy, a number of factors have to be noted: (a) that economic growth cannot be analysed exclusively in terms of physical production with the production aspect stressed to the exclusion of distribution and consumption aspects; (b) that global totals need to be broken down as far as possible because of divergent rates of growth *within* a total (e.g., the figure for industrial expansion might be increasing while certain key industries are in fact stagnating); (c) that because of severe dislocation resulting from the economic blockade against Yugoslavia 1948–52, the true test of the performance of the new style economy and the workers' councils system, was that which occurred after 1952; (d) that *rates* of growth can be statistically misleading unless we know that 'base' years are 'average' and not markedly unusual upwards or downwards.

3. Figures from United Nations, *Economic Survey of Europe*, 1956, Geneva.

4. While the economic growth in Yugoslavia for this period 1952–7 has often been described as much lower than in the rest of Eastern Europe (as in *Pravda*'s critique of Yugoslavia of 26 January 1959), such comparisons are 'dodgy' in that Bulgaria, for example, suffered less war damage and did not experience the deleterious effect of a Cominform blockade of the sort the Titoists had to endure from 1948 to 1952 in particular.

5. See Chapter 11 for the record of the 1960s in these economic activities.

6. As seen in the figures already quoted in Tables 10.10–10.12 from a lecture by J. Sirotković of the SZZPP given in Belgrade, May 1958 entitled 'The Problems of Planned Accumulation of Capital'.

Chapter 11

1. Among the most important documents of the SZZPP explaining the new plan methodology were *Prethodni Materijali Za Izradu Nacrta Plana 1961–1965* (Materials for elaborating the goals of the Plan) 29 November 1960 and *Problemi i Mogućnosti Priverednog Razvoja Yugoslavje 1964–1970* (24 July 1963).

2. For reforms in the banking and monetary area see the section 'money and banking' in Chapter 9.
3. Tragically, exactly the same thing happened twenty years later in 1984–6: see Chapter 12.
4. See B. McFarlane, 'Communist Economic Planning Over last Decade' in T. H. Rigby & J. Miller (eds), *The Disintegrating Monolith*, Canberra, ANU Press, 1965.
5. Confederation of Yugoslav Trade Unions, *How do the Working Collectives Distribute Created Value*, 1984, Belgrade; Horvart, 1971a, pp. 113 ff.
6. For example in the documents listed in note 1.
7. Confederation of Yugoslav Trade Unions, *op. cit.*
8. Figures in this chapter are from Institute for Economic Investments (1965), from *SG*, 1965, 1970 and National Bank of the Federal People's Republic of Yugoslavia, *Annual Report*, 1970.
9. Bogdan Šekler, 'Self-Management and the Health Service', *Yugoslav Review*, no. 6, 1970.
10. Ibid., p. 39.
11. See articles on education strike fall-out by Popov, on continuing illiteracy and educational opportunity by Z. Kučavić in *Praxis*, nos 3–4, 1971.
12. P. Ugrižović, 'Self-Management Behind the Scenes', *Yugoslav Review*, nos. 7–8, 1970, pp. 14–15.
13. Ibid., p. 15.
14. Published in the Social Democratic paper *Die Neue Gesellschaft*, nos. 5–6, 1969.

Chapter 12

1. In a speech in the Federal Assembly (*Politika*, 3 November 1971), leading party figure M. Todorović admitted to serious economic difficulties facing Croatia and the whole nation, and promised a 'complex, long-term plan', which would 'put an end to unfavourable trends of development'.
2. See the discussion in Chapter 13 on the 'Agro-Commerc' affair.
3. *Kajmak*: a Yugoslav delicacy, akin to cheese, made from the cream rising to the top of milk boiled in vats: a sort of scalded cream.
4. In 1975 regulations required firms who made good profits to *plough back* a much higher percentage in new investments. This ensured even higher investment in Croatia and Slovenia, where such were usually located, rather than for Macedonian, Montenegrin and Serb factories.
5. M. Čirović, *Novac i Stabilizacija*, Savremena Administracija, 1982, Belgrade, p. 87.
6. Ibid.
7. 'Aktuelni Problemi Privrednih Kretanja i Ekonomske Politike Jugoslavije 1974–75', published in *Ekonomist*, No. 4, 1974.
8. I. Perešin, 'Stara Nova, Naša i Njihova Inflacija', *Ekonomski Pregled*, vol. 26, nos 5–6, pp. 335–7.

9. D. Vojnić and M. Korošic, 'Problemi Inflacije v Jugoslavija', *Ekonomski Pregled*, vol. 26, nos 5–6, pp. 241–50.

10. Z. Pjanić gives a full account of this in *Anatomija Kriza* (Ekonomski Politika, 1986) and in *Socialist Thought and Practice* 2, May 1984. B. Bosković (1984) covered the earlier developments in 1982–4.

11. Z. Pjanić, op. cit., pp. 117–37, exposes this 'line of defence' as hollow and self-serving.

12. Published in *Borba*, 11 July and 27 July 1983.

13. Especially noteworthy was criticism of regional étatism, but the authors were at pains to establish the legitimacy of their views by reference to earlier sentiments expressed by the XI and XII Congresses of the League of Communists. In particular, the idea of *social control* over the banking system and opposition to heavy-handed treatment of workers' councils by some étatist elements in the Republics were expressed.

14. As explained by Stojan Stojčevski of the Presidium of the Yugoslav Confederation of Trade Unions in an interview with R. Puchkow, see 'Unions mobilise workers to fulfil economic stabilisation plan', *World Trade Union Movement*, no. 1, 1985, pp. 14–17.

15. A Yugoslav discussion which reviewed the implications of the 13th Congress of the SKJ and the work of the Assembly Chambers of the federal parliament in drawing up a 'Resolution on the Country's Socio-Economic Development in 1987' by J. Vuković was printed in *Yugoslav Life*, vol. 32, nos 11–12, November 1986–January 1987, pp. 1–2. Interestingly the measures discussed there are identical with those recommended in the OECD, *Annual Report on Yugoslavia* for 1986 (OECD, 1986, pp. 4–14).

16. *Yugoslav Life*, vol. 32, nos 11–12, loc. cit.

17. During late February Prime Minister Mikulić told Parliament on several occasions that foreign credits were needed for medium and longer-term loans for new production facilities, exports and transport infrastructure (*Financial Times*, London, 27 February 1987). He noted also that such loans would be increasingly difficult to get due to the failure of the Five Year Plan and Western complaints about the state of Yugoslav law protecting patents and technology transferred from the West.

18. *Financial Times*, London, 16 March 1987.

19. *The Times*, London, 24 November 1987.

20. M. Korošić and D. Vojnić, loc. cit.

21. M. Kalecki, 'A Theory of Hyperinflation', *Manchester School of Economics and Political Science*, 1958.

22. See Chapter 13, section on 'Agro-Commerc' affair.

23. The report was an inter-disciplinary study with a strong preference for Yugoslavia's orientation towards Europe and integration further into the world economy. It is *Jugoslavija u Svetskoj Privredi Na Pragu 21 Veka*, Informator, Zagreb, 1986.

Chapter 13

1. A. F. Burns, *The Decline of Competition*, was the classical empirical study of the United States; for the United Kingdom an important influence in raising consciousness about concentration was E. A. G. Robinson, *The Structure of Competitive Industry*, Cambridge, Cambridge University Press, 1937.
2. Implications and analysis of this are in McFarlane, 1973.
3. This case was discussed in J. Pjević, 'Dilemma of Iskra: co-operation or classical export?' *Borba*, 26 October 1964.
4. See also the comment in note 15 of this chapter.
5. B. M. Ward also argued that if technologies of different firms within Yugoslav industry are different, the optimization position of the industry will not be reached because the equilibrating movement due to workers' council behaviour will not yield equalizations of marginal products between firms.
6. See Eric Neumann, *The Origins and History of Consciousness*, Princeton, N.J., Princeton University Press, 1954, pp. 436-4. Other contributors in this area from an earlier time include T. Burrows and Hans Szyr.
7. E. Neumann, op. cit., pp. 440-1.
8. Ibid., p. 441.
9. See B. McFarlane, *Radical Economics*, London, Croom Helm, 1982, pp. 37-49; E. K. Hunt, 'Introduction' in E. K. Hunt and J. G. Schwartz, *A Critique of Economic Theory*, Harmondsworth, Penguin, pp. 17-19. In an earlier article, 'Orthodox Economic Theory and Capitalist Reality', *Monthly Review*, February 1968, pp. 50-55, Hunt found seventeen abstract assumptions were needed to ensure the optimality theorems of neo-classical economics held up, but he quoted K. J. Arrow and others showing some of these seventeen were incompatible with each other.
10. For the SKJ advocacy of this see 'Resolution of the Ninth Congress of the SKJ' (March 1969) and for an academic see Horvart (1964), pp. 119-20, 218.
11. T. W. Hutchison, 'The Crisis of Abstraction' in his *Knowledge and Ignorance in Economics*, Oxford, Basil Blackwell, 1977, pp. 62-97.
12. Ibid., pp. 80-1.
13. P. Sraffa, *The Production of Commodities by Means of Commodities*, Cambridge, Cambridge University Press, 1960.
14. M. Dobb, *On Economic Theory and Socialism*, London, Routledge & Kegan Paul, 1955, p. 123.
15. I make this comment in the full awareness that the modern American robot student can draw various functions and optimizing loci of points to find the equilibrium of a 'Yugoslav style' firm.
16. Joan Robinson, *The Economics of Imperfect Competition*, London, Macmillan, 1933; R. Triffin, *Monopolistic Competition and General Equilibrium Theory*, Cambridge, Mass., Harvard University Press, 1940; E. H. Chamberlain, *Monopolistic Competition*, Cambridge Mass., Harvard University Press, 1933.

17. See note 16 for literature on this issue of the causes and nature of excess capacity.
18. In what follows my difference in approach with the WVM is the familiar one between neo-Marxists and 'bourgeois' economists, namely, I emphasize macro-economic questions (distribution of income between classes and so forth) as a determining influence upon micro-relations, whereas the latter derive macro-relations—e.g. income distribution—from micro ones. For further discussions see Kalecki (1965), also M. Kalecki, 'Class struggle and the distribution of national income', *Kyklos*, vol. 24, 1971; B. McFarlane, 'Michal Kalecki's economics', *Economic Record*, vol. 47, 1971. See, as well, J. Vanek, 'Decentralization under workers' management', *American Economic Review*, vol. 59, 1969; D. M. Nuti, Review of B. Horvart's 'Essay on Yugoslav Society', *Economic Journal*, vol. 80, 1970.
19. R. G. Goodwin (1983b) also has this assumption in *Essays in Linear Economic Structure*, op. cit., p. 140.
20. Goodwin, ibid., p. 141; M. Kalecki, *Essays in Dynamic Economics*, London, Allen & Unwin, 1954, pp. 12–20.
21. We could now drop the assumption of stable capitalists' consumption and show it is unnecessary. If it rises when profits rise, we can make m_1 and m_2 not only dependent on monopolistic factors but rather on how much of the increase of profit is saved and how much consumed. The change is likely to be small in relation to the size of changes in profit.
22. See the discussion in Horvart, 1971a, pp. 108–13.
23. R. Marris, *The Economics of Managerial Capitalism*, London, Macmillan, 1964.
24. A. Wood, *A Theory of Profits*, Cambridge, Cambridge University Press, 1975.
25. Jan Vanek, 1972, ch. 4.
26. J. K. Galbraith, *The New Industrial State*, London, Hamilton, 1967.
27. A. Wood, *A Theory of Profits*.
28. D. Blondel, 'Mort et résurrection de la pensée économique', *Le Monde*, 2–9 April, 1986.
29. Michel Agietta & Anton Brender, *Métamorphoses de la societé salariale*, Paris, Calmann-Levy, 1984.
30. During the March–April 1987 strikes, when the government put up prices by 20 per cent and cut wages by 40 per cent (*Le Monde*, 25 March 1987), one worker interviewed said that the strike at his Zagreb plant was against the government, not the enterprise (*Le Monde*, loc. cit.); evidently the workers take jobs with firms for job security while getting wages to live above subsistence in a black labour market.
31. Even such an excellent 1987 textbook as Stefano Zamagni's *Micro Economic Theory* (Oxford, Basil Blackwell) declined to take up the self-managing firm (p. 452), settling instead for Aoki's 'cooperative game theory' of the firm, and simply avoiding the serious implications of abandoning the neo-classical concept of the 'market' for Adam Smith's wider one.
32. See Chapter 10.

Chapter 14

1. In April 1954 Tito unexpectedly announced towards the end of the Serbian Communist Party Congress being held in Belgrade that under certain circumstances Yugoslavia would consider joining the European Defence Committee. This created diplomatic uproar and pleased the Americans but only a few weeks later, Foreign Minister Koča Popović, while mentioning the possibility of Soviet aggression against Yugoslavia, did not mention anything about the military aspect of the Community—only the 'political . . . economic and cultural integrity of Europe'. The disappointed United States was only partly mollified by Yugoslavia signing a mutual defence pact with Greece and Turkey, two NATO countries, on 9 August 1954.

2. Tito's policy of 'active neutralism' was actually used by the Kremlin in its general strategy of easing international tension after the death of Stalin. It assisted in the preparation of the 1954 Geneva Conference. It helped to bridge a gap between Communist nations and regimes in Egypt, Indonesia and India. Tito's trip to the Far East preceded identical trips by Khruschchev and Bulganin. The Yugoslav Communists' views were similar in all important respects to the line on international policy emerging from the 20th Congress of the CPSU and can be said to have been initiated by Yugoslavia's SKJ.

3. Richard Lowenthal argued at the time that Tito was concerned to back Khrushchev in his struggle against the surviving Stalinists such as Molotov and Kaganovich in the Soviet government and this is why he took a hesitant attitude to the uprising and to the second Soviet intervention (see Lowenthal, 'Tito's gamble', *Encounter*, October 1958). Later this assessment was proved correct. (Mićunović, 1980, ch. 21).

4. Chinese leaders, in an article reprinted in *Pravda*, 10 June 1958, wrote that the Titoists were 'revisionists being used as spies by imperialists'; Khrushchev's speech before the Romanian CP Congress (published in *The New Road*, Bucharest, 5 June 1958) called Yugoslav Communists 'agents of the class enemy inside the labour movement'.

5. On 31 October 1971 Dr Anton Vratuša, a member of the FEC, addressed the 'Group of 77' nations in Peru. In his speech (*Politika*, 1 November 1971) he said that income per head in the developing countries had increased sixteen times more than in the Third World, and that the outflow of capital from the latter was rapidly approaching the size of the inflow. Yugoslavia proposed a change in basic principles inside UNCTAD and international monetary institutions, and the establishment of mutual credits among developing nations. This move annoyed some of the Third World bloc as well as the Americans.

6. In 1973 a shrill quarrel broke out with Italy over Trieste. Yugoslav local officials put up notices saying 'Socialist Federal Republic of Yugoslavia' on the border in an area which was not under Yugoslav sovereignty, although for twenty years *de*

facto control had been agreed with Italy. The Italians replied with a diplomatic note referring to the area as 'Italian territory', but withdrew the note verbally after a Yugoslav protest. The issue was used by the Slovenians at their Party Congress to warn all of Yugoslavia's neighbours that the country's sovereignty and independence would be defended, a statement believed to be aimed largely at Italy.

7. The failure of Iraq and Libya to pay Yugoslav construction firms for roads that they had built for these clients has caused anger in Yugoslav official circles and the wider public.

8. R. Vukadinović, 'Strategi sigurnosti mediterranskih zemalja' (Strategic security of Mediterranean countries), *Politička Misao*, vol. 23, no. 1, 1986, pp. 121-30.

9. This view was expounded to the author in Belgrade at the Centre for Strategic Studies in October 1987. A statement quoted above appears in *CSS papers*, no. 1, 1987, of the Centre, p. 30.

10. Ibid., p. 31.

11. Centre for Strategic Studies, Belgrade, 'West Europe in the Contemporary World', *CSS Papers*, no. 1, 1987, p. 22.

12. Ibid., pp. 32-7.

13. Dimitrijević, 'Ljudska Prava u U.N.' ('Human Rights in the U.N.') *Arkiv Za Pravne i Društvene Nauke*, vol. 69, no. 3, July–September 1983, p. 184.

14. Ibid.

15. 'Konvencija U.N. o pravu mora u svetlosti borbe za zovi medunarodni ekonomski poredalu', *Arkiv Za Pravne i Društvene Nauke* (Law and Social Science Archive), vol. 69, no. 3, July–September 1983, p. 185.

16. A recent book by leading public servant and economist Janez Stanovnik criticized the IMF in strong terms. He said in Chapter VI of his *Svet U Dugovima i Medunarodni Monetarni Fond* (Novi Sad, Dnevnik, 1985) that the IMF demanded state withdrawal from markets and a step-by-step approach to a 'real' foreign exchange value for the dinar. Yugoslavia believed that stability would not be possible with a lower rate of economic growth, while the IMF argued that there can be no stability unless foreign investment and free markets were being constantly opened up. Hence Yugoslavia and the IMF 'had very different views about the concept of economic development'.

Chapter 15

1. The arrival of many delegates at various political assemblies from non-blue collar areas became so obvious that Tito complained that 'one of the greatest weaknesses of the League of Communists is that there are relatively few workers and direct producers in its ranks. It is inconceivable that with the growing development of self-management attended by an expanded circle of self-managers as delegates to self-management bodies, there have been, until

recently, no fresh flow of industrial workers' (J. B. Tito, *Socialist Thought and Practice*, January–March, 1969, p. 35). Significantly too, at the 2nd Congress of Self-Managers held in Sarajevo in 1971, only 80 out of 1,200 delegates could be classified as 'blue-collar', something which created wide discussion in the Belgrade press at that time.

2. In 1968 Professor Joan Robinson noted that 'the Czechoslovak reform is intended to give the workers an interest in the efficiency and discipline of the enterprise in which they work without going the whole length of giving them equity in it on the Yugoslav model. The wage fund is measured so that bad management would not be the disaster for a group of workers that a bankruptcy may be under capitalism'. (J. Robinson, 'Socialist Affluence' in *Socialism, Capitalism and Economic Growth: Essays in Honour of Maurice Dobb*, ed. C. H. Feinstein, Cambridge, Cambridge University Press, 1968). Evidently a similar comment could apply to the 'disaster' for Yugoslav workers which was described in Chapter 12, the occasion of blocked wage funds, illiquidity of firms and bankruptcies in Yugoslavia in 1968–71 and earlier.

3. Interest rates (or, in Yugoslavia of the 1950s and 1960s, 'tax on working capital') were abolished in their old form in 1970. This stimulated a role for management in considering new investment in the more underdeveloped area by in fact subsidizing profit rates. The federal investment funds available for these areas, already abolished as a *central* fund administrated by the Yugoslav Investment Bank in 1964, were further reduced after 1970.

4. As noted years ago by Maurice Dobb in *On Economic Theory and Socialism*, London, Routledge & Kegan Paul, 1955, Chapter 3. See also the events described in McFarlane (1984a) and Cobelić & Stojanović (1966), Bajt (1971, 1986). In 1967 Joan Robinson noted that 'in Yugoslavia the investment system has evidently got out of hand, and the authorities, instead of trying to get a grip on the plan again, have resorted to a temporary all-round credit squeeze' (Joan Robinson, 'Socialist Affluence', op. cit., p. 182). It hardly needs to be pointed out that a series of such *ad hoc* squeezes could only give the rhythm of Yugoslav economic activity a cyclical character.

5. It has become increasingly obvious that there have to be in place certain institutional arrangements about resource-flows and investment allocation before 'deregulation' and its 'market signals' can work properly. These include some clear locus-points of decision-making; sufficient funds for quick expansion of plant at enterprise level; suspicion of 'centralized proletarian power by managers and resistance to it' and some concern for dynamic efficiency as well as static resource optimization. Comments along these lines have been made by W. Brus in *The Market in a Socialist Economy* (London, Routledge, 1972) and by Nove (1983).

6. See note 4 above.

Bibliography

* Indicates works of useful reference which have not been used directly in this book.

Adamović. L. 1983. Yugoslavia and the international economic environment: In *Ekonomski Odnosi Jugoslavije Sa Inostranstvom*, Belgrade, Informator.

Adizes, I. 1971. *Industrial Democracy: Yugoslav Style*. New York, Free Press.

Adler-Karlsson, G. 1969. *Functional Socialism*. Stockholm, Prisma.

—— 1968. *Western Economic Warfare 1946-67*, Uppsala.

Afansyev, Y. 1987. Energy of historical knowledge. *Moscow News*, 11 January 1987.

Amacher, R. 1972. *Yugoslavia's Foreign Trade*. New York, Praeger.

Amnesty International, 1985. *Yugoslavia: Prisoners of Conscience*. London, Amnesty.

Aoki, M. 1980. A model of the firm as a stockholder–employee co-operative. *American Economic Review*, vol. 70, September.

Auty, Phyllis 1965. *Yugoslavia*. London, Thames and Hudson.

—— 1970. *Tito: A Biography*. London, Longman.

Bajt, A. 1986. 'Economic growth and factor substitution: what happened to the Yugoslav economic miracle? *Economic Journal*, vol. 96.

—— 1971. Investment cycles in European socialist economies. *Journal of Economic Literature*, vol. 9.

Bakarić, V. 1960. *O Poljoprivredi i Problemima Sela*. Belgrade, Kultura.

—— 1968. Etatizam-Samoupravljnje. *Socializam*, nos 1–2.

Basaraba, P. 1967. Changes in the organisation and management of banks. *Yugoslav Survey*, Belgrade, no. 4.

Berković, E. 1969. Differentiation of personal income. *Yugoslav Survey*, Belgrade no. 9.

Bibić, A. 1986. Interesi i politika. *Politička Misao*, no. 1.

Bićanić, R. 1973. *Economic Policy in Socialist Yugoslavia*. Cambridge, Cambridge University Press.

*Bombelles, J. T. 1968. *Economic Development of Socialist Yugoslavia*. Stanford, Hoover Institution.

Borkenau, F. 1972. *World Communism*. Ann Arbor, University of Michigan.

Bošković, B. 1984. The programme of economic stabilization. *Socialist Thought and Practice*.

Bottomore, T. 1979. *Political Sociology*, London, Hutchinson.

Broekmeyer, M. J. 1970. *Yugoslav Workers' Self-Management*. Holland, Dordrecht.

—— 1977. Self-management in Yugoslavia. *Annals of the American Academy of Political and Social Sciences*, May.

Centre for Strategic Studies, 1987. West Europe in the contemporary world. *Papers*, no. 1. Belgrade.

Ciliga, A. 1940. *The Russian Enigma*. Westport, Hyperion.

228   *Yugoslavia*

Citrić, I. 1971. Naše seljgastvo i njegov polozaj u socijalzmu danas. *Praxis*, nos 3–4.

Confederation of Yugoslav Trade Unions 1964. *How Do the Working Collectives Create Values?* Belgrade, CTUY.

Constitution of the Socialist Federal Republic of Yugoslavia 1986. Belgrade.

Cviic, K. F. 1974. Dissent and defiance in Yugoslavia. *The World Today*, May.

Čirović, M. 1982. *Novac i Stabilizacija*. Belgrade, Savremena Administracija.

Čobelić, N. 1959. *Ekonomska Razvoja Yugoslavije 1947–1956*. Belgrade.

—— & Stojanovic, R. 1966. *Teorija Investicionih Ciklusa u Socialističkoj Privredi*. Belgrade, Rad.

Dahl, R. 1971. *After the Revolution: Authority in Good Society*, Part II. Yale, Conn., Yale University Press.

Davies, R. W. 1958. *The Development of the Soviet Budgetary System*. Cambridge, Cambridge University Press.

Deakin, F. W. D. 1971. *The Embattled Mountain: Mission to Tito*. Oxford, Oxford University Press.

Dedijer, V. 1953. *Tito Speaks*. London, Weidenfeld & Nicolson.

Dimitrije Tucović Kombinat Sečera 1964. *Nacrt Predloga Statuta*. Belgrade.

Djilas, M. 1957. *The New Class*. New York, Praeger.

—— 1959. *Anatomy of a Moral*. London, Thames & Hudson.

—— 1962. *Conversations with Stalin*. London, Hart-Davis.

—— 1969. *The Unperfect Society*. London Methuen.

—— 1972. *The Unperfect Society*. London, Unwin Books.

—— 1981. *Tito*, London, Weidenfeld & Nicolson.

Djordević, J. 1962. *Birokratija i Birokratizam*. Belgrade, Kultura.

—— 1966. A contribution to the theory of social property. *Socialist Thought and Practice*.

Dmitrijević, D. & Macesic, G. 1973. *Money and Finance in Contemporary Yugoslavia*, New York, Praeger.

Domandžić, A. 1965. Customs tariff. *Yugoslav Survey*, vol. 19.

Dubravčić, D. 1970. Labour as entrepreneurial input. *Economica*, vol. 37.

Duričić, A. 1965. Local communities. *Yugoslav Survey*, vol. 19.

Economics Faculty, Belgrade University 1983. Round table on long term stabilization. *Economski Anali*, vol. 28.

Estrin, S. 1983. *Self-Management: Economic Theory and Yugoslav Practice*. Cambridge, Cambridge University Press.

—— & Ben-Ner, A. 1986. What happens when unions run firms. *Flinders University Economics Seminar Series*, 24 July 1986.

Fabinc, I. and Kalogjera, D. 1987. Processes in the contemporary world. *Socialist Thought and Practice*.

Federal Assembly of Yugoslavia 1977. *The Associated Labour Act*. Belgrade.

Federal Planning Commission (SZZPP) 1957. *Draft Plan for the FPRJ for 1957–61*, Belgrade, SZZPP.

—— 1960a. *Prethodni Interno Materiali Za Izrada Nacrt Plana 1961–65*. Belgrade, SZZPP.

—— 1960b. *Osnovi Pravci Privrednog Razvoja Yugoslavija u Periodu 1961-65 God*. Belgrade, SZZPP.

—— 1963. *Problemi i Mogućnost Privrednog Razvoja Jugoslavije 1964-70*, vols 1-5. Belgrade, SZZPP.

—— 1964. *Nacrt Resolucjie o Smernicu Za Izradu Društvenog Plana Jugoslavije Za Period 1964-70*. Belgrade, SZZPP.

Fehrer, F., Heller, A. & Markus, G. 1983. *Dictatorship over Needs*. Oxford, Blackwell.

Fehrer, F., & Heller, A. 1983. Class, democracy, modernity. *Theory and Society*.

Fisher, J. 1968. *Yugoslavia: A Multi-Nation Country*. San Francisco.

Furubotn, E. 1974. *The Economic Theory of Property Rights*. Cambridge, Mass., Bolinger.

Golajanin, M. 1967. Credit and money control. *Yugoslav Survey*, no. 3.

Goodwin, R. M. 1983a. *Essays in Dynamic Economics*. London, Macmillan.

—— 1983b. *Essays in Linear Economic Structures*. London, Macmmillan.

Grdšić, I. 1986. Discussion. *Politička Misao*, no. 1.

Green, R. 1983a. The scourge of monetarism. *Contributions to Political Economy*, vol. 3, Cambridge.

—— & Wilson, A. 1982. Planning and workers' control. In T. Topham (ed.), *Planning and Planners*. Nottingham, Spokesman Books.

—— 1983. The future course of planning. In Eve, M. & Musson, D. (eds), *The Socialist Register*. London, Merlin.

Gregory, M. B. 1973. Regional development in Yugoslavia. *Soviet Studies*, vol. 25.

Hegedus, A., Heller, A., Markus, M. & Vajda, M. 1976. *The Humanisation of Socialism: Writings of the Budapest School*. London, Alison & Busby.

Hočevar, T. 1968. *The Structure of the Slovenian Economy*. Slovenia Studija, NY.

Hodges, D. C. 1981. *The Bureaucratization of Society*, Boston, Mass., University of Massachusetts Press.

Hodgson, G. 1984. *The Democratic Economy: A New Look at Planning, Markets and Power*. Harmondsworth, Penguin Books.

Horvart, B. 1962. *Methodological Problems in Long-Term Development Planning*. Belgrade, Institute for Economic Research.

—— 1964. *Towards a Theory of Planned Economy*. Belgrade, Institute for Economic Research.

—— 1969. *An Essay on Yugoslav Society*. White Plains, NY, International Arts and Science Press.

—— 1971a. Yugoslav economic policy in the post-war period. *American Economic Review* (supplement), vol. 61.

—— 1971b. Business cycles in Yugoslavia. *East European Economies*, vol. 9.

Institut Za Ekonomiku Investicija 1963. *The Optimum Size of the Firm*. Belgrade.

—— 1965. *Investicijie 1947-63*. Belgrade.

International Labour Office 1962. *Workers' Management in Yugoslavia*. Geneva, ILO.

Ireland, N. & Law, P. 1982. *The Economics of Labour-Managed Enterprise*. London, Croom-Helm.

Ivanović, B. 1962. *Application to the I-Method in the Problem of Estimating the Degree of Economic Development*. Institute for Economic Research, Belgrade.

Jakić, M. 1965a. Proportions in the economic system. *Kommunist*, 11 March 1965.

—— 1965b. Changes in Bor copper works. *Socialist Thought and Practice*.

Jakšić, M. 1985. The theory of modes of production. *Journal of Contemporary Asia*, vol. 15.

Jelić, B. 1961. Characteristics of the Yugoslav economic planning system. *Yugoslav Survey*.

Jones, D. C. & Svejnar, J. (eds) 1985. *Advances in the Economic Analysis of Participatory and Labor-Managed Firms*. Connecticut, Jai Press.

Jovanović, B. 1965. Reform of the credit and banking system. *Yugoslav Survey*.

Jugoslavenska Investiciona Banka 1957, 1963, 1971. *See* Yugoslav Investment Bank.

Kalecki, M. 1965. *Towards a Theory of Growth of Socialist Economy*. Oxford, Blackwell.

Kardelj, E. 1956. *Speech to the Federal Assembly on Hungarian Events*. 7 December 1956, Yugoslav Information Service, Belgrade.

—— 1960. *Problems of the Socialist Policy in the Countryside*. Belgrade, Edn. 'Jugoslavija'.

—— 1961a. *Report of Vice-President Kardelj to the Federal Peoples' Assembly*. Belgrade, Edn. 'Jugoslavija'.

—— 1961b. *Speech on the Discussion of Income Distribution*. Belgrade, Edn. 'Jugoslavija'.

—— 1961c. *Socialism and War*. London, Methuen.

—— 1962. Basic principles of the new constitution. *Yugoslav Survey*.

—— 1968. Radnička klasa, birokratizam i SKJ. *Socijalizam*, nos 1–2.

—— 1974. Socialism and the policy of non-alignment. *Socialist Thought and Practice*, vol. 14.

Kidrič, B. 1950. *Privredni Problemi FNRJ*. Belgrade.

Koloja, J. 1964. *Workers' Councils: The Yugoslav Experience*. New York, Praeger.

Kovać, O. 1987. System and policy of Yugoslavia's economic relations with foreign countries. *Socialist Thought and Practice*.

Kovačević, M. 1958. *Communal System of Yugoslavia*. Belgrade, Savremena Administracija.

—— 1969. Enterprise rules and regulations. *Yugoslav Survey*.

Lazarević, B. 1965. Turnover tax. *Yugoslav Survey*.

League of Communists of Serbia 1985. *Socijalizam i ekonomske zekonitosti*. Belgrade Ekonomska Politika.

League of Communists of Yugoslavia (SKJ) 1958. *Draft Programme of the League of Communists: Seventh Congress*. Belgrade.

—— 1964. Eighth Congress of the SKJ: Speeches and Documents. *Review of International Affairs*, 20 December 1964.

—— 1974. Tenth Congress of the League of Communists. *Socialist Thought and Practice*. Special Issue, June–July 1974.

Lewis, P. (ed.) (1984). *Eastern Europe: Political Crisis and Legitimation*. London, Croom Helm.

Lindbeck, A. 1975. *Swedish Economic Policy*. London, Macmillan.

Ljubičić, N. 1974. The concept of nation-wide defence. *Socialist Thought and Practice*, vol. 14.

*Macesich, G. 1964. *Yugoslavia: The Theory and Practice of Development Planning*. Charlottesville. University of Virginia Press.

McCain, R. 1982. Empirical implications of worker participation. In Jones & Svejnar, 1985.

McFarlane, B. 1966. Yugoslavia's crossroads. In J. Saville & R. Miliband (eds), *The Socialist Register*. London, Merlin.

—— 1971. Regional planning in Yugoslavia. In G. J. R. Linge & P. J. Rimmer (eds), *Government Influence and the Location of Economic Activity*. Canberra, ANU Press.

—— 1973. 'Price level and excess capacity in socialist economics. *Australian Economic Papers*, June.

—— 1984a. Political crisis and East European economic reform. In Lewis, 1984.

—— 1984b. Economic planning: past trends and new prospects. *Contributions to Political Economy*, vol. 3, Cambridge.

—— 1985. Review: Self-Management: Economic Theory and Yugoslav Practice', by S. Estrin, *Economic and Social Democracy*.

—— & Gordijev, I. 1964. Profitability and the Soviet firm. *Economic Record*, December.

Maclean, Fitzroy, 1966. *Eastern Approaches*. London, Cape.

Mandel, E. 1967. Yugoslav economic theory. *Monthly Review*, April.

Marinković, R. 1986. *The Hidden State*. Universitetska Riječ, Titograd.

Marjanović, J. (ed.) 1976. *The Collaboration of Draža Mihailović*. Archiv. Pregled, Belgrade.

Meade, J. E. 1972. The theory of labour-managed firms and profit-sharing. *Economic Journal*, vol. 82.

—— 1974. Labour-managed firms in conditions of imperfect competition. *Economic Journal*, vol. 84.

Medinica, V. 1968. A survey of the major results achieved in the implementation of Yugoslavia's 1966–70 social plan. *Yugoslav Survey*.

Mićunović, V. 1980. *Moscow Diary*. London, Chatto & Windus.

*Milenkovitch, D. D. 1971. *Plan and Market in Yugoslav Economic Thought*. New York, Praeger.

*Moore, J. H. 1980. *Growth with Self-Management: Yugoslav Industrialization 1952–1975*. Stanford, Calif., Hoover Institution.

Mrksa, S. (ed.), 1963. *Integracija u Privredi*. Zagreb, Informator.

National Bank of the Federal Peoples' Republic of Yugoslavia. *Annual Reports*, 1960, 1964, 1970.

Neuberger, E. 1959. The Yugoslav investment auctions. *Quarterly Journal of Economics*, vol. 83.

Niketić, R. & Pejović, M. 1958. *Investment Handbook for Enterprises*. Belgrade.

Nove, A. 1983. *The Economics of Feasible Socialism*. London, Allen & Unwin.

OECD 1970–86. Country Yearbooks: Annual Reports on Yugoslavia, Paris.

Pečuljić, 1967. *Klase i Savremnosti Drustvo*. Belgrade.

*Pejovich, S. 1966. *The Market-Planned Economy of Yugoslavia*. Minneapolis, University of Minnesota Press.

—— & Furubotn, G. 1970. Property rights and behaviour of the firm in a socialist state. *Ziertschrift für National-Okonomie*.

Perešin, I. 1974. 'Stara Novca, Naša i Njihova Inflacija', *Ekonomski Pregled*, vol. 26, p. 335–7.

Perlman, F. 1973. *Revolt in Socialist Yugoslavia*. Detroit, Black and Red Books.

Pertot, V. 1966. Stabilizacija u uslovima disparitetnih odnosa troskova proizvodnje. *Ekonomist*, vol. 19, Belgrade University.

Pjanić, Z. 1986. *Anatomija Krize*. Belgrade, Ekonomika.

Popovic, K. 1959. *Report of the State Secretary for Foreign Affairs to The Peoples' Federal Assembly*. Belgrade, edn. 'Jugoslavija'.

Popović, M. 1949. O ekonomskom odnosima izmedu socialistickih drzava. *Kommunist*, no. 4, 1949.

—— 1961. *New Developments in Yugoslav Social Relations*. Belgrade, edn. 'Yugoslavija'.

Popović, N. 1970. *New Class in Crisis*. New York, Syracuse University Press.

Proutt, P. 1985. *Market Socialism in Yugoslavia*, Oxford, Oxford University Press.

Remington, R. 1978. Yugoslavia: the partisan vanguard. *Studies in Comparative Communism*, vol. II, no. 3.

Roundtable Discussion 1968. 'O problemima upravlyanja i raspodele y samo-upravno-robno privredit. *Ekonomska Prezudeca*, July.

Rusinow, D. 1977. *The Yugoslav Experiment: 1948–1974*. London, Royal Institute of International Affairs.

—— 1984. Yugoslavia. Paper delivered to London School of Economics Seminar on East European Countries, London.

Samardžija, M. 1968. Metodološke i društvene osnove teorije raspodele dohodka. *Gledišta*, vol. 19.

Savezni Zavod, Za Privrednog Planirenja 1960a, 1960b, 1963–64. *See* Federal Planning Commission.

Secretariat of Information of SFRJ Assembly, 1977. *The Associated Labour Act*. Belgrade, Prosveta.

Šibek, I. 1986. Discussion. *Politička Misao*. no. 1.

Sirc, L. 1979. *The Yugoslav Economy under Self-Management*. London, Macmillan.

Sirotković, J. 1951. *Planiranje Proširenje Reprodukcije u Socializmu*. Zagreb.

—— 1961. *Problemi Privrednog Planiranja u Jugoslaviji*. Zagreb.

—— 1966. *Planiranje u Sistema Samoupravljanja*. Zagreb.

Socialist Philosophy Group, London 1986. *Market Socialism*. Fabian Pamphlet.

Spiljak, M. 1984. Internal and external policy of Yugoslavia. *Socialist Thought and Practice*, May.

Spulber, N. (ed.) 1961. *Study of the Soviet Economy*. Bloomington, Indiana University Press.

Stallerts, R. 1981. The effect of capital intensity on income in Yugoslav industry. *Economic Analysis and Workers' Management*, vol. 15.

Stanovčić, N. 1986. Discussion. *Politička Misao*, no. 1.

State Bank of the USSR, 1927. *The State Bank of the USSR*. Moscow.

Stephen, F. H. 1978. Bank credit and investment in the Yugoslav firm. *Economic Analysis and Workers' Management*, vol. 12.

—— 1980. Bank credit and the labour-managed firms. *American Economic Review*, vol. 70.

Stojanović, R. 1970. *Veliki Ekonomski Sistemi*. Belgrade, Institute for Economic Research.

Stojanović, S. 1967. Etatisticki mit socijalizma. *Praxis*, vol. 3.

*Sukijasović, N. 1968. *Foreign Investment in Yugoslavia*. New York, Oceania.

Sulyok, B. 1966. The socialist banking system and the Hungarian Banks. *New Hungarian Quarterly*.

Suvar, S. 1970a. Neither power nor dependence on power. *Socialist Thought and Practice*, July–September.

—— 1970b. *Presek Jugoslovenske Drustva*. Belgrade.

Sweezy, P. 1958. The Yugoslav experiment. *Monthly Review*, March.

—— 1964. Peaceful transition from capitalism to socialism. *Monthly Review*.

Šik, O. 1967, 1968. *Plan and Market under Socialism*. White Plains, N.Y., International Arts and Sciences Press.

Šoškic, B. (ed.)1983. *Sauvremene Problemi Ekonomske Stabilizacije*. Titograd, Montenegrin Academy of Social Sciences.

Štaubringer, Z. 1974. *Tito: Građanin Sveta*. Belgrade, Radnicka Stampa.

Tadić, B. 1986. *Sukovi Među Nevrstanim Zemljamama*. Institute for International Politics and Economics, Belgrade.

The Economist, London 1971. Another way. *The Economist*, Supplement 21–7 August 1971.

Tišma, T. 1986. Finansiranje Federacije. *Finansije* May–June.

Tito, J. B. 1956. *Speech at Pula on Hungarian Events*. Belgrade, Information Service, Yugoslavia.

—— 1960. *Speech to First Congress of Workers' Councils*. Belgrade, Information Service, Yugoslavia.

—— 1971. *The Essential Tito* (ed. H. M. Christman). Newton Abbot, Devon, David & Charles.

—— 1974. Speech at the Tenth Congress of the SKJ. *Socialist Thought and Practice*, nos 1–2.

Trifunović, B. 1987. Enforcement of the decisions of the Thirteenth Congress of the SKJ. *Socialist Thought and Practice*, no. 1.

Uvalić, R. 1962. Funkcije tržista i plana u socijalstičkoj privredi. *Ekonomist*, vol. 15, University of Belgrade.

Vanek, Jan 1972. *The Economics of Workers' Management: A Yugoslav Case Study*. London, Allen & Unwin.

Venek, Jaroslav 1969. Decentralization under workers' management: a theoretical appraisal. *American Economic Review*, vol. 57.

—— 1970. *The General Theory of Labour-Managed Market Economies*. Ithaca, NY, Cornell University Press.

Venek, Jaroslav 1973. The Yugoslav economy viewed through the theory of labour management. *World Development*, vol. 1, no. 9.

Vasić, F. 1963. Investment in the post-war period. *Yugoslav Survey*, vol. 15.

Vidaković, Z. 1970. *Drustvena Moć Radnicke Klase*. Belgrade.

Vućković, M. 1956. Preduzece i kredit. *Ekonomiski Anali*, vol. 2, University of Belgrade.

—— 1963. The recent development of the money and banking system of Yugoslavia. *Journal of Political Economy*, vol. 81.

Vuković, D. 1968. Price formation and social price control. *Yugoslav Survey*, no. 1.

Vuković, M. 1967. Dodašnja inflaciona u Jugoslaviji. *Ekonomist*, vol. 20, University of Belgrade.

Wachtel, H. 1973. *Workers' Management and Wage Differentials in Yugoslavia*. Ithaca, NY, Cornell University Press.

Ward, B. M. 1957. Workers' management in Yugoslavia. *Journal of Political Economy*, vol. 65.

—— 1958. The firm in Illyria: market syndicalism. *American Economic Review*, vol. 48.

—— 1967a. *The Socialist Economy*. Ithaca, NY, Cornell University Press.

—— 1967b. Marxism–Horvatism: a Yugoslav theory of socialism. *American Economic Review*, vol. 57.

Wiles, P. 1961. Communist economics and our economic textbooks. In Spulber, 1961.

Yugoslav Bank for Foreign Trade 1960. *Annual Report*. Belgrade.

Yugoslav Investment Bank (Jugoslovenska Investiciona Banka) 1957, 1963, 1971. *Annual Reports*, Belgrade.

Yugoslav Investment Bank 1964. *Vesnik*, July–August.

Yugoslav Survey 1987. No. 1, Belgrade.

*Zaninovich, M. G. 1968. *The Development of Socialist Yugoslavia*. Baltimore, Maryland, John Hopkins University Press.

Index

DATE DUE

The Library Store   #47-0103